W9-BXP-349

Ethics and Values in Archaeology

Ethics and Values in Archaeology

Edited by
Ernestene L. Green

THE FREE PRESS
A Division of Macmillan, Inc.
NEW YORK

Collier Macmillan Publishers
LONDON

The Free Press
A Division of Macmillan, Inc.
866 Third Avenue, New York, N. Y. 10022

Collier Macmillan Canada, Inc.

Printed in the United States of America

printing number
1 2 3 4 5 6 7 8 9 10

Library of Congress Cataloging in Publication Data

Main entry under title:

Ethics and values in archaeology.

Includes index.
1. Archaeology—Moral and ethical aspects—Addresses, essays, lectures. I. Green, Ernestene L.
CC175.E83 1984 930.1'01 83-48644
ISBN 0-02-912750-5

Contents

Contributors

E. CHARLES ADAMS, Littleton, Colorado

ANNETTA L. CHEEK, National Park Service, Department of Interior, Washington, D.C.

HESTER A. DAVIS, Arkansas Archaeological Survey, University of Arkansas, Fayetteville, Arkansas

ROBERT C. DUNNELL, Department of Anthropology, University of Washington, Seattle, Washington

BRIAN M. FAGAN, Department of Anthropology, University of California, Santa Barbara, California

T. J. FERGUSON, Albuquerque, New Mexico

JAMES E. FITTING, Soil Systems Inc., Atlanta, Georgia

RICHARD I. FORD, Museum of Anthropology, University of Michigan, Ann Arbor, Michigan

DON D. FOWLER, Historic Preservation Program, University of Nevada, Reno, Nevada

GEORGE C. FRISON, Department of Anthropology, University of Wyoming, Laramie, Wyoming

DOROTHY M. GODDARD, Tonto National Forest, USDA Forest Service, Phoenix, Arizona

DEE F. GREEN, Southwest Region, USDA Forest Service, Albuquerque, New Mexico

ERNESTENE L. GREEN, Northern Region, USDA Forest Service, Missoula, Montana

PAUL F. HEALY, Department of Anthropology, Trent University, Peterborough, Ontario, Canada

BENNIE C. KEEL, National Park Service, Department of Interior, Washington, D.C.

RUTHANN KNUDSON, Woodward-Clyde Consultants, San Francisco, California

CLEMENT W. MEIGHAN, Department of Anthropology, University of California, Los Angeles, California

MARTIN E. MCALLISTER, Tonto National Forest, USDA Forest Service, Phoenix, Arizona

CHARLES R. MCGIMSEY III, Arkansas Archaeological Survey, University of Arkansas, Fayetteville, Arkansas

FRED PLOG, Department of Anthropology, New Mexico State University, Las Cruces, New Mexico

L. MARK RAAB, Department of Anthropology, California State University, North Ridge, California.

KAREN D. VITELLI, Classical Archaeology, Indiana University, Bloomington, Indiana

LESLIE E. WILDESEN, Cultural Resources Research and Planning, Portland, Oregon

JOSEPH C. WINTER, Department of Anthropology, University of New Mexico, Albuquerque, New Mexico

J. SCOTT WOOD, Tonto National Forest, USDA Forest Service, Phoenix, Arizona

Introduction

Ernestene L. Green

THE PAST 15 years has seen a rapid expansion in archaeology, probably more than at any other time in the history of the discipline. While this expansion has produced many benefits, it has also resulted in increasingly diverse values and conflicting ethics. Archaeology has moved out from academia into the worlds of business and government. Largely because of this, there has been an increase in the total amount of archaeological work done annually, an increase in the total number of practicing archaeologists, and, consequently, a greater diversity of personal goals and values.

The archaeologist's world today is different from what it was 15 years ago. To use an ethnographic analogy, we have gone from the homogeneity of a village society—characterized by a similarity of value orientation and world view—to the heterogeneity characteristic of an urban society. In the past, most archaeologists worked in the academic world and experienced a generally similar professional environment. The focus was inward, toward the university and professoriat, and ethical expectations reflected this. One was expected to be intellectually honest, not to harm one's students or colleagues, and not to damage the archaeological resource by trafficking in artifacts or digging without serious purpose. Accountability was to one's peers only, not to any segment of the world outside academia. Advancement was through academic approval, and scholarly behavior was appropriately awarded.

Today we work in at least three worlds—those of government, business, and academia. One of the results of extending out of the traditional milieu is that archaeology has encountered sets of values and ethics very different from those of academia. An example is the conflict between the values and objectives of business management and those of traditional research management. Archaeologists had not previously dealt with such business concepts as profit requirements, cost and pricing, contract time requirements, labor costs, fringe benefits, and so on. Traditionally, an archaeologist worked until the research project was finished. The main concern was that the quality of work satisfied professional research standards, not a business client's financial and time constraints. The organization was that of an association or alliance of colleagues, not a hierarchical business structure.

As archaeologists began interacting and working with people who were not socialized into the academic value system, they were challenged by new questions. What is the intrinsic value of archaeology? Why spend time and money on something which does not produce energy, food, shelter, or clothing? Suddenly archaeologists had to justify their professional existence.

Another shock to our value system came when archaeological resources had to compete with others for the use of the same location. The archaeological resource was not necessarily considered by businessmen and land managers to be as important or valuable as other resources. This came as quite a surprise to those of us who had considered archaeological remains to be priceless.

These challenges to the profession and conflicts with other systems of values could not be ignored. The response, however, was not always the same. Perhaps the most common reaction was to attempt to integrate the new values into the traditional framework. Sometimes the fit was acceptable, but in other cases the conflict could not be reconciled and the result was stress to the fabric of the discipline.

Another frequent response was compartmentalization: traditional values were used when dealing with archaeological work or other archaeologists, while other value orientations were adopted when dealing with business matters, politics, or the arena of agency management.

A third reaction was to reject the new ethics and values. This response was possible only in areas of academia isolated from cultural resource management and politics. To ignore the new orientation is not a choice for those who have to interact with it.

A much rarer response was to reject traditional archaeological values on the grounds that they were not functional in the "real world." When this happens, good archaeology obviously suffers.

At the same time that archaeology has been challenged from without, the growth of cultural resource management (archaeology and history in government and business) has produced changes within. The job of managing cultural resources on public lands involves different objectives, approaches, and tasks, and additional knowledge and skills, compared to those of traditional academia. An action which is best for the resource today may be different from that which was thought best 20 years ago. For example, it may be best now to conserve a site rather than to excavate it, which was the usual approach two decades ago. Archaeologists had long thought that they had an inherent professional right to test or excavate a site. It came as a surprise to many that the government agency which manages the land containing the site has the legal right to manage the site, even if this means preventing excavation in order to conserve the resource. Thus, traditional values have been challenged and have been changing to meet new situations. These events have highlighted and increased the importance of professional responsibility to the discipline and to other professionals.

We also have responsibilities to the public interest which we have so diligently created and cultivated. For at least the past two decades, archaeologists have emphasized among themselves the need for greater efforts to bring the nation's cultural heritage to the American public. We have cultivated the information media and exhorted our colleagues to make knowledge of past cultures more available to the lay audience. The resulting increase in television and newspaper accounts of archaeology has been a reward, but this also brings greater responsibility to respond to the growing interest in prehistory by the American people.

Since the late 1960's there has been increasing legislation concerning public agency management of prehistoric resources on agency land and the impact of projects on cultural properties. The enactment of such laws shows an increased public interest in America's cultural background. Millions of public dollars have been spent annually on archaeological work by Federal and state agencies. The use of tax dollars for archaeology obviously increases the profession's obligations and responsibilities to the public.

With increased management of cultural resources by governmental agencies has come the growing awareness that these resources do not belong to individuals who would take artifacts for their own collections. Theft and vandalism of archaeological materials from public land is a crime against the American people. The archaeological profession's support of efforts to reduce this vandalism and looting is another way of showing responsibility to the public as well as to the resource.

The chapters in this volume are organized around the themes of responsibilities to the public and responsibilities to the profession. The specific issues selected for treatment reflect, in the editor's opinion, those problems and ethical concerns most critical to the discipline today. These topics have been discussed at national and regional meetings, have been the subject of articles, and in some instances relate to cases investigated by ethics and standards committees of professional societies.

Ethics is defined by Webster's Dictionary both as a system of moral values governing a profession, and as an individual's standards of behavior. The essays in this volume concern both the professional system or code of ethics and individual ethics as they relate to the professional code.

Two ethical codes or statements have national circulation. The later and more extensive one is that of the Society for Professional Archaeology. This code, which consists of over 30 items, is divided into archaeologists' responsibilities to the public, to colleagues, and to clients. The earlier statement, published in *American Antiquity* (Champe et al., 1961), consists of five separate items and focuses on responsibilities characteristic only of the academic world. Obviously the field has become more complex in the last two decades.

The issues examined in this book are sensitive. Professional ethics and values reflect the ways in which individual professionals define themselves and want others to think of them. Therefore, they become synonomous with our characterization of ourselves and basic to our sense of self-worth. Change may threaten our self-image, but failure to change may be more damaging, both to that self-image and to our reputation among other professionals and the public. Neither the editor nor the individual authors want to preach, pontificate, or moralize; rather, they aim to recognize the conflicts and dilemmas which have developed in the discipline today and to provide recommendations to deal with them. That is the spirit in which this volume was written.

Ethics and Values in Archaeology

PART I

Background

1

The Search for an Ethic in Archaeology: An Historical Perspective

Leslie E. Wildesen

THE GENERAL TOPIC of ethics and standards for the practice of archaeology is not new. One reason for the founding of the Society for American Archaeology in 1934 was to provide a forum for the dissemination of "professional" archaeology to interested "non-professionals"; another was to "further the profession of archaeology" (Anonymous 1935: 142, 144). Some early scholars developed and defended standards of documentation and reporting (i.e., standards of archaeological practice) that not only were rigorous for their time but that remain as models of scholarly effort today (e.g., Bandelier 1881, 1892; Gladwin et al. 1937; Haury 1950; Kidder 1924; Rouse 1939; Squier and Davis 1848; Willey 1953; see Willey and Sabloff 1980, *passim*).

What is new is the fervor and urgency of the present discussions, and the frequency with which they are carried on by outside parties, including the mass media (Clary 1978; Fisher 1977; Holden 1977; Large 1977). Another change is that during the last decade archaeology has become an applied science as well as a theoretical one, and the application of archaeological findings has come to have real world consequences in public and corporate decision making (Mayer-Oakes 1978; Wildesen 1979).

Whereas early archaeology could be characterized as a calling, engaged in by a small guild of practitioners whose ideas were validated (or not) by their peers on the basis of the "calibre" of the proponent (Woolley 1930, quoted in Daniel 1967:8), today archaeology meets all six of Flexner's classic criteria for a "profession," including the criterion of "practical application" (Flexner 1915). Archaeology has long been characterized by "intellectual operations coupled with large individual responsibilities, . . . raw materials drawn from science and learning, . . . an educationally communicable technique, . . . tendency toward self-organization, and . . . increasingly altruistic motivation,'' the other five criteria (Cogan 1955:106).

To some extent, ''ethics'' has always been part of archaeology in practice. Archaeologists are expected to refrain from trafficking in stolen antiquities and to promote the application of scientific methods, including adequate documentation, to the scholarly study of past cultures (Anonymous 1935; Champe et al. 1961). Today's archaeologist also is expected to exhibit a ''conservation ethic'' and to ''actively support conservation of the archaeological resource base'' (Lipe 1974; Society of Professional Archaeologists 1976). Thus, advocacy is added to scholarship as an apparent requirement for the complete archaeologist.

Given the explosive growth of archaeology in the past few decades (measured in number of degrees awarded, projects conducted, and practitioners employed, and amount of publicity generated), it is perhaps inevitable that archaeologists have initiated an explicit and comprehensive search for rational, enforceable codes and standards that define their responsibilities in the modern world. As in other professions, the existence of such codes is perceived as an excellent way to explain oneself to outsiders, and to inculcate students and junior colleagues with the seriousness of the career step they are about to take (Drinker 1955; Fitts and Fitts 1955; Wagner 1955; see Chalk et al. 1980, *passim*). That is, a code serves to define ''group norms'' in a way that mere possession of an advanced degree and some field experience cannot (MacIver 1955).

Three general issues are basic to the ethical standards of any profession and can be phrased as relatively simple questions: (1) Who is an archaeologist? (2) To whom or what is an archaeologist accountable for his or her actions? (3) What is an appropriate level of accountability in general, and in any specific situation? Archaeology's focus on things (sites, artifacts) and the recent emphasis on conservation may separate archaeology from many sister disciplines (e.g., law, medicine, engineering, geology) (Wildesen 1980). Certainly, archaeologists' commitment to their ''resource'' is different from lawyers' commitments to their clients, or engineers' commitment to petroleum or highways.

Archaeology and archaeologists are not alone in their dilemma, however. Other disciplines, such as history, architecture, archives management, museology, art history, landscape architecture, and architectural history, have developed or are developing a conservation ethic. These and other humanities are allied with archaeology in the attempt to identify, protect, and maintain elements of the cultural heritage that members of these disciplines (and sometimes the public) perceive as important. It is instructive, therefore, to review the historical development of ethical standards and codes in some of these allied disciplines to provide a perspective on the current ethical struggles within archaeology. In addition, because the historical development of an idea affects its present status and future potential, the following comparative review is intended to illustrate the historical dynamics of ethical struggles in the cultural resource professions.

The following treatment of ethics in archaeology is explicitly comparative and historical. Because other chapters in this book provide detailed discussions of specific problem areas, the discussion here is intentionally broad, and citations are limited. Although archaeology long has been imbued with "nobility of purpose," it is important to understand "the situation within which noble purposes must be pursued" (Monypenny 1955: 102). The rest of this chapter outlines something of the nature of that "situation" during the last century.

Who Is an Archaeologist?

This question always means, who is a *real* archaeologist? The distinction being drawn is not between archaeologists and lawyers or historians, but between archaeologists as members of a peer group (the "guild") and those who may lay some claim to being archaeologists but who are not accepted by the peer group. Therefore, the answer seeks to distinguish between "archaeologists" and members of any of the following categories: amateur archaeologists, avocational; archaeologists, interested laymen, journalists, pot hunters, relic collectors, vandals, dealers, grave robbers, local "historians," adventurers, and movie stars. The answer to the question is important to most archaeologists and, increasingly, to funding entities and others who base their assessment of the integrity of the *profession* on their assessment of the integrity of its individual *members*. By implication, the question "Who is an archaeologist?" includes the question, "How can you tell?"

In the early days of archaeology, the answer to both questions was simple: an archaeologist was one who did archaeology. "Doing archaeology" also was defined simply: it consisted of finding exotic artifacts, bringing them home to put on display, and writing a book about one's adventures. Usually, the archaeologist also described something of the "newly discovered civilization" whose members had made the artifacts. People whom we now seek to reject as "real" archaeologists—Belzoni, Bandelier, Lord Elgin, Boucher de Perthes, even Schliemann— were in their own time widely accepted as scholars, scientists, and revealers of wondrous facts about "lost" cultures. Today, the best of these predecessors are considered remarkable amateurs; the worst of them, grave robbers and thieves. Clearly, the answer to the question varies through time, with intellectual fashion and other factors.

One key factor is extent of formal education and training. None of these early archaeologists ever participated in a graduate seminar on method and theory in archaeology, or took a summer field school. Thus, none of them ever learned the "right" way to do field archaeology or to interpret their finds. In fact, all of them did something other than archaeology (*sensu stricto*) for a living, and none of them were academics.

Similar conditions prevailed in early architecture, history, and museology. Buildings were designed and built, histories were written, and collections acquired and displayed without benefit of formal academic training, monthly paychecks, professional organizations, scholarly journals, or other paraphernalia of modernity. Some of the practitioners devoted their lives to building and landscape restoration, and wrote treatises describing the "right" way to accomplish these tasks; the names of Ruskin, Downing, Olmsted, and Viollet le Duc come to mind. Historians similarly wrote treatises, founded museums, and discoursed on method, as the writings of Turner, Parkman, and Schoolcraft show.

In fact, such conditions were not limited to the humanities, but prevailed throughout the learned disciplines until almost (and in some cases, after) the turn of the century. For example, the premier issue of *Science* (July 3, 1880), listed 17 "well known and esteemed scientists" who supported the new publishing venture. Of these, only four were cited as "Dr.," and it is likely that most of those were doctors of medicine rather than physics, chemistry, geology, or other "sciences."

Scholars and others with interests in particular topics founded numerous societies in the late 19th century as a vehicle to share their interests. Historical societies had existed in the United States since before 1800. The American Institute of Architects was founded in 1857, the Archaeological Institute of America by 1880, the American Historical Association by 1890, and the American Society of Landscape Architects by 1900. Of these, only the American Institute of Architects purported to distinguish real from self-appointed architects, and to have as its object the elevating of the architectural profession "as such" and the improvement of its members (Cummings 1955: 11). Of course, architects were the only group that had clients as well as protégés and patrons.

Thus, 19th-century answers to the question, "Who is a(n) ______?" were largely self-centered. Schliemann was an archaeologist because he said so; Eliot and Downing and Olmsted were landscape architects for the same reason. Most 19th-century scholars whom we revere today were simply considered important thinkers in their time, not specialists in a particular discipline or practitioners of a specific method. Boas, Darwin, Huxley, Marsh, Tyler, Worsaae, and others were in this class—without benefit of formal training, supervised experience, or professional organizations.

Around the turn of the century, some of these early pioneers created and staffed academic departments; the self-taught thus became the teachers of the next generation of scholars. Training emphasized proper methods; graduates of these academic programs were held in greater esteem among their fellow graduates than were contemporary self-taught practitioners. Professionalism had taken root in the humanities, as it had started to in the "hard" sciences. Anthropology, history, landscape architecture, architecture, and other disciplines (including forestry and soil science) now met Flexner's criterion that "technique" be imparted in an educational program, rather than by on-the-job training.

At this time, the concerted search began for ways to distinguish the legitimate from the illegitimate practitioner in archaeology and nearly every other related discipline. Clearly, level and type of formal education played an important role in this process. Concurrently, some disciplines began to develop codes of professional standards, including state licensing programs monitored by professional societies whose members met the standards and held state licenses. For example, engineers and architects, two groups with both an academic and a client-centered practice, struggled with codes of behavior that included training requirements, and proper attitudes toward students, colleagues, and clients. These groups tried to instill in clients a respect for society members (as distinguished from nonmembers). Especially with the advent of licensing based on educational requirements, self-taught practitioners clearly were at a disadvantage both in academia and in the marketplace.

Archaeology was largely shielded from similar concerns because of its purely academic base. Until at least the late 1960's, peer pressure and the "grapevine" were sufficient to distinguish a "real" archaeologist from various imposters. Departments were in essence self-accredited, on the basis of the quality of research and publications that faculty and students ultimately produced. No clients, and therefore no competition, were involved. Friction over research results was limited to arguments about the relevance of theoretical approaches, and theoretical approach was associated closely with an individual or an academic department, not the profession as a whole.

Historians shared, and still share, this orientation. Academic historians, if not the public, can easily distinguish themselves from "popular" historians on the basis of degree of methodological rigor and type of theoretical approach to their research. Thus, both popular historians and amateur archaeologists have written "best sellers" that have little effect on the mainstream of historical or archaeological (academic) thought.

The key factor here is that, until recently, these two classes coexisted quite happily. Pop writers got rich while academic scholars produced new facts and theories, and each group ignored the other. No important policy decisions hinged on the findings of the individual researcher, no funding programs involved real competition among departments, and no "resources" were destroyed because of the variation in theoretical approach of an individual researcher.

Today, all these things have changed in archaeology and, to a growing extent, in history. The type and direction of national and local policies affecting archaeological and historical sites depend on the kind of recommendations made by archaeologists and historians, which in turn depend on the background, training, experience, and interests of individual practitioners. Research funds no longer are channelled to local academic departments on the basis of their assumed expertise, but are subject to competitive award. Competition is open to individuals and groups from the academic and private sectors, and some nonprofit foundations. These changes, designed to incorporate existing standards of fairness and democracy, have created a new need for archaeologists to define the threshold of training and experience that can unambiguously separate the "real" archaeologist from the imposter.

The response has been predictable: a new organization, the Society of Professional Archaeologists, was developed by a self-appointed group, who in turn created standards that all *new* members must meet in order to belong; government agencies developed standards that all *new* employees or contractors would have to meet. Both sets of standards strongly emphasized education and experience, and were oriented toward outside parties as a means of documenting the integrity of members and employees, respectively. Thus, archaeologists finally caught up with architects, who had faced these problems over a hundred years earlier; by and large, both groups found the same kinds of solutions.

To Whom or What Is an Archaeologist Accountable?

Most scholars, including archaeologists, hold themselves accountable to such abstract entities as knowledge, science, and the advancement of humankind. Many archaeologists include the general public and/or interested lay citizens on their list because public dollars support their research. The list of entities to which archaeology as a profession is accountable rarely has been formalized, however, and no set of procedures for selecting among potentially conflicting responsibilities has been developed. In the past, unlike other professions (such as engineering), loyalty to employer per se was not an issue; archaeologists got a teaching or museum job and held it until retirement. Unlike chemists, archaeologists did not need to resolve conflicts about patent rights or publication priority. Unlike historians, archaeologists rarely faced issues of outright plagiarism or falsification of data. In the absence of these issues, the "scholar's code" seemed to suffice.

Other disciplines faced some of these issues from the turn of the century onward. Should architects also be involved in the building trades or in real estate? How should a mechanical engineer designing a new product to code specifications resolve a conflict between duty to the consumer and loyalty to the employer? What should a landscape architect tell a client who demands a landscape design that violates current aesthetic principles or that will result in massive long-term maintenance costs? Should a museum curator also be an active private collector of the kinds of objects contained in the museum collection he or she manages? The level of education and training achieved by a practitioner is not relevant to these issues; hence, organizations began to develop standards of conduct, formal lists of responsibilities and ultimately, formal lists of "do's and don'ts" for their professions.

As long as one feels accountable only to abstracts like "science," such lists are not needed. Differences in theoretical or methodological approach or data interpretation are considered part of the dialectic of scholarship. These differences lead to new knowledge, new methods, and new theories, and only the scholarly community is directly affected. Thus, it doesn't really matter, in any comprehensive way, whether an individual scholar is "ethical" so long as the general scholarly code is observed (e.g., avoidance of plagiarism).

Add clients, competition for funds, conflicts between entities to whom one is accountable, and investigation by parties outside the profession, however, and the picture changes dramatically, as archaeologists are beginning to discover. Recently, archaeology has followed in the footsteps of other disciplines that have developed codes of ethics that include specific statements about each class of entity to which the practitioner should be accountable. Chemists should "respect and maintain the confidentiality of the employer's trade secrets" (Chalk et al. 1980: 178); architects should "guard equally the interests of the contractor as well as those of the client" (Cummings 1955: 10); lawyers owe their clients "absolute candor, unswerving fidelity, and undivided allegiance" (Drinker 1955: 45). Archaeologists should "actively support conservation of the archaeological resource base" (Society of Professional Archaeologists 1976).

These lists are very useful in describing the fundamental principles of a profession to outsiders, and function to define group norms much as the Boy Scout's Code does. Virtually none of these lists guides the professional in choosing between items on the list, which is where most conflicts arise (Chalk et al. 1980: 102). All items on the list are presumed to be of equal importance; decision criteria are in the realm of personal opinions. Appeals to "knowledge," "science," and other abstractions are expected to resolve conflicts between listed responsibilities (see, e.g., Meighan 1982).

Lists of responsibilities also change through time, responding to changes in the "social, economic, and political environment" of the particular discipline (Chalk et al. 1980: 103). Thus, the search for *a* code of ethics in any profession is futile. The conflict between modern medical practice and ethical prohibitions on abortion contained in the 2500-year-old Hippocratic Oath are well known. Less well known, but equally instructive, is the 1979 reformulation of the code of ethics for archivists as a result of the blurring of formerly distinct lines between "archivists" and "manuscript curators" (Society of American Archivists 1979). The new code explicitly recognizes potential conflicts between corporate archivists and their employers. The former are responsible for maintaining the research potential of documents under their care; the latter may wish to destroy documents that could be embarrassing or contain evidence of illegal activities. Again, although the list recognizes that multiple responsibilities exist, it contains no criteria to help the archivist choose among them.

Such conflict-ridden situations are new to archaeologists and cause much anguish within the profession (see Plog 1980). From an historical and comparative perspective, these situations develop when the "accountability equation" is expanded beyond abstractions and collegial relations with professional peers—that is, when decisions between conflicting priorities have "real world" consequences. Given that an archaeologist has responsibilities both to apply scientific research methods to human skeletal material and to respect contemporary Native American feelings about dignity of human burial, what rules guide the archaeologist's choice? Is it possible for two archaeologists to be equally "ethical," while resolving such a conflict in different ways? This is the essence of the third question now facing archaeologists.

What Is an Appropriate Level of Accountability?

In some professions, this queston is answerable in the courts: alleged wrongdoers are subject to civil or criminal proceedings, fines, loss of license to practice, and a host of lesser sanctions. A "wrong" decision by a practitioner (that is, one not in accordance with the current code) thus has serious "real world" consequences, especially in professions such as engineering and law. The purpose of such sanctions is to protect the public (and, ultimately, the reputation of the profession) from the actions of quacks, incompetents, and crooks.

Such remedies are not available in the humanities and social sciences. Almost none of the pertinent learned or professional societies have adopted internal rules to guide a member to the "right" choice among competing responsibilities, and none has a legally enforceable mechanism that prevents violators of the code from continuing to practice their craft. Some groups, including historians, geographers, and archivists, either have no ethical code at all or no means of implementing it (Chalk et al. 1980).

The problem with existing ethical codes for archaeologists, including that of the Society of Professional Archaeologists, is precisely that they provide no guidance in answering this third important question. A subscriber to the code (i.e., a member of the group) can be sanctioned for violating one portion of it, but the choice about which item on the list should receive highest priority is by and large left to personal discretion. Although ethnographers doing fieldwork are told they owe primary responsibility to the people they study, their only option when faced with a conflict between that requirement and security restrictions is to refuse to do the research (Chalk et al. 1980); some archaeologists apparently espouse similar solutions to resolving conflicts, as Meighan (1982) illustrates (See also the essay by D. Fowler in this volume—ed.).

Clearly, the proper level of general accountability in any profession cannot be determined in the absence of guiding methods and criteria. If general criteria cannot be developed, how is an individual to be guided in specific cases? It is one thing to state that sociologists must not "use faculty powers to gain sexual favors" from students or that chemists should "apply only for those positions in which [they] have a sincere interest" (Chalk et al. 1980), but quite another to require that archaeologists should "be sensitive to" Native American concerns (Society of Professional Archaeologists 1982). How is the "ethical" archaeologist to translate this requirement into action?

In fact, most current controversy about archaeological "ethics" revolves around defining the proper level of accountability in specific cases. Given the tendency of archaeologists to theorize and generalize, it is no wonder that this issue is so thorny. Like anthropologists, perhaps archaeologists should recognize that a kind of cultural relativism operates in ethics, as elsewhere in archaeological method and theory: that is, there may exist a set of equally equitable, applicable, and ethical decisions for a given category of conflicts. The "right" answer may depend on the specific circumstances of time, place, and individual participants in the conflict.

As with the other two basic ethical questions, solutions to these problems will not be forthcoming until they affect "real world" activities—that is, until the answers *matter*. Recent events suggest that the level of accountability now is a question that matters to archaeologists, and the example of other professions suggests that archaeologists now will make the effort to develop methods for answering it.

Conclusion

As the preceding discussion shows, the search for an ethic in archaeology is neither new nor completed. Archaeology lags behind most of the more established "applied" disciplines, but is ahead of most of the other humanities and social sciences in the search for answers to the moral and ethical dilemmas that assail members of any profession in the contemporary world. This world is one of competing and conflicting values that generate moral perplexities on an unprecedented scale. At least archaeologists now are beginning to realize the nature of the important questions and to grope toward answers.

This first step is important for several reasons. First, most writers on professional ethics agree that a major purpose for a written ethical code is to inculcate group spirit among the members of a profession, especially students and new professionals. Now that archaeology is outgrowing its guild structure, it is essential to foster that kind of group identity in an increasingly diverse and disarticulated social environment.

Second, codes of ethics and standards of conduct and practice are useful devices to communicate a more uniform set of expectations to outsiders, such as clients, employers, funding agencies, and the public. By compiling formal lists of educational requirements, acceptable business practices, and the nature of "professional" behavior, group boundaries can be defined and operationalized. Thus, the group enhances its visibility and stature in the public eye, and changes from a guild to a profession, just as many other former guilds have done. In this way, practitioners of a profession, and the profession itself, become legitimatized.

The third and most compelling reason is simply that today the nature of archaeological research has important "real world" implications that it did not 50 or 100 years ago, when it was cloistered in academia. Archaeology has climbed up out of the pit and into the public eye, and archaeologists are enmeshed in issues of public policy that have a direct bearing on the integrity of the profession and the future of their resource (and research) base. As with other disciplines, the addition of nonarchaeological actors to the archaeology drama has led to increased emphasis on ethical codes, and to increased internecine struggle. If comparisons with other disciplines have any meaning, these recent developments suggest that archaeology is in some sense coming of age, with all that that entails. Archaeologists are neither the first nor the last group of scholars to face this problem. In our search for answers, therefore, we are not alone.

2

Approaches to Ethical Problems by Archaeological Organizations

Hester A. Davis

Although discussions of ethical concerns occur at every national archaeological meeting and most regional ones, these are an informal mechanism to deal with the issues. Several professional societies have established formal mechanisms as well; specifically, formalized ethical codes and standards to which their members agree to adhere. The following essay examines the history of formal ethical codes in archaeology, their intended function, and how they have worked.

As one of the founders of the Society of Professional Archaeologists ("SOPA"), Hester Davis was instrumental in drafting the Society's Code of Ethics, Standards for Research, and Disciplinary Procedures.

The standards and codes of the Society of Professional Archaeologists and the American Anthropological Association follow Davis's essay, while the standards of the Society for American Archaeology ("SAA") are reprinted as part of this essay.

PERHAPS THERE IS safety in numbers. Surely it is easier for a group of colleagues to agree that someone's conduct is ethical or unethical than for one righteous individual to challenge another's actions. Traditionally in many professions, it has been through an organizational structure that "codes of ethics" and/or "standards for conduct" have been issued, with greater or lesser effect, follow-through, and prosecution. Traditionally, professional and nonprofessional archaeological organizations have studiously avoided making any but the blandest statements concerning members' behavior. Perhaps no more was needed; we were, as a profession, at a band level of organization (Society for American Archaeology, 1974a). In 1976, however, when the Society of Professional Archaeologists was formed, it issued a Code of Ethics, Standards of Research Performance, and Disciplinary Procedures allowing for review of activities deemed unethical or below standard. The time had come, some felt, to formalize the mechanisms and the ability to review the activities of those who called themselves archaeologists and of others who affected the finite resource base. The idea of establishing standards for conduct is not a new one, of course; the following review traces the history of national, state, and local efforts.

National Organizations

In 1935, the initial Constitution and By-laws of the Society for American Archaeology included the following statements regarding appropriate or ethical behavior by members, and action the Society could take against members whose behavior did not measure up:

> Article I, Section 3: The practice of securing, hoarding, exchanging, buying, or selling of archaeological objects for the sole purpose of individual satisfaction or of personal financial gain is declared contrary to the objects of the Society, and therefore detrimental to the Society.
>
> Article II, Section 7: The Council [of the Society] may drop from the roll of Affiliates and Fellows of the Society anyone who habitually commercializes archaeological objects or sites, or who otherwise has made improper use of his membership, or whose membership is regarded as detrimental to the Society [Society for American Archaeology, 1948: 148].

The latest published version of the SAA By-laws (Society for American Archaeology, 1977: 308–309) contains the following statements:

> Article I, Section 2: The practice of collecting, hoarding, exchanging, buying, or selling archaeological materials for the sole purpose of personal satisfaction or financial gain, and the indiscriminate excavation of archaeological sites are declared contrary to the ideals and objects of the Society.
>
> Article III, Section 4: Membership in the Society shall be denied to any person who violates accepted standards of archaeological conduct by misusing archaeological materials or sites for commercial purposes, or by failing to behave in a responsible manner with respect to the archaeological record.
>
> Article III, Section 10: The Executive Committee may, by three-quarters vote, remove from the membership rolls any member whose acts are contrary to the ideals, objects, and accepted standards of the Society as set forth in Article I and Article III, Section 4, or who otherwise makes improper use of membership in the Society. The action of the Executive Committee may be subject to an appeal to the Society at its Annual Meeting.

What, then, are the ideals, objects, and "accepted standards" to which members should refer in judging behavior? Article I of the By-laws, published in 1977, addresses this issue:

> Article I, Section 1: The objects of the Society shall be to promote and to stimulate interest and research in the archaeology of the American continents; to encourage a more rational public appreciation of the aims and limitations of archaeological research; to serve as a bond among those interested in American Archaeology, both professionals and nonprofessionals, and to aid in directing their efforts into more scientific channels; to publish and to encourage the publication of their results; to foster the formation and welfare of local archaeological societies; to advocate and to aid in the conservation of archaeological data; to discourage commercialism in the archaeological field and to work for its elimination [Society for American Archaeology, 1977: 308].

Presumably actions contrary to any of the above "objects" (e.g., discouraging publication, encouraging commercialism) would be grounds for the Executive Committee to consider removal of an individual from the membership rolls. There is no indication as to where one might go to learn of "accepted standards." In addition, the documentation of improper or irresponsible behavior is not indicated; one presumes that anyone can present information for the Executive Committee's consideration. To the best of this writer's knowledge, however, no member has ever been removed from the membership rolls of the SAA by action of the Executive Committee under Article III, Section 10, or similar earlier versions. The Executive Committee *has* been asked to "look into" actions which were considered questionable or possibly unethical by another member, but no information as to the nature of these inquiries is available in the published minutes of the Executive Committee.

The Society did publish some guidelines for "accepted standards" in 1961 (Champe et al. 1961: 137–138), after almost 10 years of debate on the part of the Executive Committee and the membership at annual meetings. Its effort, titled "Four Statements for Archaeology," is quoted in full here:

FOUR STATEMENTS FOR ARCHAEOLOGY

1. The Field of Archaeology

> Archaeology, a branch of the science of anthropology, is that area of scholarship concerned with the reconstruction of past human life and culture. Its primary data lie in material objects and their relationships; of equal importance may be ancillary data from other fields, including geology, biology, and history.

2. Methods in Archaeology

> Archaeological research depends on systematic collection of material objects together with adequate records of the circumstances of the finds and relationships among objects and their surroundings. Value attaches to objects so collected because of their status as documents, and is not intrinsic. Therefore, collecting practices which destroy data and thus prevent the scholarly goal of archaeology are censured.

Explicit permission of the property owner must be secured before excavation is undertaken. State and federal statutes regarding preservation of antiquities and permits for excavation must be scrupulously observed.

Field techniques aim at preserving all recoverable information by means of adequate descriptive records and diagrams. Although archaeologists may take only a limited sample from a site, the collection should include all classes of artifacts encountered, not excluding any category; all pertinent data, including relationships and associations; samples of faunal remains; and other data to be interpreted by scientists in other fields. The archaeologist does not discard classes of information in favor of a special interest.

Certain basic field records must be kept, including the following: (1) A map of the site showing the surface features of the site and environs as well as the location and extent of the digging. (2) Detailed written records and maps of burials, houses, and other structural or natural features, known or assumed to have significance in the cultural history of the site. (3) Stratigraphic relationships of data must be noted and preserved, either through separation in natural soil layers or by arbitrary levels established during digging. (4) A catalogue of all the specimens found indicating their location, stratum of origin, and cultural association. Specimens should be labelled, numbered, and catalogued to preserve their identity as scientific data. (5) Photographs, drawings, and other documentation necessary to clarify the technique of the work and the context and associations of the finds.

Disregard of proper archaeological methods provides grounds for expulsion from the Society for American Archaeology, at the discretion of the Executive Committee.

3. Ethics for Archaeology

Collections made by competent archaeologists must be available for examination by qualified scholars; relevant supporting data must also be accessible for study whether the collection is in a museum or other institution or in private hands.

It is the scholarly obligation of the archaeologist to report his findings in a recognized scientific medium. In the event that significance of the collection does not warrant publication, a manuscript report should be prepared and be available.

Inasmuch as the buying and selling of artifacts usually results in the loss of context and cultural associations, the practice is censured.

An archaeological site presents problems which must be handled by the excavator according to a plan. Therefore, members of the Society for American Archaeology do not undertake excavations on any site being studied by someone without the prior knowledge and consent of that person.

Willful destruction, distortion, or concealment of the data of archaeology is censured, and provides grounds for expulsion from the Society for American Archaeology, at the discretion of the Executive Committee.

4. Recommendations for Training in Archaeology

Archaeology is a scholarly discipline requiring knowledge of field techniques, competence in laboratory analysis of specimens, and the ability to

> prepare a detailed report of the investigations and their implications in archaeology. In times past, a number of leading archaeologists have acquired the necessary skills without formal training, but they, as well as archaeologists trained in scholarly techniques, have spent years in the study of archaeology as a science. The Society for American Archaeology condemns uncontrolled excavation by persons who have not been trained in the basic techniques of field archaeology and scholarship.
>
> The Society for American Archaeology recommends the following formal training as a minimum qualification for persons planning to enter archaeology as a career. Individuals engaging in archaeology as a profession should acquire the B.A. or B.Sc. degree from an accredited college or university, followed by two years of graduate study with concentration in anthropology and specialization in archaeology during one of those programs. This formal training should be supplemented by at least two summer field schools or their equivalent under the supervision of archaeologists of recognized competence. A Master's thesis or equivalent in published reports is highly recommended. A Ph.D. in anthropology is recommended but not required.

Not only are some "standards" given here, particularly for fieldwork and for training, but certain things are specifically singled out for special action by the Society: "collecting practices which destroy data and thus prevent the scholarly goal of archaeology *are censured*"; "disregard of proper archaeological methods *provides grounds for expulsion* from the Society"; "buying and selling of artifacts . . . *is censured*"; "Willful destruction, distortion, or concealment of the data of archaeology *is censured,* and *provides grounds for expulsion* from the Society"; and finally, "The Society for American Archaeology *condemns* uncontrolled excavation by persons who have not been trained" (emphasis by author). At the very least, then, the SAA provides its members with some measures of performance, gives an inkling of what is "right and wrong" in archaeological pursuits, and gives the Executive Committee the authority to expel a member.

The records of other national archaeological societies vary. For example, the American Society for Conservation Archaeology, founded in 1974, has essentially adopted the same wording as the SAA's for its Constitution and By-laws. On the other hand, the Society for Historical Archaeology, founded in 1967, makes no mention of unethical behavior and provides no mechanism for chastising its members for wrongdoing.

Until recently, then, general statements on ethical behavior and standards have sufficed for archaeologists. Control presumably was administered socially, or academically, by word of mouth, or through the good-ol'-boy-or-girl-network. In practice, however, very few people publically accused colleagues of unethical behavior for fear of professional or legal reprisals. As competition for jobs, research data, and even sites increased, and as more and more people with varying motivations and levels of training began calling themselves archaeologists, the need for more formal "control" was recognized. The idea of certifying archaeologists was considered at length by one of the SAA-sponsored seminars at the Airlie House in 1974 (McGimsey and Davis 1977: 97–105), and the SAA appointed an ad hoc committee on standards to pursue the concept. The members of this committee founded the Society of Professional Archaeologists. Only those meeting certain criteria were admitted to membership, all had to sign an agreement to abide by the published Code of Ethics and Standards of Research Performance, and a detailed procedure for review of alleged violations of the Code and/or the Standards was issued.

So now there is a detailed, defined formality available to guide ethical behavior in archaeology and a "due process" procedure to protect the accused and the accusor. The formal mechanisms for quality control in archaeological research are available—and what has been the result? Have we indeed reached the level of social organization to make these mechanisms necessary? After five years, 15–20 grievances have been filed, and one case has been taken to the Standards Board for a hearing. Of course, only those who have signed the agreement to abide by the Code and Standards can be held accountable to the Board, but the process is being used and it is working; the profession is indeed beginning to police itself. It is a slow process, however; no one likes to blow the whistle on a colleague.

Perhaps SOPA should have added another "thou shalt not" to its list: "Thou shalt not let go unreported any instance of behavior in violation of this Code." The threat of public censure is a powerful incentive for ethical behavior. The fact that accusation can result in huge financial indebtedness may account in part for the slowness with which archaeologists are taking advantage of the mechanisms for identification of unethical behavior. Powerful pressure can be applied through the screws of social control; but when applied through formal peer review as is available through SOPA, the pressure seems even more effective.

State Archaeological Councils

Most of these organizations, largely made up of practicing archaeologists, have been formed within the last five years, again with an eye to providing peer review for the greatly increased volume of archaeological research in each state. Many have adopted SOPA's Code and Standards verbatim; some have modified them to fit their own situations. Only one, to the best of this writer's knowledge, has a constituted Ethics Committee—the New Mexico Archaeological Council. Others may have ad hoc ethics committees. State investigations of individual cases of ethical violations have been made by both the New Mexico Archaeological Council and the Missouri Association of Professional Archaeologists. But formal procedures and accepted mechanisms for judgments are still undergoing modification in all known cases. For purposes of review of documentation of unethical behavior, the state councils and SOPA have some parallel and equally valid mechanisms.

State Archaeological Societies

State archaeological societies, made up largely of amateur archaeologists but with some professional members, have somewhat different views, approaches, and problems with regard to treatment of and attitude toward archaeological resources, and particularly archaeological objects. What often separates the "good guys" from the "bad guys" is their approach to the buying and selling of artifacts at meetings. It is obvious from the previous quotes that the national organizations consider this activity unethical. Most state archaeological societies specifically disallow this at meetings but do not mention the activity as something which might influence individual membership. Several societies have experienced problems with misuse of membership cards (i.e., individuals gaining access to land by showing their card, thereby intimating some greater amount of training and/or "official" association than was actually the case). One society took care of this problem by ceasing to issue membership cards.

Several societies have broad "ethical" statements in their constitution or by-laws which offer some behavioral guidance, but many do not. Many of those with guiding statements do not indicate how accusations might be handled. Two examples of state societies which have made an effort to be explicit on ethical behavior and/or provide details on due process in case of accusation are Texas and California. These are worthy of examining in some detail:

Article VII of the Texas Archaeological Society's Constitution and By-laws, which is entitled "Ethics," states:

> Violation of the terms and conditions of any Texas Antiquities Statutes, as the same now exist, or shall be hereafter amended or enacted; the practice of buying and selling artifacts for commercial purposes; the disregard of proper archaeological field techniques; and the willful destruction or distortion of archaeological data, are censured and will provide grounds for expulsion from the Society upon the three-fourths vote of a quorum of the Board of Directors . . . .

There follows a lengthy detail of due process. As far as is known, only one person has had a hearing before the Board for ethical violation in the history of this Society, and that was 20 years ago.

The Society for California Archaeology has a statement on its application form indicating, "I have read the provisions of the Code of Ethics on the reverse side of this page and agree to abide by them." The preamble to the Code, which is actually called a "Code of Ethical Guidelines," states:

> Whereas, it is not the intent of the Society for California Archaeology to violate the constitutional rights of any member or citizen of the United States of America, the following guidelines shall be adhered to by the Society for California Archaeology (SCA) membership (universities and institutions included) to advise the most ethical courses of action in the various archaeological matters which may arise.

The Code includes "Ethical Responsibility to the Public," "Ethical Responsibility to Colleagues," "A Code of Scientific Ethics," and "A Code of Ethical and Professional Standards." Each section has a series of "an archaeologist shall . . ." and "an archaeologist shall not . . ." statements, similar to that of SOPA.

At the time of this writing, the Florida Anthropology Society was considering a "Statement of Ethical Responsibilities" which would be included in its Articles of Incorporation and By-laws. One section reads:

> No member shall undertake any research for which he/she is not qualified, but should seek to aid and assist the trained or professional members in the furtherance of archaeological survey, excavation, laboratory analysis, record-keeping, and other aspects of information gathering, etc.

The editor of a local archaeological newsletter in Florida (*Sun Coast Archaeological and Paleontological Society Bulletin* 14 [3]) has this response:

> As for the word "qualified" in this guideline, what we would like to know is this: Just who determines who is or is not qualified to conduct archaeological excavations, site surveys, record keeping, research, etc.? *Research,* for their information, is the *God-given right of every individual* of any age of reason who is desirous of furthering their knowledge in any subject, science, or whatever! According to our legal sources, there can be no plausible excuse or explanation for the inclusion of such unrealistic, dictatorial, and unconstitutional requirements in these articles. . . .
>
> Lest they forget, F.A.S. is not S.O.P.A. . . ., where stringent guidelines for standards of professional performance are a prerequisite to membership! It is, instead, a symbiotic organization whose very existence is dependent upon the goodwill and membership of its predominant avocational archaeologists!"

This reaction is actually not far different from that of some professional archaeologists when the idea of certification first was suggested. The predominantly amateur organizations must be willing to deal with differences of opinion stemming from different views of archaeological data (the public versus the private, in essence). In fact, agreement on appropriate behavior relative to archaeological resources already has been reached in many state archaeological societies. The trauma of documentation and review of inappropriate behavior in the context of state societies has almost never occurred.

Summary and Conclusion

By and large, national, state, and local archaeological organizations have some general statements to guide their members in ethical behavior, but the development and implementation of mechanisms for the review of unethical behavior have been slow. Only the Society of Professional Archaeologists requires signed agreement to a code and provides a specific mechanism for reviewing violations to that code.

It certainly seems appropriate for professional organizations to take responsibility for the behavior of their members. Considering that some unethical behavior actually destroys finite scientific data, it is a wonder that it has taken professional archaeologists so long to provide themselves with a workable measure of performance with some teeth in it. On the other hand, public censure or expulsion from membership in a professional organization could mean the end to a professional career, and that action is not to be taken lightly by an accusor or an organization. The SOPA due process procedures, and those known for state and local organizations, are reflective of a democratic society where one's peers review documentation and make judgments. It is the best system we know of; it should be used when it is needed; it has worked when it has been used.

3

Code of Ethics

Society of Professional Archaeologists

1. The Archeologist's Responsibility to the Public
   1.1 An archeologist shall:
      (a) Recognize a commitment to represent archeology and its research results to the public in a responsible manner;
      (b) Actively support conservation of the archeological resource base;
      (c) Be sensitive to, and respect the legitimate concerns of, groups whose culture histories are the subjects of archeological investigations;
      (d) Avoid and discourage exaggerated, misleading, or unwarranted statements about archeological matters that might induce others to engage in unethical or illegal activity;
      (e) Support and comply with the terms of the UNESCO Convention on the means of prohibiting and preventing the illicit import, export, and transfer of ownership of cultural property, as adopted by the General Conference, 14 November 1970, Paris.
   1.2 An archeologist shall *not*:
      (a) Engage in any illegal or unethical conduct involving archeological matters or knowingly permit the use of her/his name in support of any illegal or unethical activity involving archeological matters;
      (b) Give a professional opinion, make a public report, or give legal testimony involving archeological matters without being as thoroughly informed as might reasonably be expected;
      (c) Engage in conduct involving dishonesty, fraud, deceit or misrepresentation about archeological matters;
      (d) Undertake any research that affects the archeological resource base for which he/she is not qualified.
2. The Archeologist's Responsibility to her/his Colleagues
   2.1 An archeologist shall:
      (a) Give appropriate credit for work done by others;
      (b) Stay informed and knowledgeable about developments in his/her field or fields of specialization;

First published in 1976 and reprinted by permission of the Society of Professional Archaeologists.

(c) Accurately, and without undue delay, prepare and properly disseminate a description of research done and its results:

(d) Communicate and cooperate with colleagues having common professional interests;

(e) Give due respect to colleagues' interests in, and rights to, information about sites, areas, collections, or data where there is a mutual active or potentially active research concern;

(f) Know and comply with all laws applicable to her/his archeological research, as well as with any relevant procedures promulgated as duly constituted professional organizations;

(g) Report knowledge of violations of this Code to proper authorities.

2.2 An archeologist shall *not*:

(a) Falsely or maliciously attempt to injure the reputation of another archeologist;

(b) Commit plagiarism in oral or written communication;

(c) Undertake research that affects the archeological resource base unless reasonably prompt, appropriate analysis and reporting can be expected;

(d) Refuse a reasonable request from a qualified colleague for research data;

(e) Submit a false or misleading application for accreditation by or membership in the Society of Professional Archeologists.

3. The Archeologist's Responsibility to Employers and Clients

3.1 An archeologist shall:

(a) Respect the interests of his/her employer or client, so far as is consistent with the public welfare and this Code and Standards;

(b) Refuse to comply with any request or demand of an employer or client which conflicts with the Code and Standards;

(c) Recommend to employers or clients the employment of other archeologists or other expert consultants upon encountering archeological problems beyond her/his own competence;

(d) Exercise reasonable care to prevent his/her employees, colleagues, associates and others whose services are utilized by her/him from revealing or using confidential information. Confidential information means information of a non-archeological nature gained in the course of employment which the employer or client has requested be held inviolate, or the disclosure of which would be embarrassing or would be likely to be detrimental to the employer or client. Information ceases to be confidential when the employer or client so indicates or when such information becomes publicly known.

3.2 An archeologist shall *not*:
(a) Reveal confidential information, unless required by law;
(b) Use confidential information to the disadvantage of the client or employer;
(c) Use confidential information for the advantage of himself/-herself or a third person, unless the client consents after full disclosure;
(d) Accept compensation or anything of value for recommending the employment of another archeologist or other person, unless such compensation or thing of value is fully disclosed to the potential employer or client;
(e) Recommend or participate in any research which does not comply with the requirements of the Standards of Research Performance.

4

Standards of Research Performance

Society of Professional Archaeologists

THE RESEARCH ARCHEOLOGIST has a responsibility to attempt to design and conduct projects that will add to our understanding of past cultures and/or that will develop better theories, methods, or techniques for interpreting the archeological record, while causing minimal attrition of the archeological resource base. In the conduct of a research project, the following minimum standards should be followed:

1. The archeologist has a responsibility to prepare adequately for any research project whether or not in the field. The archeologist must:
   - 1.1 Assess the adequacy of her/his qualifications for the demands of the project, and minimize inadequacies by acquiring additional expertise, by bringing in associates with the needed qualifications, or by modifying the scope of the project:
   - 1.2 Inform himself/herself of relevant previous research;
   - 1.3 Develop a scientific plan of research which specifies the objectives of the project, takes into account previous relevant research, employs a suitable methodology, and provides for economical use of the resource base (whether such base consists of an excavation site or of specimens), consistent with the objectives of the project;
   - 1.4 Ensure the availability of adequate staff and support facilities to carry the project to completion, and of adequate curatorial facilities for specimens and records;
   - 1.5 Comply with all legal requirements, including, without limitation, obtaining all necessary governmental permits and necessary permission from landowners or other persons;
   - 1.6 Determine whether the project is likely to interfere with the program or projects of other scholars and if there is such a likelihood, initiate negotiations to minimize such interference.
2. In conducting research, the archeologist must follow her/his scientific plan of research, except to that extent that unforeseen circumstances warrant its modification.

First published in 1976 and reprinted by permission of the Society of Professional Archaeologists.

3. Procedures for field survey or excavation must meet the following minimal standards:
   3.1 If specimens are collected, a system for identifying and recording their proveniences must be maintained.
   3.2 Uncollected entities such as environmental or cultural features, depositional strata, and the like, must be fully and accurately recorded by appropriate means and their location recorded.
   3.3 The methods employed in data collection must be fully and accurately described. Significant stratigraphic and/or associational relationships among artifacts, other specimens, and cultural and environmental features must also be fully and accurately recorded.
   3.4 All records should be intelligible to other archeologists. If terms lacking commonly held referents are used, they should be clearly defined.
   3.5 Insofar as possible, the interests of other researchers should be considered. For example, upper levels of a site should be scientifically excavated and recorded whenever feasible, even if the focus of the project is on underlying levels.
4. During accessioning, analysis, and storage of specimens and records in the laboratory, the archeologist must take precautions to ensure that correlations between the specimens and the field records are maintained, so that provenience, contextual relationships, and the like are not confused or obscured.
5. Specimens and research records resulting from a project must be deposited at an institution with permanent curatorial facilities.
6. The archeologist has responsibility for appropriate dissemination of the results of his/her research to the appropriate constituencies with reasonable dispatch.
   6.1 Results viewed as significant contributions to substantive knowledge of the past or to advancements in theory, method, or technique should be disseminated to colleagues and other interested persons by appropriate means, such as publications, reports at professional meetings, or letters to colleagues.
   6.2 Requests from qualified colleagues for information on research results ordinarily should be honored, if consistent with the researcher's prior rights to publication and with her/his other professional responsibilities.
   6.3 Failure to complete a full scholarly report within 10 years after completion of a field project shall be construed as a waiver of an archeologist's right of primacy with respect to analysis and publication of the data. Upon expiration of such 10 year period, or at such earlier time as the archeologist shall determine not to publish the results, such data should be made fully accessible for analysis and publication to other archeologists.

6.4 While contractual obligations in reporting must be respected, archeologists should not enter into a contract which prohibits the archeologist from including his or her own interpretations or conclusions in contractual reports, or from a continuing right to use the data after completion of the project.

6.5 Archeologists have an obligation to accede to reasonable requests for information from the news media.

7. Archeologists have a responsibility to prevent the publication of precise site locations whenever such publication might lead to vandalism of the sites.

5

Ethics for Archaeology

Society for American Archaeology

COLLECTIONS MADE BY competent archaeologists must be available for examination by qualified scholars; relevant supporting data must also be accessible for study whether the collection is in a museum or other institution or in private hands.

It is the scholarly obligation of the archaeologist to report his findings in a recognized scientific medium. In the event that significance of the collection does not warrant publication, a manuscript report should be prepared and be available.

Inasmuch as the buying and selling of artifacts usually results in the loss of context and cultural associations, the practice is censured.

An archaeological site presents problems which must be handled by the excavator according to a plan. Therefore, members of the Society for American Archaeology do not undertake excavations on any site being studied by someone without the prior knowledge and consent of that person.

Willful destruction, distortion, or concealment of the data of archaeology is censured, and provides grounds for expulsion from the Society for American Archaeology, at the discretion of the Executive Committee.

From "Four Statements for Archaeology," J. L. Champe et al. 1961, *American Antiquity* 27:137–39. Reprinted by permission of the Society for American Archaeology.

6

Statements on Ethics

Principles of Professional Responsibility

Adopted by the Council of the American
Anthropological Association May 1971

Note: *This statement of principles is not intended to supersede previous statements and resolutions of the Association. Its intent is to clarify professional responsibilities in the chief areas of professional concern to anthropologists.*

Preamble

Anthropologists work in many parts of the world in close personal association with the peoples and situations they study. Their professional situation is, therefore, uniquely varied and complex. They are involved with their discipline, their colleagues, their students, their sponsors, their subjects, their own and host governments, the particular individuals and groups with whom they do their field work, other populations and interest groups in the nations within which they work, and the study of processes and issues affecting general human welfare. In a field of such complex involvements, misunderstandings, conflicts and the necessity to make choices among conflicting values are bound to arise and to generate ethical dilemmas. It is a prime responsibility of anthropologists to anticipate these and to plan to resolve them in such a way as to do damage neither to those whom they study nor, in so far as possible, to their scholarly community. Where these conditions cannot be met, the anthropologist would be well-advised not to pursue the particular piece of research.

The following principles are deemed fundamental to the anthropologist's responsible, ethical pursuit of his profession.

1. Relations with Those Studied

In research, an anthropologist's paramount responsibility is to those he studies. When there is a conflict of interest, these individuals must come first. The anthropologist must do everything within his power to protect their physical, social and psychological welfare and to honor their dignity and privacy.

a. Where research involves the acquisition of material and information transferred on the assumption of trust between persons, it is axiomatic that the rights, interests, and sensitivities of those studied must be safeguarded.
b. The aims of the investigation should be communicated as well as possible to the informant.
c. Informants have a right to remain anonymous. This right should be respected both where it has been promised explicitly and where no clear understanding to the contrary has been reached. These strictures apply to the collection of data by means of cameras, tape recorders, and other data-gathering devices, as well as to data collected in face-to-face interviews or in participant observation. Those being studied should understand the capacities of such devices; they should be free to reject them if they wish; and if they accept them, the results obtained should be consonant with the informant's right to welfare, dignity and privacy.
   Despite every effort being made to preserve anonymity it should be made clear to informants that such anonymity may be compromised unintentionally. (November 1975)
d. There should be no exploitation of individual informants for personal gain. Fair return should be given them for all services.
e. There is an obligation to reflect on the foreseeable repercussions of research and publication on the general population being studied.
f. The anticipated consequences of research should be communicated as fully as possible to the individuals and groups likely to be affected.
g. In accordance with the Association's general position on clandestine and secret research, no reports should be provided to sponsors that are not also available to the general public and, where practicable, to the population studied.
h. Every effort should be exerted to cooperate with members of the host society in the planning and execution of research projects.
i. All of the above points should be acted upon in full recognition of the social and cultural pluralism of host societies and the consequent plurality of values, interests and demands in those societies. This diversity complicates choice-making in research, but ignoring it leads to irresponsible decisions.

2. Responsibility to the Public

The anthropologist is also responsible to the public—all presumed consumers of his professional efforts. To them he owes a commitment to candor and to truth in the dissemination of his research results and in the statement of his opinions as a student of man.

a. He should not communicate his findings secretly to some and withhold them from others.
b. He should not knowningly falsify or color his findings.
c. In providing professional opinions, he is responsible not only for their content but also for integrity in explaining both these opinions and their bases.
d. As people who devote their professional lives to understanding man, anthropologists bear a positive responsibility to speak out publicly, both individually and collectively, on what they know and what they believe as a result of their professional expertise gained in the study of human beings. That is, they bear a professional responsibility to contribute to an "adequate definition of reality" upon which public opinion and public policy may be based.
e. In public discourse, the anthropologist should be honest about his qualifications and cognizant of the limitations of anthropological expertise.

3. Responsibility to the Discipline

An anthropologist bears responsibility for the good reputation of his discipline and its practitioners.

a. He should undertake no secret research or any research whose results cannot be freely derived and publicly reported.
b. He should avoid even the appearance of engaging in clandestine research, by fully and freely disclosing the aims and sponsorship of all his research.
c. He should attempt to maintain a level of integrity and rapport in the field such that by his behavior and example he will not jeopardize future research there. The responsibility is not to analyze and report so as to offend no one, but to conduct research in a way consistent with a commitment to honesty, open inquiry, clear communication of sponsorships and research aims, and concern for the welfare and privacy of informants.
d. He should not present as his own work, either in speaking or writing, materials directly taken from other sources. (October 1974)
e. When he participates in actions related to hiring, retention and advancement, he should ensure that no exclusionary practices

be perpetuated against colleagues on the basis of sex, marital status, color, social class, religion, ethnic background, national origin, or other non-academic attributes. He should, furthermore, refrain from transmitting and resist the use of information irrelevant to professional performance in such personal actions. (November 1975)

4. Responsibility to Students

In relations with students an anthropologist should be candid, fair, non-exploitative and committed to their welfare and academic progress.

As Robert Lekachman has suggested, honesty is the essential quality of a good teacher; neutrality is not. Beyond honest teaching, the anthropologist as a teacher has ethical responsibilities in selection, instruction in ethics, career counseling, academic supervision, evaluation, compensation and placement.

a. He should select students in such a way as to preclude discrimination on the basis of sex, race, ethnic group, social class and other categories of people indistinguishable by their intellectual potential.
b. He should alert students to the ethical problems of research and discourage them from participating in projects employing questionable ethical standards. This should include providing them with information and discussions to protect them from unethical pressures and enticements emanating from possible sponsors, as well as helping them to find acceptable alternatives (see point i below).
c. He should be receptive and seriously responsive to students' interests, opinions and desires in all aspects of their academic work and relationships.
d. He should realistically counsel students regarding career opportunities.
e. He should conscientiously supervise, encourage and support students in their anthropological and other academic endeavors.
f. He should inform students of what is expected of them in their course of study. He should be fair in the evaluation of their performance. He should communicate evaluations to the students concerned.
g. He should acknowledge in print the student assistance he uses in his own publications, give appropriate credit (including co-authorship) when student research is used in publication, encourage and assist in publication of worthy student papers, and compensate students justly for the use of their time, energy and intelligence in research and teaching.

h. He should energetically assist students in securing legitimate research support and the necessary permissions to pursue research.
i. He should energetically assist students in securing professional employment upon completion of their studies.
j. He should strive to improve both our techniques of teaching and our techniques for evaluating the effectiveness of our methods of teaching.

5. Responsibility to Sponsors

In his relations with sponsors of research, an anthropologist should be honest about his qualifications, capabilities and aims. He thus faces the obligation, prior to entering any commitment for research, to reflect sincerely upon the purposes of his sponsors in terms of their past behavior. He should be especially careful not to promise or imply acceptance of conditions contrary to his professional ethics or competing commitments. This requires that he require of the sponsor full disclosure of the sources of funds, personnel, aims of the institution and the research project, and disposition of research results. He must retain the right to make all ethical decisions in his research. He should enter into no secret agreement with the sponsor regarding the research, results or reports.

6. Responsibilities to One's Own Government and to Host Governments

In his relation with his own government and with host governments, the research anthropologist should be honest and candid. He should demand assurance that he will not be required to compromise his professional responsibilities and ethics as a condition of his permission to pursue the research. Specifically, no secret research, no secret reports or debriefings of any kind should be agreed to or given. If these matters are clearly understood in advance, serious complications and misunderstandings can generally be avoided.

Epilogue

In the final analysis, anthropological research is a human undertaking, dependent upon choices for which the individual bears ethical as well as scientific responsibility. That responsibility is a human, not superhuman, responsibility. To err is human, to forgive humane. This statement of principles of professional responsibility is not designed to punish, but to provide guidelines which can minimize the occasions upon which there is a need to forgive. When an anthropologist, by his actions, jeopardizes peoples studied, professional colleagues, students or others, or if he otherwise betrays his professional commitments, his colleagues may legitimately inquire into the propriety of those actions, and take such measures as lie within the legitimate powers of their Association as the membership of the Association deems appropriate.

Addenda

The following amendments to the Principles of Professional Responsibility have been approved by the Council of the American Anthropological Association:

1. Relations with those studied:
   - c.(1) Despite every effort being made to preserve anonymity it should be made clear to informants that such anonymity may be compromised unintentionally. (November 1975)
   - c.(2) When professionals or others have used pseudonyms to maintain anonymity, others should respect this decision and the reasons for it by not revealing indiscriminately the true identity of such committees, persons or other data. (May 1976)

3. Responsibility to the discipline:
   - d. He should not present as his own work, either in speaking or writing, materials directly taken from other sources. (October 1974)
   - e. When he participates in actions related to hiring, retention and advancement, he should ensure that no exclusionary practices be perpetuated against colleagues on the basis of sex, marital status, color, social class, religion, ethnic background, national origin, or other non-academic attributes. He should, furthermore, refrain from transmitting and resist the use of information irrelevant to professional performance in such personnel actions. (November 1975)

The Role and Function of the Committee on Ethics has been amended by the Council as follows:

- (i) Grievance Procedure:
  - (3)(c) If in the opinion of a majority of the Committee there exists a probable cause for action involving a genuine and serious instance of questionable ethics in terms of policies and standards of the Association, the Committee would recommend that further action be taken by the Board. (May 1976)

The Grievance Procedures have been amended by the Executive Board as follows:

1. Notification of all Parties to the Complaint

   The chairperson shall send Form Letter #2 (see Appendix B) and a copy of the complaint to those individuals whom the COE has identified as parties to the complaint. This is the case where the complaint is to be pursued further by the COE. In the event the complaint will not be pursued further by the COE because the alleged violation occurred before the pertinent standard had been adopted by the AAA, or no pertinent standard could be identified by the Preliminary Analysis Subcommittee or some other reason, the complaint will be transmitted to the Executive Board with COE's recommendation and a draft response to the complainant. (November 1976)

7

The Way to Somewhere: Ethics in American Archaeology

Joseph C. Winter

"Would you tell me, please, which way I ought to go from here?"
"That depends a good deal on where you want to get to,"
said the Cat.
"I don't much care where," said Alice.
"Then it doesn't matter which way you go,"
said the Cat [*Carroll 1960: 88*].

What role do an investigator's ethics and values play in the study of human behavior and the interpretation of the material remains of that behavior? Most archaeologists think that their observations record a reality which is discoverable and knowable through sensory perception outside their personal value system. We think that our interpretations of these data, after we have observed them, are based on a rigorous, unbiased thought process and scientific approach.

Although we rarely do so, it is worth asking to what extent our values influence our scientific investigations, the research questions we pose, the explanations of reality we accept, and how we perceive and relate to reality. Specifically, to what extent do our ethical systems and value constructs affect our performance of archaeology? These issues are the subject of the following essay.

IN *A Philosopher Looks At Science* (1959), John Kemeny argues that Alice's question and the Cat's answer express "precisely the eternal cleavage between science and ethics" (Gardner 1960: 89). Science cannot tell us where to go, Kemeny concludes, but once the decision is made because of economic, religious, political, or other reasons that are based on value statements, it can tell us the way to get there. This interpretation of the role of ethics is as valid for archaeology as it is for nuclear physics, genetic engineering, or any other field of scientific endeavor—more so, perhaps, since archaeology is a social science in which human behavior is studied by researchers who possess all of the frailties, emotions, and other limitations of the very subjects they are investigating.

Ethics include any and all sets of moral principles and values that govern individual and group behavior (White 1959: 216). At the group level, ethics are the laws, mores, traditions, and other codes that regulate individual actions and maintain group welfare. At the individual level, ethics take the form of value statements (e.g., commands, assertions, conclusions) that involve right, wrong, desirable, undesirable, good, bad, and related behavior, such as destroying data is wrong. The question of whether something is right or wrong is obviously a preoccupation of humans and our cultures, and every day we make hundreds (if not thousands) of decisions that are based on value statements.

Ethical beliefs differ from scientific assertions, in that the latter can be tested, while it is impossible to demonstrate whether the former are true or false. Also, whereas science is the search for knowledge about general truths or laws through the formulation and testing of hypotheses, ethical (or moral) philosophy is the search for the principles that underlie value statements and the reasons for their existence. Science is concerned with developing methods that examine reality; ethical theory is concerned with how humans view the nature of reality, why they attach values to it, and their behavior in relation to it.

Schools of Ethical Theory

Although there is very little agreement among ethical philosophers about definitions, questions, assumptions, and similar matters, there are six basic schools of ethical theory, at least as defined by Hill (1950). These theories range from a total denial of the intelligible meaning of value statements, to a social process view of ethics, to theological, metaphysical, and intuitive theories that refer moral concepts to deities or immutable principles. The skeptical end of the continuum asserts that there are no logical meanings to value statements, since they are emotive expressions and the products of irrational impulses. Certain ways of behaving are more sensible than others, but for the logical positivists and other skeptics there are no "real" underlying meanings to moral standards.

While the skeptics deny that there are any absolute meanings to value statements, they are aware of the relationship between ethics and authority. This identification of morals with moral judges is the basis of approbative ethical philosophies. As interpreted by these philosophies, morals and other values serve a very practical purpose: they guide our actions, which are always based on someone's or some institution's approval (or disapproval). For Durkheim (1933) and other social approbative theorists, the approval and disapproval of society form the basis of ethics and determine individual behavior. For most of the world's religions and the theological approbative theorists, it is the omniscient approval of deities and other supernatural beings that guides us.

In contrast to the skeptical and approbative philosophies, process ethical schools of thought argue that good, bad, and other value statements possess an objective existence apart from emotions, humans, and gods. For some "processual" theorists, the reality of goodness takes the form of goals toward which individual humans, cultures, and/or species progress. For others, the unfolding process of life itself and our basic humanity constitute the good. Despite their differences, all process theorists share in the belief that the basic meaning of value statements can be found in vital, ongoing processes. Obvious examples are the evolutionary and Marxist schools; others include the pragmatists and humanists. For Darwin (1876: 612), Spencer (1895: 15), Huxley (1929: 52–53), and other early evolutionists, the whole process of human evolution can be viewed in ethical terms. Morgan (1877), Tylor (1871), Frazer (1914), and more recent evolutionary archaeologists, such as White (1959), also associate the progression of ethics with the progressive evolution of cultures. Because of their influence on archaeology, White's views will be discussed in more detail later.

Humanistic ethical theories include a wide range of views, all of which share the belief that the meaning of right, good, and other value statements can best be understood in relation to basic human processes and lives. The philosophers of the Enlightenment and Renaissance viewed humanism as an ethical system concerned with the interests, achievements, and dignity of human beings, rather than with abstract beings and theological problems, or with organic and social human processes. For others, such as Fite (1924), the individual and his or her needs and relationships are the basis of value systems, with egoistic motivation the primary moral determinant.

Closely related and developing out of humanism is the school of ethical thought which proposes that good refers to desire, feeling, and other psychological states, while right involves their promotion. For the hedonists, something is good if it promotes pleasure; for the affective theorists, goodness lies in the satisfaction of a variety of desires besides pleasure.

The metaphysical and intuitive schools of ethical theory believe that goodness, evil, and other values possess an absolute existence outside of the approval of society or gods, and human goals. The metaphysical theorists believe that goodness is associated with a Natural Law, and that the Absolute *is* Goodness. In human terms, good and right consist in fulfilling one's being and self-hood. Finally, most metaphysical philosophers believe that the eternal Self is reproduced in the finite, individual self.

The intuitive theorists link the ends of the continuum by agreeing with the skeptics that it is impossible to understand the meaning of goodness and other values, but by nonetheless asserting the existence of values. Right, wrong, good, bad, and other values possess a reality yet are irreducible to any definable cause (e.g., natural or cultural processes, the approval of deities, adaptive processes, progress, desire). Rather, they just *are* and thus can be known only through intuition.

Ethics in Archaeology

Broadly speaking, archaeological views of ethics typically fall within two systems of moral philosophy: Approbative and evolutionary. Levy-Bruhl (1905), for example, expanded on Durkheim's theory that society holds the key to morality and attempted to develop a science of morals which described and interpreted the nature, origin, and function of ethical facts. Similarly, Malinowski (1944), Benedict (1946), and many other cultural archaeologists have attempted to determine how various cultures create and control, or at least affect, moral systems. More recently, a number of applied anthropologists have become very concerned with how their own cultural backgrounds affect their professional value systems. Spradley and Rynkiewich (1976), Nash (1976), Maquet (1964), and Nader (1976), for example, have concluded that no anthropologist or other scientist can escape the influence of his or her cultural values and personal biases. Even the choices of what we study and the research priorities our profession sets reflect these underlying values.

Although some anthropologists argue that ethics and the methods and theories of anthropology should be carefully separated, most applied anthropologists believe that it is impossible and undesirable to do so. For Rynkiewich (Spradley and Rynkiewich, 1976), our personal ethics are essential guides for our choices and behavior. For Maquet (1964) and Nash (1976), the scientific attitude of impersonal objectivity should be totally rejected, since our very presence as applied anthropologists means that we are the instruments of someone else's programs. For Bastide (1973), applied anthropology in and of itself is a biased, subjective approach that is merely one aspect of the larger Euro-American strategy of transforming the behavior and reorganizing the cultures of indigenous populations.

This attitude that our own cultural background influences our choices and behavior has been carried over into archaeology through the writings of Fitting, Trigger, and Winter. Fitting (1973: 12) is convinced that archaeological truth is determined by the cultural context in which it occurs, while Trigger (1980: 662) argues that one of the most important factors shaping the long-term development of North American archaeology is the traditional Euro-American stereotyping of Native Americans. The problems that we research and the conclusions that we reach about the development of Indian cultures are influenced by the prevailing views and prejudices in American society concerning Indian cultures. For this author (Winter 1980), cultural resource management itself is a continuation of the centuries-old conflict between the Euro-American and Indian cultures over resources. That is, our cultural resource laws and policies regarding preservation and excavation, our other forms of management of scientifically significant resources, and our perceptions of Indian cultures and sites as objects of study all reflect definite cultural biases. Although the social approbative theorists have had a major impact upon cultural anthropology, which in turn has affected archaeology, the evolutionists—especially White (1959) and other cultural materialists—have had the most effect upon archaeology. Evolutionary theories have affected not only our paradigms and methods, but also our ethical approaches.

As proposed by White (1959: 217), there are two major types of ethical systems: absolutist and relativist. In an absolute system, something is right because it *is* right, regardless of the context or consequences of the situation. Absolute ethical systems are based on absolute truths, which usually have a supernatural basis. Thus lying is always wrong because God has decreed it.

Relativist ethical systems, in contrast, are not supernatural and have no absolute truths. Right and wrong are still present, but they are situational, depending on the context of the action and its effects upon the individual and/or group. Thus lying can be right if it promotes individual or group welfare. White (1959: 217) argues that a scientific view of culture (as well as the underlying scientific approach) requires a relativist ethical approach, since each group's ethical system (including that of the scientist) is related to that group's social, technological, and environmental situation. He also takes the view that as societies evolve and change, so do their ethical systems.

White's belief in the appropriateness of a relativist stance for anthropology is an example of a major ethical dilemma confronting archaeology and other fields of science. Although there should be no question about the utility of the scientific method as a means of effectively understanding cultures and human behavior, these is also no question that much of what is called science in archaeology (as well as in many other fields) is actually composed of value statements. Many of our hypotheses, theories, scientific assertions, research imperatives, so-called laws, and methodologies are bound together in a particular ethic that is meaningless in absolute terms. Thus White uses the theory of evolution to support his particular way of viewing it and his relativist approach to studying it, as do Alland (1967), Harris (1968), and other believers in evolutionary theory and the adaptive ethic. Harris has been especially critical of approaches that do not agree with his cultural materialist views, and he is convinced of the "methodological priority of the search for the laws of history in the science of man" (1968: 3). Accordingly, middle-range theory is irresponsible, eclecticism is an excuse for laziness, and the basic principle of cultural materialism requires that researchers assign priority to the study of cultural evolution (1968: 3–4).

The epistemology and methodology of Harris (1968), White (1959), and others have clearly been influenced by the very principles they hope to prove, and as such as based at least in part on untested value statements. Although he is not an anthropologist, Odum (1971) has taken this situation to its logical extreme. According to Odum, energy is the basis of all matter and therefore is also the basis of all political, public, and scientific issues. Thus human survival (as well as its study) depends upon our awareness of energy systems and budgets, and our ability to adapt our ethics, scientific studies, and other actions to the changing demands of these systems. Odum believes that the key to human survival is a system that joins humans and nature in an energy ethic that follows natural laws.

Although not always as obvious, this mixing of research imperatives, values, and theory with scientific methodology underlies much of contemporary American archaeology. A form of the energy ethic, in fact, is the very basis of cultural resource management and historic preservation. Accordingly, Lipe, along with most archaeologists, believes that the survival of our profession depends upon an ethic that preserves the data base or at least slows down its attrition (1974: 213). Lipe and other historic preservationists favor a number of ethical guidelines that involve conservation (e.g., emergency salvage excavations should be undertaken only as a last resort and then only with a strong research orientation). And although Lipe does not espouse "defining problem orientation narrowly or associating it with some particular one of the basic research paradigms now current in the field," he believes "that the researchers must feel a drive to contributing to the solution of some substantive or methodological problem or problems" (1974: 243).

The conservation ethic is only one of a number of interrelated value systems that are currently part of normal archaeological science. Thus we also have "processual" archaeology, which demands rigorous use of covering laws, and requires that objectives and methods be based on a scientific framework aimed at describing and explaining historic events (Watson, LeBlanc, and Redman 1971: xiii). Although processual archaeology is not in and of itself a value system, since it purports to be a scientific approach to the study of cultural processes, its assumptions and approaches involve value statements. Also, the intellectual demands and research imperatives of the processual approach are quite rigid and often take the form of commands. Thus Binford writes that we *must* seek explanations in systems terms for classes of historic events (1962: 22) and that we *must* be able to isolate cultural systems and study them in their adaptive milieu (1964: 136). The closely related "behavioralist" school takes an equally assertive stance in stating that the cultural formation processes *must* be considered when deducing test implications, interpreting absolute dates, and designating proveniences (Schiffer 1976: 186).

The point of this discussion is not to denigrate any one researcher or approach, but rather, to show that value statements (ethics) pervade all aspects of archaeology, from our rationale for doing it, to the manner in which we survey, excavate, and analyze data, to the goals, methodologies, and research imperatives that govern our research and professional relations. Once we have recognized the presence of value statements in archaeology, it should be possible to separate them from the scientific approach, which is absolutely essential if we are to understand behavior in Western terms. How do we make this separation when value statements are so pervasive?

Kemeny (1959) has proposed that the way out of this ethical morass is to recognize that science can only provide us with a means of achieving goals and objectives, such as eradicating cancer and explaining human behavior. The definition of the goals, and the decision as to which goals and methods are appropriate, cannot be made on scientific grounds, since they are based on moral and other ethical values. Thus the Cat and Alice dialogue—nonscientific, ethical values are used to tell us where to go; then science can be used to get there.

Kemeny's argument (1959) is based on the assumption that it is actually possible to separate value statements from science. This assumption is not accepted by all philosophers of science and morals. Certain ethical philosophers, such as George Schueler at the University of New Mexico, argue that ultimately all science rests on evaluative principles, since scientists assume that it is valuable to know the truth about reality. Also, every branch of science develops its own internal values and basic research imperatives, which are dictated by the methods of the science itself. One such value is that a sound scientific approach depends on the availability of one's experimental data for verification. Thus it is bad to be secretive, just as it is bad to destroy all samples of a rare compound or all archaeological sites of a particular type.

Research imperatives blur the distinction between science and values further because they are based on community priorities about which problems are worthy of consideration. The questions asked by the evolutionists, materialists, processualists, and behaviorists, and the assertive demands that they must be asked, are research imperatives.

Schueler's interpretation of research imperatives is very similar to

Kuhn's (1962) proposal that the ultimate authority of science is not so much its rational methodology and rules, but the consensus of the scientific community. The key to Kuhn's argument is his concept of a paradigm, which is composed of "universally recognized scientific achievements that for a time provide model problems and solutions to a community of practitioners" (1962: x). In the "Postscript" to his 1962 work, he distinguished between two aspects of a paradigm: (1) the disciplinary matrix which includes the "entire constellation of beliefs, values, techniques, and so on shared by the members of a given community," and (2) exemplars, the "concrete puzzle-solutions which, employed as models or examples, can replace explicit rules as a basis for the solution of the remaining puzzles of normal science" (1970: 178,182,187). Thus the paradigm contains a collection of methods, assumptions, laws, examples, values, and beliefs that form a supertheory or world view (Gutting 1980: 2). Because the ultimate judge of a paradigm's content and worth, and of the choice between competing paradigms, is the scientific community, Kuhn concludes that this community is the fundamental locus of authority. Scheffler (1967), Fitting (1973), and others have interpreted this to mean that Kuhn is proposing that science is basically irrational and subjective, since its authority is based on human judgments rather than impersonal, objective rules and methods.

Assuming that Kuhn is correct about the ultimate locus of authority, does this necessarily mean that science is basically irrational and that a distinction between science and ethics is not possible? Many authors disagree with Kuhn and believe that it is possible to separate values and science. Gutting (1980: 8), for example, argues that the judgment of the scientific community can still be rational, since it is "informed by logical arguments based on methodological rules, including some shared by all scientists at all times." Popper (1970) notes the constant criticism of basic questions in science, and states that only beginning students and technicians uncritically accept the prevailing dogma. Others believe that science is much more varied and self-critical than Kuhn asserts, and that there are several alternative approaches and theoretical orientations present at all times (Feyerabend 1970; Barbour 1980).

However these arguments are interpreted, we are still left with the problem that all science is ultimately based on the value statement that it is worthwhile for one reason or another (the greater good, a scientist's ego, the intellectual challenge, the fear of the unknown, etc.) to study the meaning of reality. Despite this problem and the question of whether research imperatives and paradigms ae subjectively based, it is this author's belief that our ethical system must guide our scientific inquiries. Otherwise, we are left in a relativistic chaos in which it is impossible to evaluate the results of our research objectively. Moreover, one need not see the situation as an either/or choice between total subjectivity and irrationality, on the one hand, and total objectivity, on the other. The value of Kuhn's and Schueler's interpretations is that they force us to recognize how value statements can influence and even enter into our assumptions, methods, research priorities, etc. They demonstrate that instead of uncritically accepting what we are taught in graduate school, what we read in the popular texts and journal articles, and what we develop as a result, we should continually ask ourselves whether our work expresses an objective, rational approach or someone's (our own included) personal values. As Popper has challenged, "if we try, we can break out of our framework at any time" (1970: 56). In this way it should be possible to separate the more obvious values from science.

The problem of separating ethical ends and underlying values from scientific means is at the core of historic preservation, model building, teaching, the selection of research questions, and other aspects of modern archaeology. Let us assume, for example, that an archaeologist is interested in using a mitigation/excavation project in the Central Rio Grande Valley to investigate late prehistoric and historic economic change among the Pueblo Indians. Innumerable ethical questions have to be addressed both before and during the research project. First of all, how does the archaeologist define reality and the scientific method? Why is it worthwhile for him or her to investigate economic change? Why does the project have to occur in a mitigation context, and how does this context affect the manner in which the project is designed and carried out? What effects will the resulting development activities have on the local community and the archaeologist's personal life? Why should the sites be excavated rather than preserved? Why should a processual, behavioral, cultural ecological, or other approach be used? Why should students be used (or not used)? Why should the archaeologist excavate the burials at the sites (or not excavate them)? Should the Indian and non-Indian informants be paid? Why should the archaeologist obtain the landowner's permission and peer consensus? Should the project be cost-effective? Why should a sample approach be used, and which sites should be selected? How extensively should the results be published? These and many other questions will obviously influence how the project is designed and carried out, and what the data will be used for. The scientific method can be used to design the project and to offer alternative approaches, as well as to carry out the project, but it cannot decide which ends should be met and which alternatives should be used, since these are based on economic, political, social, and other reasons grounded in values.

A Humanistic Ethical System

Since ethics are an essential aspect of archaeology, and archaeology is concerned with human behavior, it is this author's opinion that a humanistic ethical system is the most appropriate one for archaeology. As discussed previously, a skeptical approach is probably the *ideal* ethical atmosphere for science, since it attempts to delete value statements and create a total laboratory situation that is free of biases, psychological values, intuition, etc. Unfortunately, such an atmosphere is impossible, and it is naive (and dangerous) to assume that archaeology can occur in an ethical vacuum. Thus any ethical system is probably better than the total absence of values that skeptical negativism advocates.

A humanistic ethic in archaeology focuses on understanding basic human processes and individual human beings. In a sense, all archaeologists are humanists, since we are all concerned with human behavior. However, most archaeologists attempt to paint the picture of humanity with broad strokes, by discovering and explaining the chronological outlines of cultural developments, the underlying adaptive and evolutionary processes, the economic and stylistic changes, etc. This is a productive and necessary approach to the study of the species and its individual cultures, but it often ignores the interests, achievements, and dignity of individual human beings, and the problems that confront them in their daily lives. It also often overlooks the fact that as human beings, members of specific cultures ourselves, our ability to understand other humans and cultures is impaired by our perceptions, emotions, cultural biases, research imperatives, and other value-based factors.

A humanistic ethic in archaeology therefore attempts to: (1) separate value judgments from the scientific approach whenever possible; (2) recognize that this is never totally possible, and that all of our assumptions, methods, and research imperatives are based to some degree on value judgments; (3) recognize that all of our actions have an effect on the people that we are studying; and (4) recognize that the perceptions and beliefs of these people concerning the structure and meaning of reality can be a useful way for us to understand not only their cultures but also reality.

American archaeologists are often involved in culturally and politically sensitive conflicts in which groups representing different segments of Anglo-American society compete with each other, with archaeologists, with Native Americans, and with other groups for control of land, archaeological sites, scientific data, and even the interpretation of these data; we should be careful to recognize the influences of our actions upon these various groups, and to act in a humanistic, ethically responsible manner.

A humanistic approach that respects the rights and dignity of our students, peers, and informants helps to assure that we do not compromise those rights in our attempts to obtain knowledge for the greater good of humanity. This ultimate goal of knowledge is commendable, but if in striving for it we treat those with whom we interact as scientific means, then we are defeating our purposes (Hansen 1976: 133).

Finally, a humanistic approach is a very useful and productive way to perceive reality. As noted in an earlier article that dealt with Indian/archaeologist relations, a humanist approach may enable us

> to see the sites from the Indians' (or other culture's) perspective, which can be radically different from ours, yet just as legitimate. Instead of viewing a site merely as a source of scientific data, we can also appreciate it through the Indians' world views. This chance to perceive a common part of reality from a different culture's perspective is an especially useful way to understand that culture and its value system. It is also a useful way to understand reality. Whether the site is "real" in a historic sense, such as grandfather's grandfather's village, or "real" in a mythical sense, such as a mountain peak where Raccoon danced to become a doctor, it provides a way of perceiving existence through both the non-Western Indian and the Western scientific perspective [Winter 1980: 125].

In this context, "perceiving" is not used to mean understanding or explaining in scientific terms. Perceiving is the everyday, normal way of relating to and interacting with reality, without understanding it. Our senses are physical ways that we perceive existence. Imagination, myth, religion, and other value systems that believe rather than explain are other ways that we perceive. It can be very useful to appreciate how other individuals and cultures perceive and relate to reality. By "trying the intimate experiences of another upon oneself" (Levi-Strauss 1967: 16), we can better appreciate both the other one (and other culture) and ourselves.

This role of ethics (i.e., to allow us to interact with and relate to the rest of existence) is an essential aspect of the human experience. Perhaps we are wrong and our science is wrong, and reality is nothing more or less than "a nonsense tale told by an idiot mathematician" (Gardner 1960: 15). Perhaps the only absolute is the death sentence that all life labors under. But even if the inner core of existence is meaningless, do we not still use laughter, myth, religion, and even science as ways of interpreting reality's surface?

Summary and Conclusion

Ethics include the moral codes and value statements that influence almost every aspect of human behavior. Archaeologists often study prehistoric and historic value systems as they are expressed in art styles, tool types, and architectural features. At a more basic level, our assumptions, research imperatives, methods, and related behavior are affected by (and affect) the values of the groups and cultures with whom we interact. The Judeo-Christian religious background of our culture, and our training in evolutionary theory, among other things, have influenced the way we perceive reality and the values that we attach to it.

Since a totally amoral scientific atmosphere is impossible, it is essential to realize how our value systems affect our research, our professional lives, and the people with whom we deal. Most of our research decisions are based at least in part on value statements. It is only after these decisions have been made on ethical grounds that a scientific approach can be used to understand human behavior. Also, only after values have been removed from, or at least identified in, our research imperatives can we obtain unbiased data.

The values and activities of other archaeologists, students, employers, employees, developers, Indians, land managers, and other people are integral components of American archaeology. It is therefore recommended that our ethical system have a strong humanistic orientation, so that their rights and dignity are respected. A humanistic approach will also provide us with opportunities to better perceive other people and their cultures, as well as ourselves and our cultures.

PART II

Responsibilities to the Profession

8

Achieving Professionalism through Ethical Fragmentation: Warnings from Client-Oriented Archaeology

L. Mark Raab

This essay goes to the heart of one of the major ethical problems in archaeology today—whether work done under contract should serve primarily the client's interests or the research needs of the discipline. As the profession has struggled with this conflict over the past several years, we have realized that the question is not whether to serve one or the other exclusively, because most projects include both interests, but rather, how much emphasis to place on each and which gets priority on a particular project.

All archaeologists hope that this conflict will not lead to ethical and moral fragmentation in the profession, but a uniform approach to which most archaeologists could subscribe has yet to emerge. Currently, the decision about how to reconcile research interests and client's needs is a personal one. The preferred response is to meld the two, but the extent to which this is possible varies with the project.

WHAT ENDS SHOULD the archaeologist serve? Do archaeologists in private enterprise have ethical imperatives that differ from those of colleagues in academia or government? Or, regardless of the institutional base, do "applied" archaeologists have different ethical and professional obligations than "pure" researchers? These questions matter because certain answers to them urge a professional and ethical relativity that might well split the discipline into insular, mutually antagonistic realms. This essay attempts to show that ethical and professional values in archaeology are undergoing rapid change, that certain arguments from "client-oriented" archaeology about dealing with this change do not make sense within a valid theory of professional ethics, and that a more useful consensus should be built upon a unifying core of disciplinary needs and values.

Indications of Change

Indications of change in archaeology are pervasive. The proximate cause is the advent of cultural resource management ("CRM") archaeology (King et al. 1977; Schiffer and Gumerman 1977; Goodyear et al. 1978). There are a number of ways to measure the impact of CRM archaeology, but perhaps none is more telling than Wendorf's (1979: 642) analysis of how this program has absorbed the discipline's "human capital":

> In 1974–1975, 39 of the 216 proposals submitted to NSF [National Science Foundation] were for North American archaeology, representing 18% of the total; by 1977–1978, however, the number of North American proposals had declined to only 21 out of 347 submitted, or only 6% of the total. Of 100 proposals submitted in the fall of 1979, only 3 were for North American archaeology, and this at a time when the number of archaeologists coming into the profession from our graduate schools is rapidly increasing. What has happened is clear. Almost all archaeologists with interests in North America have become so completely involved in one or another aspect of the archaeological conservation effort that it has consumed all of our research time.

The employment of this work force has occurred largely outside universities and museums. While academic hiring sharply declined in recent years, an increasing number of archaeologists took jobs with private firms or the government. Along with increased diversity of employment, archaeologists found themselves subject to divergent institutional values and objectives. Predictably, these changes are now challenging traditional ideas about professionalism and ethics.

In some quarters, for instance, there is frank skepticism that problem-oriented research is compatible with the demands of bureaucracy and business (e.g., MacDonald 1976, Keel 1977, Kinsey 1977, Willey and Sabloff 1980: 262). Others (e.g., Fitting 1978, 1979a, b, c; Patterson 1978) have suggested that archaeology can play a legitimate and useful role in an applied form, even if it is not directed toward traditional research goals. (See also the essay by Dunnell in this volume—ed.) Still others (e.g., Gumerman 1973; Schiffer and Gumerman 1977; Goodyear et al. 1978; King and Lyneis 1978; Raab et al. 1980) have attempted to show that the research ethic and CRM archaeology are not only compatible but mutually dependent for their well-being.

Attempts to deal with changes in the profession have become as complex as the problems. The comment on ethics contained in the Society for American Archaeology's "Four Statements for Archaeology" (Champe et al. 1961) bears about the same relation to recent statements on ethics by the Society of Professional Archaeologists (SOPA 1981) as a biplane does to a Boeing 747. (The "Four Statements for Archaeology" and the SOPA Code of Ethics and Standards for Research are reprinted in this book—ed.) The SOPA statements on ethics contain 30 specific do's and don'ts connected with the interests of the public, the archaeological profession, and the client. Not only are we warned about many more specific problems, we are explicitly reminded that archaeologists must look beyond their own interests to those of the public and the entities that hire them.

Despite its detail, however, the SOPA Code of Ethics reaffirms many of the scholarly values contained in the Four Statements. The requirements of scientific honesty, competence, and responsible treatment of archaeological remains are long-standing values. But, just as clearly, there are nondisciplinary interests represented. Ethical tenets allocated explicitly to *public, colleague,* and *client* interests represent a much more circumspect and differentiated view of ethical obligations than in the past. Therein lies a problem of ambivalence. Whose interests within this tripartite division are most important? Clearly, they are all legitimate, but should they all get equal attention?

The prospect here is not a conflict between good and evil but one between ethical priorities—priorities that are not necessarily addressed in codified morality. In fact, without an *underlying theory of ethics,* upon which ethical codes are built, there is little hope of avoiding ethical anarchy in archaeology. The examples of the Four Statements and SOPA's Code of Ethics attempt to deal with ethical problems by constructing a laundry list designed to thwart specific professional abuses and to recognize specific interests. Unfortunately, without a coherent principle to tie this list together, attempts to apply ethical codes will just as easily provoke ethical fragmentation as ethical consensus. The debate about client-oriented archaeology is an instructive example of conflict that is already with us as a result of ethical ambivalence.

Client-Oriented Archaeology and Ethical Relativity

Client-oriented archaeology is based on the concept of ethical relativity by analogy with established professions. Ethical relativity refers to the idea that the practice of archaeology can be separated, at least ideally, into different types, or goal orientations, each with its distinctive moral and professional imperatives. This idea provides one answer to the question of how to assign ethical priorities to the interests we can identify in modern archaeology: ethical constraints are considered relative to one's employment situation. Fitting (1978: 13) describes the ethical position of the client-oriented archaeologist working for corporate or governmental clients as an

> orientation . . . directed toward the client, the person who is financing the project. This is a position analogous to that of the doctor, the lawyer, and the engineer. In this instance, the professional consultant is concerned with the interests of the client. If the client wishes to build a dam or a power plant, the goal of the archaeologist should be to provide an objective evaluation of the potential danger such a project might have on archaeological resources. The moral imperative is the objective evaluation, not the preservation, of the resources no matter how the archaeologist personally feels about the resources.

Similarly, Patterson (1978: 134) argues that

> Any increases in archaeological knowledge and satisfaction of individual research goals are simply secondary effects, no matter how important. . . . Contract archaeology is really no different than professional consulting in other fields, such as ecology and engineering. Consultants are engaged to solve client problems, not research goals of the consultant.

Taken at face value, this kind of analogy may appear attractive to some. But is it really valid? In the first place, it is questionable whether professionals in other fields serve their clients in the ethically simplistic way portrayed by Fitting and Patterson. All of the professions mentioned recognize responsibilities that transcend the client's particular needs. Second, there are specific archaeological issues that cast doubt on the analogy. Consider two of these:

1. I'm okay, you're okay: the idea of a distinctively client-oriented approach implies that there can be many different but equally valid approaches to professional archaeology. This idea implies that it is no more unethical to be client-oriented than it is, say, to be research-oriented. Unfortunately, as has been argued in detail elsewhere (Raab et al. 1980), the client orientation defense rests on the position that *technical* studies are appropriate when serving a client's needs. The term "technical" refers to application of existing information in a comparative and descriptive framework, rather than to work designed to advance knowledge through *research.* The idea of applied technical information is one readily drawn from analogy with other professions.

Our opposition to this view rests on the conclusion that we cannot eschew research in contract studies because (a) archaeologists do not have a body of adequate technical data anything like that in medicine or law, (b) it is completely unrealistic to expect an academic or "pure" research arm of the discipline to supply such a technical base, and (c) most of our rapidly disappearing archaeological resources will be dealt with by contract studies in the long run. In short, agreeing to satisfy a client's needs by means of narrow technical studies is not necessarily the same thing as protecting the resource base or seeing to it that invaluable potential for intellectual advance is not squandered. With such issues at stake, many would not agree that one approach is as good as another.

2. Doctors, lawyers, engineers and archaeologists—professionals all. We are flattered to be in the company of such prestigious professionals. And if those professionals' ethics center on the relationship between themselves and their clients, why shouldn't ours? The answer is that we would be assuming that our clients are just like theirs; i.e., those with whom we have face-to-face contact and from whom we take professional fees. Unfortunately, the case is not nearly that simple when (a) we are frequently dealing with public money; (b) regardless of who is paying, the work is being done in the first place because of public policy (laws, government directives); and (c) we are dealing with an irreplaceable resource that is humankind's cultural heritage.

One facile generalization should not creep in here. These issues do not sort themselves neatly into categories of Good Guys in Academia and Bad Guys in CRM. A lesson to be learned from client-oriented archaeology, practiced in both academia and the corporate world, is that it is too easy to put on professional blinders in the name of a single legitimate interest in archaeology. Fitting (1978: 13) proposed the concept of client-oriented archaeology to counter a tendency of some archaeologists to ignore the client's needs in order to promote their own research interests:

> Contracts were often viewed as an alternative to the National Science Foundation as the stress from too many applicants was being felt by that organization. Reports which were generated by such projects were often directed toward the ends of the archaeologists who generated them, rather than the client who sponsored them. Can an evaluation of site significance be objective if, by determining a site is significant, the archaeologist will be generating additional personal revenue, or support for students and facilities by mitigation?

There is little doubt that such abuses occur, and they need serious attention. But suggesting a client-oriented approach as an answer to the problem may only create another equally bad problem; the responsibility will merely shift from one narrowly defined interest to another.

The fundamental problem here is a reactionary tendency in which one counters a problem by narrowly defining spheres of interest and then attempting to protect those interests within an adversarial relationship. Schemes of this type encourage separatism rather than mutual problem solving, conflict rather than consensus. Client-orientation is only one kind of extremist reaction. Willey and Sabloff's conclusion (1980: 262) that "there is probably more reason, *at the moment,* to be pessimistic than optimistic" about successful combination of the research ethic and CRM undoubtedly reflects a widespread fear in the discipline, particularly in its academic sector. Retreat into mutually suspicious orientations in the name of high but narrowly defined principle is a real danger that could fragment the discipline.

Resisting an urge to take the easy way out may be difficult. It would be easy to accept an analogy between archaeology and professions such as law, medicine, and engineering for the reasons given earlier. We should be careful, however, not to preclude the possibility that archaeology as a profession may have ethical and professional dimensions that do not parallel those of the other fields. It may be that archaeologists will have to take the more difficult path of finding their own solutions to their own problems (cf. Plog 1980: 11). It would also be easy to conclude that questions of ethics and professionalism are merely the foil of a self-serving group; e.g., of client-oriented archaeologists. It should be clear, however, that retreat into a variety of insular professional role models is a real possibility, including extreme academic or research orientations.

A Functional Theory of Professional Ethics

An analysis of ethics and professionalism in archaeology might benefit from an examination of a theory of professional ethics. This is a subject with an immense literature dispersed among many fields, including philosophy, religion, sociology, and anthropology (see, e.g., Cassell 1980 for a recent bibliography). The point can be made succinctly, however through a brief review of Moore's (1967: 318–319) functional characterization of professionalism and professional ethics, a characterization that seems to contain many points of agreement among students of the topic:

1. The professional possesses esoteric knowledge, based on specialized training of exceptional duration. The knowledge is useful according to values held in the particular society.
2. The professional is set apart from the laity by various signs and symbols, but by the same token is identified with his peers—often in formal organization.
3. In the use of his exceptional knowledge, the professional proceeds by his own judgment and authority, and thus enjoys autonomy, restrained by responsibility.

"Autonomy, restrained by responsibility" is the essential point. In return for authority and autonomy, the professional subscribes to ethics. In addition to setting explicit standards of behavior, these codes facilitate the interaction of professional and client by establishing a relationship of trust:

> The fundamental rationale for codes of competence and ethical performance adopted by professional associations is to insure *responsibility* in re-

> turn for the *trust* of the client. In the nature of the role relationships, the client cannot judge the details of competence or performance; he can only judge results. And since superior knowledge does indeed carry power, the client needs to be protected from exploitative misuse of the asymmetrical power distribution [Moore 1967: 323].

The functional relationships of this scheme provide a blueprint for analyzing the ethical requirements of a profession. In that analysis we need to understand clearly who is supposed to benefit by the practitioner's knowledge—in other words, who is the client—and what kind of behavior will in fact hurt or help the client's interests. That observation may seem obvious, but it turns out to need closer attention than we might think. Much like the analogy between archaeology and more mature professions, it would be easy to derive a superficial conclusion from Moore's model. It is easy to imagine clients as consisting of nothing more than individuals or organizations with problems to be solved. Professionals in the fields of law, medicine, engineering, and plumbing, to name a few, typically conceive of clients in that way and are able to serve them on the basis of the personal and individual problems that need solution. Since the scope of these problems typically is restricted to the persons or organizations seeking help, it is logical to frame the professional service as a more or less closed relationship between professional and client. This arrangement works because the issue of harm and benefit is largely confined to the client's individual situation. Clearly, something of this sort is intended by client-oriented archaeology. The fundamental error in this interpretation, however, is a much too narrow assessment of whose interests are necessarily involved in archaeological matters.

The theory of professional ethics as a device to protect legitimate interests will work if we understand whose interests are really at stake. Before we can determine what a fundamental theory of archaeological ethics ought to be, we should take a close look at such interests.

Whose Interests Are at Stake?

Whose interests are at stake in archaeology? The question invites an avalanche of responses, citing a list of particulars of interminable length. A more telling way to approach the question might be to look at the *archaeological record:* a fragile, finite, irreplaceable and rapidly disappearing source of information about the past. The facts it contains are crucial because they not only shape the possible interests that archaeology can serve, but also indicate how it must go about meeting its obligations. It makes little sense to talk about interests in archaeology without coming to grips with archaeology's essential potentials and limitations.

A quintessential archaeological potential is discovery of the human cultural patrimony. Indeed, one could argue as Plog (1974) does that archaeology's distinctive contribution to recovery of our past is an ability to deal with human behavior over long expanses of time. That ability is both a distinctive characteristic and a specific responsibility of archaeology. And that responsibility is not entirely one of self-estimation. If it were, we would not see archaeologists supported by public policy and funding through university and museum positions, National Science Foundation grants, and huge CRM programs operating at various levels of government. However we approach the archaeological record, we are always dealing with *somebody else's* heritage as well. For this reason it seems ethically dubious for archaeologists and clients to construe their dealings as a closed relationship without immediate extrinsic significance.

If appeals to a shared human heritage are not impressive, consider the state of the archaeological record. Projections of worldwide population growth and its effects promise massive environmental alterations, including unprecedented loss of archaeological records. While the proportions of destruction vary, North American archaeologists recognize that destruction has reached crisis proportions for many regions of this country (Davis 1972; Lipe 1974). McGimsey (1972: 3) warned some time ago that those of us alive now will probably be the last to see the archaeological record of regions of the United States in a reasonably complete state. Given that systematic knowledge of the archaeological record is perforce comparative and cumulative, treatment of the record by anyone for any purpose diminishes an already dwindling resource, inherently constraining what all of us can hope to know. This inescapable character of our data base dictates that all interests in archaeology are directly affected by what each of us does.

Parenthetically, the character of our data base should caution us about analogies between archaeology and other scientific fields. If we wanted to hazard a parallel between archaeology and physics or chemistry, however, we might suggest that chemists and physicists would be in our position if elements that they wished to manipulate experimentally were being steadily destroyed, never again to be available.

The nature of archaeological things, both intellectual and material, encompasses many legitimate interests in archaeology. Again, diverse lists could be compiled, but the SOPA Code of Ethics gets to the crux of these interests: the public, at large and in segments; our colleagues in archaeology and in the sciences and humanities generally; and entities in need of information for environmental planning purposes. But it should be apparent that we have a complex, multifaceted client composed of all these elements, following the dictum of looking at who is harmed or helped. The same theory suggests that the role of ethics ought to be one of establishing modes of professional behavior that best allow an equitable balance of interests. In fact, the central ethical *desideratum* of the discipline might well be to achieve such an end through the following principles.

The first and most fundamental obligation of archaeology is to approach its subject matter on the basis of rigorous inquiry; i.e., on the basis of *research* aimed at answering meaningful scientific and humanistic questions, thereby advancing knowledge. Particularly under the onslaught of contract archaeology, there is increasing awareness of the strategic importance of maintaining research in all kinds of archaeological work, regardless of its funding source.

> I fear that we can never prevent the petrification of bureaucracy, but we can mitigate its effects by insisting that the evaluation of all proposals for archaeological work rest within the profession. . . .
>
> If we can retain the research ethic, if we can retain a clear idea of the goals of our profession, and if we can maintain the freedom in which to strive for these goals, then the florescence of American archaeology may be just beginning [Wendorf 1979: 643].

> Whatever success contract work eventually will achieve depends on the intellectual input of the whole profession. A cultural resource management program without intellectual goals or a theoretical framework will be doomed to failure in the long run [Willey and Sabloff 1980: 262].

These views are hardly in sympathy with Patterson's (1978: 134) conclusion that, "Any increases in archaeological knowledge and satisfaction of individual research goals are simply secondary effects [to a research contract], no matter how important." To agree to such a concept would rob archaeology of its most essential product by crippling its ability to serve anyone's interests except perhaps sellers of a narrow technical service.

Given the diverse values attached to archaeological studies, it is difficult to argue that archaeologists are the only people who should profit from research. Archaeologists have a direct and immediate responsibility to relate the results of their research to interests in need of it. Foremost among these interests is the public. Perhaps environmental laws and regulations are the most formal vehicles through which public interests are currently met (King et al. 1977; McGimsey and Davis 1977; Schiffer and Gumerman 1977). Still, these private and governmental clients are merely one segment of the public. It is worth stressing again that, despite entering into a business relationship, the archaeologist and client are both subordinate to public policy. Yet this fact does not release the archaeologist from responsibility to the client. Potential ethical conflicts should always be considered *before* entering into a specific contract (Raab et al. 1980). Once an archaeologist has agreed to a contract, he or she owes prompt, cost-effective, and technically and intellectually defensible work.

It is particularly important that one explain research needs to the client, showing why research is necessary to evaluate the resources and devise a meaningful plan for managing them. The scope of the research should of course be appropriate to the project and not merely a vehicle for self-aggrandizement. Once more the idea of an equitable balance of interests comes in: advancement of archaeological knowledge allows more enlightened management of environmental impacts, while preserving the best possible data base for the future. Fortunately, there is a large body of evidence to show that this goal is not utopian but practical in most cases, *if* we avoid polarization of interests (King et al. 1977; Schiffer and Gumerman 1977; Goodyear et al. 1978; King and Lyneis 1978).

Other public interests are being less successfully met. Contract workers are well aware (e.g., Woodbury and McGimsey 1977) that they are failing to communicate to the public the vast amount of archaeological information that is accumulating. The same problems exist with publicly funded museums, universities, and the National Science Foundation. If we expect to be allowed to carry out research in the public's name, we must expect "autonomy restrained by responsibility;" responsibility includes meeting a wide range of public needs and interests with the fruits of our research.

The greatest ethical emphasis here is on *balancing and harmonizing research interests and public interests*—if not out of idealism, then out of recognition that the public will not indefinitely support an archaeology bent on satisfying only its own curiosity. At the same time, there must be recognition by archaeologists (of all professional approaches), clients, and the public of the fundamental role of research in this whole scheme. Archaeology done without intellectual goals wastes our common data base. No matter how effective our public-outreach programs, without research results we convey only science fiction and bad history. And our clients' interests will likewise be damaged by our inability to supply them with information that can accurately predict the consequences of their archaeological resource programs. For this reason we must be particularly careful that the discipline does not develop an applied arm that is really no more than a caricature of research.

Conclusions

Few of us eagerly seek the role of moralist. Ideas about ethics and professionalism presented here inevitably contain ample potential for misunderstanding. Despite the pervasiveness of moral ideas, however, we seem headed toward professional and ethical fragmentation rather than consensus. The impulse is a wholly understandable one. Our newfound involvement in public policy urges effective professionalism. The desire for a quick professional "fix" may lead us to accept dubious professional analogies with other fields instead of examining whether archaeology has distinctive problems that require their own solutions. Calls for tougher ethical codes and professional licensing, reflecting many legitimate interests in archaeology, do not necessarily offer guidance in how to weld disparate values into a coherent professional and ethical structure. The irony is that we could become ever more "professional" while we fragment into insular domains based upon employment. It would be easy to sample codes of ethics and professionalism for the parts that best suit our personal objectives, while ignoring others altogether. Without recognition of a pandisciplinary ethical consensus, that trend seems inevitable.

Another reaction leading to fragmentation is simply to reject the premise that archaeology is a profession and to repudiate any interest in seeing it become one. For some, professionalism may be a code word for attacks on intellectual freedom (a point that should indeed make us cautious), while codes of ethics that enjoin one to refrain from being evil add insult to potential injury.

More frequent than both of these responses perhaps is simple apathy, resulting from failure to see how overt professionalism has a real bearing on doing archaeology. Reactions of this kind are probably more frequent in academic, or "pure," research settings (despite the fact that most archaeologists in these positions use publicly derived funds) since pressures to justify one's work on grounds of explicit professionalism are generally less urgent there. To take such a retreatist position, however, denies the whole profession the critical introspection that it needs to answer ethical questions. It also could be interpreted as a sign that academically oriented archaeologists do not need to be as concerned about ethical matters as their colleagues in contract research.

The academic sphere faces its share of ethical problems, some of which defy separation from CRM. It is pointless to try to determine whether the academic or CRM sectors of the discipline are "really" to blame for a given problem: "there are no ethical problems that are unique to contract archaeology; the problems are problems of archaeological ethics" (Plog 1980: 12). Only extreme myopia can allow us to work on the same global data base and still imagine that what we do in the various corners of archaeology has no essential impact on the rest of the field.

All this skirts the obvious question of whether ethical codes and standards of research performance do any real good. Adoption of codes and standards, such as those of SOPA and the SAA, *may* do some good *if* they prompt archaeology to seek an underlying consensus of values, an intangible end that is difficult to achieve. When the discipline was smaller and less differentiated, we probably were much closer to such a consensus. This older moral outlook is still sound, if limited, and can be expanded to incorporate the discipline's new roles in public policy archaeology by continuing to stress the importance of research results but also emphasizing, in a balanced way, a variety of public and client needs. There is no question that balancing these interest is an exceedingly complex job whose success requires a concerted effort to build a disciplinary consensus on ethics.

9

The Ethics of Archaeological Significance Decisions

Robert C. Dunnell

No concept in cultural resource management has proved more vexing than that of the significance (in a legal and regulatory sense) of archaeological resources. In each instance of significance assessment, the archaeologist is caught in a moral dilemma. On the one hand, there is the certain knowledge that not all resources can be saved. On the other is the recognition that evaluations of significance could determine whether specific sites will be destroyed and, thereby, the nature of the archaeological record for future generations. The following is a searching and insightful probe of reasons why significance has been such a difficult concept in archaeology.

Most archaeologists would probably agree that with the increasing importance of cultural resource management, the concept of significance has become more than a technical matter. It is an issue with ethical overtones. Compared with some other ethical concerns, however (e.g., theft of cultural resources and responsibilities to the public), there is less agreement about which approach is most beneficial to the resource. (cf. significance decisions in Raab's essay "Toward an Understanding of the Ethics and Values of Research Design in Archaeology.")

It is a presumptuous and intimidating task to write on any moral issue within archaeology. Archaeologists are often deeply and emotionally committed to particular approaches, research strategies, and problem-solving techniques, and there is much diversity in each of these areas. We seem to prize freedom to explore *our own* ideas above all else. In this context, it is virtually impossible to argue rightness and wrongness without offending nearly everyone almost all of the time. In certain kinds of limited research, and certainly during particular periods in our history, it has been possible for investigators to ignore or even deny the moral implications of archaeological research. The rapid development of cultural resource management (CRM) during the last decade has brought that era of ignorant bliss to a close. The public mandate, professional concerns over data generated in this framework, and the enormous increase in the quantity and scope of fieldwork have thrown moral and ethical issues into uncomfortably high relief. The appearance of the Society of Professional Archaeologists and the American Society for Conservation Archaeology, as well as formal codes of ethics, attest to this concern. The very hub of moral concerns is the notion of archaeological significance because, to a greater or lesser extent, virtually all management decisions depend on these admittedly judgmental assessments.

This essay first identifies the dominant moral issue entailed in contemporary notions of significance and then attempts to show that both current practice and contemporary concepts are in conflict with widely held notions of moral obligation. In effect, if we take ethics to represent standards of acceptable professional behavior, our ethical standards are not congruent with archaeological morality. Finally a general strategy to minimize this disparity is offered.

The analysis and certain of the conclusions offered herein are at odds with contemporary trends in CRM and in archaeology generally; they imply different behavior on the part of archaeologists than is now customary. Indeed, this author has but recently come to embrace what still seems an uncomfortably radical view of the moral imperatives of CRM and significance assessment. No effort is made here to provide a moral justification for any particular extant approach or even the status quo. Rather, current practice and standards are analyzed in terms of widely held moral values. The development of ethics is necessarily accomplished by disciplinary consensus. The limited objective of this essay is to stimulate a serious examination of the ethical issues entailed by "significance."

The Moral Issue

In many disciplines, especially the sciences, moral issues typically arise in conjunction with the products of research because those products have practical applications, not all of which may have been intended or foreseen by the researcher. In other fields, notably those which use living research subjects, moral issues are associated with the necessity and conduct of research. Neither of these types of moral issues is very important in archaeology. Although archaeological research has sometimes been used to forward particular political and sociological goals (e.g., the Indian Land Claims cases in this country), most archaeological research has little or no value in practical application at the present time. Similarly, although ethno-archaeologists clearly deal with living subjects and living groups often have historical, emotional, or symbolic ties to segments of the archaeological record, most archaeological research does not involve living subjects directly. The dominant moral issues facing archaeology arise from the fact that it employs a *nonrenewable* phenomenon, each element of which makes a unique contribution, as a research subject. As a consequence, the moral and ethical issues facing archaeology as a discipline are somewhat different from those of many other scholarly and scientific fields.

Recognition of the nonrenewable character of the archaeological record has led to the development of what is termed the "conservation ethic" (Lipe 1974). Although occasional concern with conservation is quite old in America (e.g., Squier and Davis 1848; Peden 1955), the elevation of conservation to a disciplinary conviction is a much more recent phenomenon. Initial concern focused on efforts to protect known elements of the record from exploitation by individuals. While this concern has continued to the present, a major shift toward concern with incidental destruction of archaeological materials has characterized archaeology since mid-century. The Depression-era projects, aside from those generated by the Tennessee Valley Authority, were only marginally concerned with conservation issues. Individual investigators occasionally made decisions based on threat to the resource, but many archaeological sites were destroyed that were not otherwise threatened (Setzler, 1943; Quimby 1979). It was the loss of major segments of the Missouri Valley that generated the first truly conservation-oriented programs (Stephenson 1963). The impact of urban sprawl and agricultural practices (e.g., Davis 1972; Ford et al. 1972) were still later components.

Protective legislation reflects these changes in concern. The Antiquities Act of 1906 provided limited protection for selected elements of the record but did not address incidental destruction. The Reservoir Salvage Act (1960) and Historic Preservation Act (1966), founded in the River Basin Survey program of the Smithsonian, began to address incidental destruction of the record in a limited way and mandated active resource identification and mitigation of impacts. Executive Order 11593 and more recent legislation greatly extended these activities, recognized the desirability of avoidance of impact, expanded the range of mitigative responses, and clearly established conservation of a valued resource as the rationale for protection. Protective legislation was actively supported by the archaeological community. Conservation must be regarded as both the central component and legal rationale of CRM (e.g., Fowler 1982; McGimsey 1972; Schiffer and Gumerman 1977).

Of some importance is the fact that all of the protective legislation provided for regulated professional access to the archaeological record. In spite of this, until large-scale government funding in the 1970's, the main effect of the legislation was to protect the archaeological resource from everyone but the archaeologist. The large public investment has begun to change this situation, with the accountability implied in "research designs" being perhaps the best evidence of this change

(Goodyear et al. 1978; Grayson 1978; Raab, this volume). While archaeologists may display a strong conservationist attitude to the outside world with respect to archaeological materials, it is not clear that a conservation ethic guides our own use of the record to a similar degree.

The notion of archaeological significance plays a key role in CRM. Significance is *the* link between archaeological values and practice. Once particular threatened resources have been identified (and one could argue that even the notion of what constitutes a resource is strongly conditioned by some general notion of significance), some assessment of their significance is required by law. *All* future actions and attitudes toward those resources are predicated on this judgment. The real question thus becomes, *"Is the assessment of significance of archaeological resources founded in a conservation ethic?"* In general, the answer probably is yes. Most archaeologists seem to conceive of these decisions as preserving elements of the archaeological record for the future. But as the extensive and often contentious debate centered on the notion of significance (e.g., King 1971; Lipe 1974; Glassow 1977; McGimsey and Davis 1977; Moratto and Kelley 1977, 1978; Raab and Klinger 1977, 1978; Schiffer and Gumerman 1977; Sharrock and Grayson 1978; Thompson 1978; Weinland 1981) suggests, archaeologists find this loose and mechanistic connection inadequate for, by its very nature, any management decision influences the potential persistence of the resource. Certainly those charged with implementing CRM legislation find it wanting in terms of public accountability.

Much of the debate seems to hinge on the interpretation of conservation. Conservation can be given an absolute interpretation—conservation is its own justification (e.g., M. Wright 1982)—but this interpretation seems inconsistent with the intent of the enabling legislation from both public and archaeological perspectives. The very inclusion of significance assessments in the legal machinery presumes that not all archaeological resources have equal value. If it is to be effected in the real world, conservation has to be for some purpose and for one or more constituencies. It is purpose and constituencies that establish value. Universal criteria such as resource integrity (Bobrowsky 1982) and situational criteria such as relation to research problems (e.g., Lipe 1974; Schiffer and House 1975) have been suggested.

Dunnell and Dancey (1978) and others (Moratto and Kelly 1978) have suggested that at least two different frameworks, or sets of values, are used in assessing significance, and that these correspond with two different purposes of conservation. Humanistic values are those typically thought of as our cultural heritage. In this framework, archaeological materials are conserved because they have symbolic value to humanity generally and to particular groups of individuals as part of their history. There can be no doubt that this is the dominant public rationale. Just as certainly, these values played a critical role within the profession during the period in which much of the modern legislation was written. In fact, had there not been this kind of commonality between the constituencies lobbying for protective legislation and those of the legislators responsible for its enactment, we would not have CRM on the scale we see today. Traditional culture history had a strong humanistic component that bridged the gap between the archaeological and lay communities.

Unfortunately, just as modern legislation was being established, the nature of archaeology as a discipline began to shift from a dominantly humanistic rationale to a scientific one. Thus a second framework, that of scientific values, came to be used in making assessments of significance. In this framework, the archaeological record is valuable not because of symbolic connections with living people, but because it is a source of empirical information about the nature of humanity, in particular about how people change. In fact, it may be the only such source of information we will ever have. The frame of reference for conservation has become a *general* one delimited by what we know about the record rather than one focused on the relation of a particular resource to particular values. Currently, probably no one but archaeologists values the archaeological record as a source of information because of the limited practical value of archaeological results to date. Nonetheless, given the high value generally accorded scientific knowledge by society at large, it is not unreasonable to suppose that the public has a vested interest in conservation within this framework, even if archaeologists must be the custodians of that interest until our results warrant public appreciation.

Can the discipline ethically limit its interpretation of conservation and significance to one frame or the other? On the one hand we are the willing custodians of a body of empirical information that may prove to have significant benefits for humanity as a whole. We are certainly the custodians of our research materials and those of our colleagues, now and into the future. Like it or not, we have an obligation to conserve the archaeological record in scientific terms. But the humanistic values must be served as well. If public interest and our acceptance of large quantities of money and legislative support predicated on "heritage" conservation are not morally persuasive, then simple recognition that such funding and legislation are likely to be withdrawn if those values are not recognized should be sufficient encouragement. Without the support generated by the humanistic values, the scientific values cannot be served.

Conflict between these two sets of values is not as great as might be supposed. As Dunnell and Dancey argued (1978), the scientific values, when interpreted through significance assessments, demand conservation of a considerable segment of the record. As a consequence, there is often a large area of overlap between the two frameworks in terms of significance decisions. Many of the same elements of the record would be conserved from either point of view, with only a small number finding justification solely in the humanistic realm and a much larger number finding justification only in the scientific realm. Making humanistic judgments is a matter of identifying and documenting constituencies that have an interest in particular resources. Beyond general guidelines of this sort, there is little possibility of hard and fast standards because humanistic values are essentially political and subject to change. On the face of it, making significance assessments within the scientific framework ought to be easier. In point of fact, it has proved to be more difficult. An analysis of the sources of difficulty and suggestions for their resolution occupy the remainder of this essay.

CRM Is Not Archaeological Research

In this author's view, the single most important source of conflict in making significance assessments lies in the apparently widespread notion that resource identification, significance assessments, and mitigation efforts (e.g., Schiffer and House 1977; Goodyear et al. 1978; Wendorf 1979; Pokotylo 1982) are research. Archaeological research is generated by a problem that one or more investigators wish to solve. The characterization of traditional archaeology as lacking problem orientation is inaccurate. What characterized traditional archaeology was a limited number of related problems, in particular chronological ones, and a great deal of implicit agreement on those problems. Viewed from today's perspective, this narrowness impoverished the archaeological record, limited archaeological knowledge in undesirable ways, and led to a certan lack of awareness of the influence of those problems on the record. Research designs were hardly necessary when there was broad agreement on what to do, how to do it, and why it was being done. Contemporary research is not qualitatively different. Much of the apparent rigor is a direct function of diversity of problems. When investigators do not agree on what's, how's, and why's, they must justify what they do to their colleagues. The need to justify, to make explicit assumptions, to identify decisions, and to link these with purpose has improved the value of archaeological research, as have the numerous and significant technical advances that new problems stimulated. Perhaps the most important product has been the general recognition that no single approach collects all data, makes all interpretations, or exhausts the value of particular data, a position that is singularly difficult to appreciate when there is only one way of doing things.

Archaeological research begins with a problem. In an attempt to solve the problem, potential data sources are selected and variables identified for documentation. The *choice* of analytic methods, collection techniques, areas, sites, etc., is necessarily predicated on the initial problem. When the formulation of the problem or the approach to problem-solving is not explicit, there is almost inevitably both a failure to obtain necessary information and inclusion of irrelevant data (Goodyear et al., 1978; Raab 1979). Development of the research design approach to problem-oriented research—which demands that problems be given empirical interpretations, and that data requirements, collection techniques, and analytic methods be explicitly chosen a priori with reference to the problem—has taken much of the slack out of archaeological fieldwork. A strict problem-oriented approach using a multistage research design (Binford 1964; Redman 1973) insures conservative use of the archaeological record. It provides a means by which an investigator can obtain all those data required and only those data required in serving a particular interest. For these reasons, it is *the* way to do most research.

CRM is not so constituted (cf. Keel 1979). The generation of a CRM project has nothing whatsoever to do with an archaeological problem. CRM is generated by nonarchaeologists and concerns potential impact on a particular piece of real estate. The initial input is spatial. The archaeologist is thus deprived of the rationales that are used, implicitly or explicitly, to make all of the decisions known to influence the quantity, quality, and nature of archaeological data. The notion of relevance that guides the selection of resources in problem-oriented research is replaced by a less well-defined notion of significance.

The Problem-Oriented Research Approach and CRM

Structurally, research and CRM and different (Keel 1979), and the appropriateness of using criteria developed in one to guide the other might well be questioned on those grounds alone (e.g., J. V. Wright 1982). If we accept the overriding purpose of CRM as conservation of the archaeological record for humanistic and scientific use, is the problem-oriented research approach to assessing significance ethical and moral?

First, search as one might, it is difficult to construe a direct warrant to fund archaeological research in the CRM legislation. The intent of the legislation is clearly conservation of resources. To a greater or lesser extent, almost all archaeological research consumes the archaeological record by virtue of the techniques of data acquisition. Indeed, one of the intents of formal research designs is to minimize this negative impact of research (Watson et al. 1971). From this perspective, the use of CRM funds to conduct archaeological research is a breach of public trust or outright, though perhaps unintentional, fraud, in that it directly contravenes the intention of the legislation. The funding of archaeological research is the responsibility of archaeologists. The public has assumed an obligation to see that the necessary research materials continue to be available for research purposes (among others), but it has not undertaken the funding of research. The burden of this misconstrual does not entirely fall on the CRM archaeologist. In an effort to supply rational justifications for CRM decisions, agencies that affect the public interest in the archaeological record often demand a research orientation in final publications, if not throughout the conduct of mitigative projects. Inasmuch as funds are always limited, moneys spent on analytic and interpretive activities that could be performed at a later date necessarily reduce proportionately the amount of record actually conserved. When analytic procedures are destructive (e.g., soil analyses), the research requirements can compel a contractor to destroy the very record he or she was charged to conserve.

One might reasonably argue that a research orientation is required to carry out CRM investigations because the nature of the resource is unknown at the outset and one must know the resource in order to conserve it (Goodyear et al. 1978). The fact that analysis may be required to carry out a conservation obligation, however, falls short of a warrant for research to structure CRM investigation and significance decisions (Keel 1979).

On the contrary, it is readily apparent that modern research standards are unnecessarily destructive of the record and contravene the conservation obligation. The very features of a problem-oriented strategy that make it so powerful in the research context insure its destructive effects in the CRM context. The use of a specific problem or set of problems to rationalize decisions that affect coverage, sampling, collecting techniques, etc., insures that the data collected will be as complete and as unbiased with respect to that problem as is possible. It also insures that these decisions will not produce information similarly suited to other problems. These pernicious effects are most apparent when one problem or several related ones serve to generate criteria in the decision-making process. Indeed, this is the basis of modern objections to traditional archaeology. Implicit recognition of the problem seems to be the motivation behind efforts to identify discipline-wide, important research questions (e.g., King 1982) and underlies many efforts in developing state plans (Heritage Conservation and Recreation Service 1980). These, however laudable in intent, do not address the basic problem, but only serve to obscure the perniciousness of the approach as a whole and, in fact, to institutionalize it.

Every archaeologist who works in North America is well acquainted with the damage done to the archaeological record by our predecessors while pursuing research. Whole classes of remains have disappeared due to the effects of state-of-the-art research. For example, the concentration of investigations on large sites and on topographically visible remains such as mounds allowed other remains to slip through cracks and be eradicated by incidental destruction. As a consequence, we have highly variable data for different periods, with only modest opportunities to correct the significance decisions of previous generations.

The chronological problems of the culture historical era led to collecting biases (mainly shaped objects and decorated or otherwise distinctive ceramics). Furthermore, technical improvements (e.g., $_{14}$C dating, archaeomagnetism) rendered earlier data collection efforts depressingly inadequate. Even when materials were acquired, the means by which they were acquired often did not permit quantitative study. Such debilities arose, not because culture history was bad, but because it was so strongly problem-oriented. Seemingly innocuous concepts such as "site," which plays a key role in CRM legislation and is usually the object of significance assessments, continue to impart a decided bias in the record (Dunnell and Dancey 1983). There is no reason to suppose that archaeology will not continue to change, as it and all other empirically oriented disciplines have in the past. Theoretical developments will change the questions we ask. Technical improvements and new analytic techniques will change data requirements. To frame significance assessments in terms of contemporary problems not only restricts the value of the record to a limited number of contemporary problems but also condemns future archaeology to the intellectual and technical limitations we have today. In short, it contravenes the futuristic implications of conservation.

As populations increase and development expands to encompass more and more of the earth's surface, CRM increasingly determines the nature of the archaeological record. The current approaches to CRM decision making cannot, in this context, be construed as ethical. Significance decisions must be seen as *sampling decisions* because they determine, more than any other decision in the whole process, which elements of the record will survive into the future. The problem-oriented research approach imparts strong systematic biases into the record, biases that we will be forced to live with in the future.

Toward a More Morally Defensible Approach

In an ultimate sense, the task of conserving an archaeological record for unknown future uses is impossible. One cannot collect all data in a manner that makes it useful for all purposes. On the other hand, it does seem possible to rethink the criteria by which significance is judged so as to minimize the impact of systematic biases arising from current interests and techniques and thus provide for the greatest possible range of future uses.

The very act of assessing the significance of a resource, no matter what criteria are employed, embodies a host of assumptions about the nature and significance of the record, assumptions that will change over time. Just as the problem provides the appropriate measure by which to judge relevance in research because it is the generating given, so the piece of real estate might be used as the standard by which significance assessments are made. The piece of real estate to be affected is the only known quantity in the CRM process. Instead of focusing on archaeological resources, it is more efficacious to focus on the unit of space, treating archaeological materials as attributes of the space rather than the reverse. This conception of the problem allows us to frame our conservation objective in straightforward sampling terms: to insure the survival of a representative sample of the remains contained within the area being treated.

This approach does not eliminate decisions based on contemporary knowledge, theory, and technique. Rather, it places these decisions in a more innocuous position within the general strategy. What constitutes a resource, how much is enough, and similar questions continue to exert a systematic influence on the representativeness of a sample. Even here, certain advantages can be gained. For example, the key question "What is the unit of observation?" can be taken to be the artifact. The representation problem is then one of insuring that the patterns of kind, quantity, and distribution are preserved in those archaeological materials that will persist beyond impact. The definition of "artifact" is crucial. Effecting a conservative approach requires that the definition be divorced from specific interests and problems.

The definition of artifact must be a theoretical one. In this context, defining an artifact as *anything which cannot be shown to be the product of natural processes* is effective. The negative phrasing is important. If artifacts were defined on the basis of current knowledge about what is the product of human action then, as knowledge increased, earlier collections would become deficient. In other words, items left out of the category "artifact" today because they are not known to be the product of human activity would be ignored or forgotten in the future if the definition of "artifact" changed. On the other hand, if artifacts were defined as the residuum of what other (physical) sciences cannot account for then, as their knowledge grew, part of what we have collected/recorded would become superfluous, but no artifacts would be ignored. In short, under the first definition, growth in knowledge will create a defective record, whereas under the second, it will *not*.

One must have units of observation, and a theoretical definition does not provide them. It only provides rules for creating them. Change in our definition of what is archaeological will be greatest at the scales of the very large and the very small. Our understanding of the world is best at the scales at which we consciously interact with our environment. Consequently, artifacts that are very small (e.g., a millimeter or so down to molecules and atoms) and very large (e.g., areal and regional patterning) must be sampled blindly. Blind sampling can be done in a spatial frame of reference because the area provides an independent control. It cannot be accomplished in a qualitative frame of reference.

Sampling immediately raises questions of how much is enough. In the best of circumstances, this is a nebulous issue because the accuracy of a sample (as opposed to its precision) is case dependent. The size of the sample necessary to represent accurately a population of attributes increases with the diversity and autocorrelation of the attributes in the space being examined. Still larger samples are required to extract spatial patterning (Jermann 1981), and this, too, varies with the complexity of the patterning. Establishing arbitrary sampling intensities is neither justifiable nor effective. It should be possible to determine sample adequacy empirically by following an incremental program in which the significance of the effect of adding additional sampling units is measured directly.

Some decisions, and therewith systematic bias, seem to enter unavoidably in determining quantity. The sample size required to represent a numerous, broadly distributed variable is much less than that required to represent a rare element or one that has a markedly patchy or localized occurrence. The only completely accurate "sample" is the population itself.

At this juncture, multistage data acquisition strategies (e.g., Binford 1964; Redman 1973; Dancey 1981) developed in the research context are helpful. There is a happy correlation between cost, areal coverage, and impact on resource and data recovery techniques. Remote methods, such as aerial photography, cover large areas at low cost without damaging the resource. Surface methods cover intermediate areas at moderate cost, with minimal damage to most elements of the record. Excavation covers only small areas, at huge costs, with total destruction of the sampled record. The kinds and quantities of information increase in the opposite direction. By using such strategies we gain some information for the whole area, a fair amount of information for large areas, and the maximum amount of information for a few areas. Implementing such nested sampling strategies requires substantive decisions on the part of the archaeologist, but if they are framed in terms of representing the patterns in kind, quantity, and distribution of artifacts, the systematic impact of those decisions can be minimized. Since sampling involves decisions, its role should be minimized to the extent possible. In fact, in terms of areal coverage, not only may sampling be undesirable from an ethical point of view, but it may be illegal as well (National Park Service 1981).

Seeing decisions as entailing systematic error has a further positive effect. It clearly emphasizes the role of avoidance and preservation. The more detailed the investigations, the more decisions that must be made. Data conserved through mitigative excavation will necessarily embody more systematic biases than data conserved by avoidance. This kind of approach forces one to make a maximum effort in decisions that result in avoidance and preservation. When CRM is seen as research, and success is predicated on knowledge of the resource, it is difficult to make full use of preservation and avoidance.

Although the primary concern here has been to treat moral and ethical issues surrounding assessments of significance, it is difficult not to address the interface between what one ought to do and what one can do. If morality identifies values, and ethics identifies the standards of behavior generated by the moral position, then ethics at least involve some consideration of the possible. Behavior is ethical when it is situationally consistent with the moral values. Certainly the approach to CRM suggested above makes a radical departure from current practice. In many, if not most, cases, it would require substantially more work than current practices. The techniques to effect such an approach already exist in some form. This view also identifies areas within archaeology that need to become the focus of development but that might not otherwise be accorded a high priority. The effectiveness of CRM is clearly tied to data collection strategies. In no other area would technical innovation be more profitable than in the development of low-cost, high-coverage technologies. Remote sensing and photogrammetry are just beginning to make important contributions in archaeology; they are the means by which most of the scientific world measures. Much can and should be done to apply recent technological advances to archaeological fieldwork. Machines could do much to increase our effectiveness (e.g., the technology for mechanical surface collection may already exist in agricultural rock pickers), with the further advantage that their biases can be calibrated in ways that are difficult to do for human beings. A continued commitment to labor-intensive fieldwork can only result in loss of more of the record simply because we cannot afford to save it or protect it.

The practical effectiveness of conservation can also be greatly enhanced (a necessity if research and CRM are dichotomized, as suggested here) if new research is undertaken only when existing sources of data are inadequate. The problem every researcher faces today is that there is no way to find out what kinds of data exist, what characteristics they have, and where they are. Until much more effective means are found for disseminating this information, we will find ourselves destroying more of the existing archaeological record than necessary and making poor use of data generated by CRM.

Summary and Conclusion

The moral imperative linked to significance decisions is the conservation of archaeological resources. The values attached to these resources derive from two different contexts, humanistic and scientific. Whereas assessing significance in the humanistic context implies the identification of the various constituencies who may value particular resources, assessing significance in the scientific framework is a matter of insuring the persistence of a representative sample of the resources of a given area. The dominant set of standards by which significance is assessed today are derived from a research orientation and measure the value of resources in terms of their contribution to contemporary problems. Although current research problems are different in kind and more diverse in number than they have been in the past, this approach to significance assessment does not differ in kind from the decisions of culture historians widely acknowledged as harmful to the record.

The problem-oriented approach, entirely appropriate to research, is inappropriate in CRM. The assessment of significance with reference to particular problems leaves marked systematic biases in the remaining record which limit the latter's scientific value and thwart conservation generally. While it is impossible to conserve the archaeological record without some influence from contemporary theory, interests, and knowledge, there are other means by which significance may be judged that minimize systematic sampling errors. While such standards are possible to employ today, the development of more cost-effective and technologically sophisticated field methods, coupled with better dissemination of information, is essential to CRM and archaeology generally.

10

Toward an Understanding of the Ethics and Values of Research Design in Archaeology

L. Mark Raab

It must be conceded that most archaeologists of those days had little sense of problem, solution, and new problem; and no sense of time whatever. They loved camping, they loved digging, they loved finding something; and the longer it lasted the better they liked it (Kroeber 1940: 2).

Suddenly he discovered that so long as his research design was superb, he never had to do research; just publish the design, and it would be held up as a model, a brass ring hanging unattainable beyond the clumsy fingers of those who actually survey and dig (Flannery 1982: 265–266).

During the past several years there has been an increasing emphasis in archaeology on designed research, the purpose of which is to allow planned, rational, and efficient control of the research process. Because of this recent emphasis, it is appropriate to examine ethical issues raised by the concept of formal research design. The following essay discusses the general value and uses of research design, as well as addressing specific issues, such as whether a research design imposes a bias on the interpretation of the data and whether the absence of a research design implies a lack of professional responsibility.

A basic premise is that there is an ethical obligation in contracted investigations to develop and follow a research design. (For another opinion, the reader is advised to see Dunnell's essay in this volume—ed.)

ARE THERE ETHICAL DIMENSIONS to research design in archaeology, or is the topic of purely scientific significance? The question may seem odd or even disturbing. The term "ethical" invokes concern about moral values. Rightness or wrongness in those terms may seem unrelated to research design, especially if one views the latter as essentially involving purely technical scientific considerations or intellectual styles and personal scholarly prerogatives. These attitudes tend to emphasize ethical issues of intellectual freedom. On the other hand, however, if linking ethics and research design is seen as begging the question of a necessary relationship between the two, we may well be apprehensive.

To some, research design may seem a code phrase, along with such terms as "behavioral," "processual," "theory-building" and "scientific," designating continuation of the battles of the New Archaeology. If one fails to embrace some explicit notion of research design, one runs the risk of being portrayed not only as intellectually out of date but as ethically retrograde as well. Lack of formal research design seems to imply lack of intellectual responsibility, as Kroeber's description of early 20th-century archaeologists illustrates. Dodging fire from that segment of the discipline, however, only brings one in range of attacks of the kind seen in Flannery's characterization of destructively "careerist" archaeologists. There, research design is the tool of slick self-promotion rather than disciplinary advancement.

The fact that such conflicting views of research design exist in archaeology today indicates at least two things. First, both ethical and scientific issues are combined in concepts of research design—often torturously so. This fact is hardly surprising. Ethical questions arise from ideas about the appropriateness of behavior: Is behavior consistent with what one *ought* to do? In archaeology, notions about what one ought to do arise from other ideas about what the discipline should be accomplishing. Research design seems to be one of the focal points for asking questions about means and ends, which brings us to a second point. If we believe that research design concepts can contribute to the advancement of archaeology, it may be useful to untangle conflicting points of view. In doing so, we may at least disarm some of the potential for ideological warfare and ethical ambiguity.

Such a task certainly is not easy. This author makes no pretense about examining all of the myriad issues involved, and offers more questions than answers about ethics. The attempt here is twofold. First, we will briefly examine the changing roles of research design, focusing on the latter's functions in archaeology's past and present approaches to inquiry. This may help us to understand the conflicting attitudes toward research design. We may then be better equipped to take up the second objective, which is to look at current debates about the purposes of research design.

The Changing Roles of Research

The history of research design in archaeology must be understood in order to appreciate contemporary ethical scientific questions. One notable aspect of this history is the quite recent advent of research as a *designed* product. Once again, the discipline's research sensibilities emerged from the milieu described in Kroeber's statement. Although that picture is perhaps too frivolous, even for the discipline's earliest efforts, it does capture a style of research that is not wholly dead in the discipline even today.

If research design was not always seen as an essential methodological or theoretical tool, there were—and are—philosophical approaches that simply do not require it or are even perhaps antithetical to it. These approaches question whether a research design is necessary or ethical. They also question the value of research design methods.

One such approach widely employed in archaeology is the "natural science" model. Hill (1972: 64–65) identifies this model as derived from a long empiricist tradition:

> The current archaeological research method is based in the empiricist school of philosophy (e.g., Hume, Mill, and Bacon), and subscribes implicitly to the metaphysical notion that every object existing in nature has a meaning or significance inherent within it—if we can but discover it. Each item contains within it (or is a manifestation of) a single truth or bit of knowledge. It is reasoned that because the item is itself real, it must have some particular reality or meaning; there is a single best way to understand or interpret it.
>
> The implication of this view for archaeology is that artifacts and features (and even artifact associations) are regarded as discrete, independent entities, each having a single primary meaning to be discovered (cf. Taylor, 1967: 122, 143; Deetz, 1968). It is our task to perceive this inherent meaning. In a sense, then, our inferences about the data are contained in the artifacts and features themselves. If we are well trained, experienced and perceptive we should, it is said, be able to recognize the inferential possibilities ("indicators") that the artifacts and associations of artifacts have (Thompson, 1958, pp. 1-5): "Indication is that quality of the evidence which describes its inferential possibilities. It is this indicative quality of the evidence which describes its inferential possibilities. It is this indicative quality of data which makes inference possible. An indication suggests a conclusion" [Thompson, 1958, p. 3].

The idea that there is an empirical reality to be *discovered* by the scientist is of paramount importance. Procedurally, this implies that research is a process of letting phenomena "speak for themselves." Armed with a research problem, even a general or implicit one, the scientist can marshal empirical observations as a logical first step in deriving explanations of the relevant phenomena. Conclusions are eventually guided by the nature of the data themselves. We should also appreciate that this empiricist stance was reinforced in archaeology by certain ideas about human behavior derived from anthropology. Rouse (1939), for example, following the ideas of certain cultural anthropologists, argued in an influential monograph that ceramic (and other) artifacts exhibit stylistic "modes" that are the expression of prehistoric cognitive templates determined by shared cultural norms. In keeping with theories of culture that stressed the normative qualities of behavior, it was thought that behavioral patterning, including material remains, was a process emergent from culture. This process and the cultural patterning of its material remains were thought to have objective reality, a reality that could be discovered and interpreted in their own cultural context.

As Hill suggests, this metaphysic has real consequences for research behavior, including research design. At the procedural level, there is little need to formulate detailed arguments beforehand about the connection between artifacts and behavior, since it is assumed that research will provide not only the relevant data but also the context in which the data are to be interpreted. A research design in this case might be seen as adequate if it indicates the nature of the research problem and the general plan of attack for gathering data. On the other hand, there are possible objections to formulating detailed hypotheses or other a priori expectations regarding potential data. In past decades, the latter practice was condemned by some (Smith 1955; Thompson 1956) as going beyond data into the realm of "speculation." After all, if data reveal themselves through investigation, the appropriate place for presentation of hypotheses and the like is the conclusion of research.

Beyond philosophy, however, we should not fail to recognize the impact of archaeology's own "culture" on attitudes toward research. Traditionally, archaeologists have placed great store in *doing* archaeology. That esteem lies behind Thompson's (1956) conclusion that we can evaluate a body of archaeological work on the basis of the reputation of the archaeologist who produced it. And reputations tended to be built through commitment to action-oriented fieldwork. In this respect, even today the discipline may not be too far removed from Kroeber's sketch. Historically, the impulse has been to get on with digging rather than to spend any considerable amount of time in intellectual analysis of possible results. This order of priorities met with no objections in an inductivist philosophy of science; on the contrary, it provided a means of evaluating the merits of research contributions.

Like the naturalist approach, the humanist approach questions the ethical foundation of research design. Although one can imagine research design as a methodological tool aimed at either humanistic or scientific objectives, it has clearly been identified with the latter. For those who are dubious of the appropriateness of any scientific approach to prehistoric cultures, research design may be seen as unnecessary at best. Hawkes (1968), for example, asserts that the methods of science produce an account of prehistory that is "ugly" and dehumanizing. This notion seems compatible with a belief that human behavior, past or present, is best explained in relation to some sort of "emic" cultural context. Once more, it is assumed that discovery of the native's cultural context is the appropriate avenue to explanation. By logical extension, attempts to control this process of discovery using a research design imposed by the investigator are seen as unwarranted bias. This point is made not to examine the relative merits of humanistic and scientific approaches, but simply to demonstrate that one ethical basis for rejecting research design is a denial of the validity of any research approach that attempts to impose the investigator's categories of data relevance on the archaeological record. The major point here is that attitudes about research design in contemporary archaeology vary greatly. No disciplinary consensus about the ethics of research design will be possible unless the existence of these divergent philosophical positions is recognized.

In the last twenty years, a large segment of the discipline has adopted an approach to research quite different than those of the natural science and humanist models. Research design as a distinct theoretical and methodological concern is the result of this change. Two questions are of major importance here: (1) What is this new approach to research design? and (2) What caused the shift in expectations about research design from the earlier inductivist stance?

One of the curious aspects of research design in archaeology today is that despite becoming an increasingly well-recognized methodological tool, there is little written by archaeologists about the concept per se (exceptions include Binford 1964; Hill 1972; Raab 1977; Goodyear et al. 1978). That is, there has been little effort to analyze the structure and function of research design as a method of inquiry. This paucity contrasts sharply with the multitude of research design works in the social sciences (e.g., Blalock 1964; Campbell and Stanley 1966; Phillips 1966) and even with recent works in cultural anthropology (e.g., Brim and Spain 1970; Pelto and Pelto 1978). Goodyear et al. (1978: 160) point out elsewhere that

> It would be useful . . . to present a number of definitions and explications of research design previously published in the method and theory literature, but they scarcely exist (see Plog 1974: 18–24). As a casual example, the words "research design" do not even appear in the subject index of *Explanation in Archaeology* (Watson et al. 1971). The same is true for Hole and Heizer's (1973) *An Introduction to Prehistoric Archaeology,* an omission that is particularly distressing since this text is commonly used at the undergraduate level. Such a void in the archaeological literature seems all the more anomalous when method and theory texts from other social science fields . . . contain explicit treatment of research design.

There are a number of research design strategies in substantive research (e.g., Hill 1966; Longacre 1970; Plog 1974; Schiffer and House 1975; Binford 1978, 1981), but the archaeological literature lacks any coherent, widely recognized research design principle. Nevertheless, such a principle seems to be taking shape in response to certain changes in the research climate of archaeology.

The principal *desideratum* here seems well expressed by Kerlinger

(1964: 17): "What is important is the over-all fundamental idea of scientific research as a controlled rational process of reflective inquiry, the interdependent nature of the parts of the process, and the paramount importance of the problem and its statement." Archaeologists seem to be moving toward research strategies that allow *planned, rational,* and *efficient control* of the research process.

To attain these goals, research designs must allow one to identify important goals in advance, specify relevant data and analytical methods, assess results against stated goals, and modify existing goals in light of results. Thus we have a recurrent cycle of inquiry which, in the long run, will provide the most reliable means of attaining specified objectives. The adoption of such a perspective reflects the emergence of a new set of research values. These values in turn have resulted from marked changes in the environment of archaeology. Consider the following.

The Emergence of Modern Science

During the 20th century, scientific inquiry, at least in the physical sciences, became distinctly *theory directed.* The Baconian empiricism of previous centuries was inadequate for the development of such concepts as Quantum Mechanics and Time-Space Relativity, whose theoretical models could not be developed from simple observation alone. At the same time, phenomena came to be characterized less in terms of simple linear causality and more in relation to complex statistical or probabilistic models.

In a series of related developments, during the 20th century, the social sciences adopted an increasingly explicit theoretical and methodological stance. No doubt this move was motivated partly by a desire to obtain some of the same legitimacy afforded the physical sciences before the public and academia. But it was also motivated by a conviction that the complexity of human behavior required more sophisticated method and theory. The result was an increasing commitment to the development of method and theory, a trend that continues to this day.

By mid-century, this social science trend began to reach archaeology, as evidenced by the advent of statistical methods in archaeology, and the necessarily probabilistic concepts of causation, data relevance and data sampling that followed. At a broader conceptual level, archaeology began its love affair with the philosophy of science. This attraction arose from an understandable interest in identifying and harnessing the conceptual tools that seemed to serve the sciences so well. From this milieu emerged a powerful commitment to *explanation of behavior by means of a body of scientific theory*.

The results of these developments were far-reaching. In contrast to the natural science model, which assumed that data emerged from the nature of the subject being studied, the new social science approach assumed that research was directed from the beginning by a problem orientation. But what kind of problem-orientation? Even the most inductive efforts are motivated by a problem at some level. Hill (1977: 79) stresses this point and offers a solution:

> A problem alone, however, is not enough—regardless of how well defined it is. We cannot collect data efficiently unless we refine our a priori ideas to the point of generating specific hypotheses or other testable propositions. Nagel (1967, p. 11) goes so far as to say that "Without . . . hypotheses, inquiry is aimless and blind." While this is a strong statement, its validity is supported by experience in all fields of science, including the social sciences.
>
> There are at least two major reasons for the fact that hypotheses are necessary to research:
>
> (1) Hypotheses provide a necessary link between problems and data. Without them, we will not know what data are important to collect, and we will miss much of the relevant data.
>
> (2) Hypothesis testing provides the only efficient means for evaluating the correctness of our inferences.

In this way the formulation of explicit hypotheses becomes the major vehicle for pursuing directed research. Hypothesis testing and the whole theoretical and methodological structure of which it is a part require a coherent form of explication. Research designs serve that function. Increasing reliance on formal research designs has developed hand-in-hand with explicit hypothesis testing. Both reflect the view that solutions to complex problems may be difficult to formulate coherently, much less carry out, without a formal vehicle for designing research.

The Emergence of Conservation Archaeology

Elsewhere, this author and others (Goodyear et al. 1978) have argued that the huge upswing in publically funded research in this country is a major stimulus to the development of research design techniques. Most of us are aware that private and public agencies are now funding millions of dollars of research each year under the terms of environmental protection statutes. What may not be as apparent is that the sheer volume of work being done, along with a desire to advance archaeological science through access to an unprecedented data base, is creating pressure to improve research design.

Of the numerous facets of this trend, two are worthy of comment here. First, contract work has forced archaeologists to develop research designs because there are simply no existing theoretical or culture-historical frameworks adequate for evaluating many of the country's archaeological resources. Second, there are encouraging signs that successful research designs can be built.

Contract work deals with an enormous topical and geographical range of archaeological problems. Archaeologists have found that archaeology as a whole is poorly prepared to deal with the challenge at hand:

> It is misleading to consider many of the research difficulties of contract archaeology apart from the general theoretical and methodological inadequacies that pervade archaeology as a whole. Archaeologists working in the contract realm receive their training in academia just as the archaeologists who are based there. Contract archaeologists do not have their memories erased when they leave the groves of Academe for the contract trenches. If contract work tends to be atheoretical, it is partly because the theories and predictive models necessary to deal with the geographically and temporally expansive scope of the contract setting *simply do not exist in archaeological science.* This general vacuum in theory insures that research will frequently be initiated in a region or about a topic for which there are a few or no prior expectations. This, in turn, often results in rote descriptions of sites and artifacts using worn-out culture-historical schemes, with analytical units incapable of explicating or measuring behaviorally significant variables. In short, a maintenance of sterile, inductive description [Goodyear et al. 1978: 161].

Some contract archaeologists have responded to this challenge in a productive way. Detailed treatment of research designs in contract archaeology is beyond the scope of this essay. Suffice it to say that both topical and regionally based designs have emerged from contract studies in the last ten years. The better of these designs have made appreciable advances in method and theory (Schiffer and Gumerman 1977; Goodyear et al. 1978).

As archaeological remains have come to be appreciated as a fragile, finite, nonrenewable resource, contract researchers have been forced to present explicit rationales for saving some resources while abandoning others to destruction. Not only must they show explicitly the kinds of problems that may be solved by studying a given class of resources, but they also must make these rationales in reference to detailed arguments about method and theory. Research should be done as *efficiently* as possible; i.e., archaeologists and the public should receive the greatest possible return on the planned loss of resources. To do otherwise would be irresponsible. All of these needs focus themselves in research designs, which become a way of articulating scientific arguments, planning an efficient research effort, and communicating with interested audiences. In contract research, many archaeologists have come to see research design as a useful tool in dealing with an increasingly complex research environment.

Professional and Scientific Accountability

Cultural resources management is but one area in which research *accountability* has intensified. The National Science Foundation is a major source of funds for archaeological research by American archaeologists. Receipt of these publically derived funds imposes a high degree of accountability in the form of de facto research designs (research proposals).

If we combine the archaeologists in this country who receive contract funds with those receiving NSF dollars, we have a large segment of the archaeological establishment, all of whom need to produce research designs. We sometimes forget that these sources of funding together constitute an historically unprecedented subsidy of archaeological research, and one that has developed only in the last twenty years. The effects on the practice of archaeology are tremendous.

Quite apart from shifts in scientific philosophy, simple accountability as regards research objectives, means, and results has done much to encourage a designed approach to research. The fiercely independent, "lone wolf" scholar may be the cherished historical stereotype, but the modern reality is the scientist who has to "sell" a designed product to a group of peer reviewers or to bureaucrats. Many archaeologists have come to see research designs as an integral part of the successful practice of professional archaeology.

Ethics

As anthropologists, we learn that a group's ethical precepts arise from culturally prescribed standards of behavior. It may come as no surprise then to recognize that within archaeology's "culture," research design has taken on ethical or quasi-ethical dimensions. We have examined how research design has been incorporated into archaeology as part of powerful intellectual, historical, and professional trends. Since research design apparently serves a complex set of needs, it would be surprising if it did not become a significant criterion in judging archaeological behavior. And there is evidence that judgments are being made across a broad spectrum of concerns.

An example is the way that research design has been linked to judgments about *professionalism*. One state council of archaeologists, whose ranks contain most of the professionals in the state, adopted a comprehensive set of performance guidelines for its members. Included in these guidelines is the stipulation that, along with other concerns, explicit research designs should be developed prior to implementation of any field research program. It was hoped that such designs would encourage the critical thought necessary to successful research, and help to communicate such thought to others with an interest in the process. There is also the implication that failure to meet this stricture is a failure to live up to high standards of performance. And those who perform badly as a result of willful neglect skirt the edge of an ethical dispute.

Another example that has arisen from cultural resource management is a recent proposal by King (1982: 35–36) for the development of National Archaeological Research Topics (NART). King conceives these to be fundamentally important research questions that all government-funded research would be required to address in some way. This proposal is sure to attract intense fire, primarily over the possibility of Big Brother in government directing archaeology. We will not consider the merits of this proposal here. What is of interest is the apparent reason for the proposal. It is King's conviction that much of what is currently called research design is actually more akin to intellectual anarchy:

> we have the "research design" I reviewed the other day . . . that described in page after page of glowing jargon how the project was to seek to characterize all the cozily nested subsystems of the suchandso cultural system with never a word about why the system was worth characterizing and no trace of assignment of priorities among the swarming host of questions that could be asked about it. It was a nightmare vision of Franz Boas in a David Clarke mask [King 1980: 247].

This is a serious misgiving about the effects of research design. Although some might not agree with King's proposed solution, the problem is apparent to many who work in contract research. At issue is squandering archaeological resources—to say nothing of time and money—in uncontrolled research schemes. There are clearly ethical dimensions to such a problem.

Academically oriented archaeologists also have misgivings about research design. It is hard to overestimate the effects of the one-person scholarly tradition in archaeology on ideas about research prerogatives. Historically, one did not need to *justify* one's work in advance as much as explain after the fact what one did. Choice of research problems and methods of attacking them were closely linked to ideas about scientific and academic freedom. Until quite recently, American archaeology had no explicit statement on ethics. "The Four Statements for Archaeology" adopted by the SAA in 1961 (Champe et al. 1961), offered a brief statement on ethics stressing that one must not infringe on the research (i.e., scholarly) rights of others or traffic in antiquities. To a large extent, The Statements reflected the underlying assumption that individual interests—the values of a community of autonomous scholar—were of overriding importance.

One can see some potential conflicts between this academic tradition and the idea of designed research. On one level, some fear the impact of the "herd" on science. Concern with research design as a methodological form may look uncomfortably close to seeking approval by head count. One may feel timid about pressing ahead without first winning widespread approval of a design. Science is then seen as little more than a public relations campaign. Add to this the fact that much work on significant problems is being done under supervision of governmental bodies, and we may have the ingredients of a disaster, if they are unmitigated by strong individualism and intellectual independence.

On a different level, there are fears about the creative core of the discipline. The forces that make for strong individualism are closely connected with creativity. Traditionally, the individual has been the creative unit in archaeology. This creativity has been most approved when it was expressed as substantive research. Flannery's criticisms undoubtedly are shared by many who see some forms of research design as overweening intellectualism that breeds elitism and contempt for those who actually collect archaeology's data. There is the clear implication that some are doing harm to the discipline by substituting intellectual posturing for work.

These examples show that there is a broad spectrum of concern about research design and behavior in archaeology. Research design is confronting the discipline with an approach-avoidance conflict. Important parts of this conflict emerge from both the "applied" and "academic" sectors. Let us consider two of these.

The Conservation Ethic

The conservation ethic has probably emerged in a more powerful way than at any other time in the history of archaeology as a result of contract work. After all, the fundamental rationale for doing contract work is to preserve archaeological data for the future. We have come to speak of archaeological *resources* precisely because of this goal. It is equally important to remember that an early argument in favor of designed research was that it would be a more rationally controlled process than older, more intuitive approaches to social science research. *The emergence of the conservation ethic made such efficiency seem not merely a point of academic interest, but an essential requirement of research striving to be as effective as possible for the time and money invested.* These interests were never divorced from abstract method and theory issues, but they were pressed into active service by an appreciable number of investigators (see examples in Goodyear et al. 1978).

Yet, some have come to see research design in contract studies as a menace rather than a solution:

> Everywhere, from project proposals to state historic preservation plans, there is an earnest faith that if only we devise "research designs" we can bring things under control. There is a deadly flaw in this notion, and King

> (1980: 237) diagnoses it accurately when he points out that a given research design may include anything from a scheme to reconstruct a river-basin-wide settlement system to a study of the edge angles of stone tools. Lacking in these designs is a strategic sense of problem formulation, from which is derived a series of subordinate studies. In place of well-thought-out priorities and interlocking study components, we too often find a grab-bag of theoretical and methodological objectives, unconnected in any logical way to management decisions and the investigative process. The shotgun approach to "banking" data for the future is one way to encourage such designs. As formal research designs become more common we may find them institutionalizing the problems we seek to avoid [Raab 1981: 8].

How do we save resources with a tool that should be an efficient expression of scientific creativity without seeing the process fossilized?

In reality, this question is not far removed from one that asks what we should do about a circumstance in which someone can be professionally rewarded for inventing designs, but not necessarily ones that will or even can be applied. The central question is whether research design is a useful tool or an intellectual pose. We are attracted to the prospect of a more rationally controlled research process but dismayed by the possibilities for misuse of the tool.

Changes in the Nature of the Archaeologist's Work

Research design also worries us because it signals real changes in the way archaeologists work. We have already examined the traditional deployment of archaeologists as individuals following individualistic goals and seeking to distinguish themselves as autonomous scholars. We should not underestimate the sheer fun and sense of freedom that was possible for archaeologists when they could pursue personal goals with a minimum of intellectual superstructure or institutional entanglement. Some of this is captured in Martin's (1974: 7) candid description of some of his own early work in the American Southwest:

> The purpose of these digs was vague. Essentially, I was digging for specimens for the Museum, and because, aside from work by Prudden in the early 1900's, little research had been done on sites of this time period (about A.D. 1000). Mostly, we dug out of curiosity, for fun, for specimens, and to write the historical details for these sites and for this time period. Actually, we added a fair amount of information to the study of cultural processes and the social groupings of the early history of the Anasazi.

Certainly archaeology continues to have its satisfactions. However, with increasing commitment to creation of a social science and solution of more complex research problems, research inevitably becomes more abstract and needs to be carried out through cooperative efforts. Rewards now seem less immediate and more attenuated by an increasingly specialized division of labor. Designed research is needed to cope with our new situation.

It may be that calls for research designs signal the end of a simpler, more innocent time in the discipline. Some may fear the increasing submergence of the individual archaeologist in corporate research efforts; the increasing dependence of the discipline on public funds (NSF as well as contract projects); and the increasing orientation toward conceptual goals that may not be widely understood because of their diversity and complexity, much less subscribed to on an emotional level.

Conclusion

Research design is a key outcome of pervasive changes in archaeology. The kinds of conflicts centering around research design will have no resolution without an understanding of the underlying stresses created by change. Some of the causes of conflict are probably a self-limiting condition. There seems little doubt that most American archaeologists are commited to a scientific archaeology. That does not mean that they reject humanistic approaches, but that their methods and objectives are primarily those of science. Increasing familiarity with formal designs in scientific archaeology will lead more and more archaeologists to view research design as a familiar methodological tool. The trends of research accountability and the need to control complex investigative processes seem likely to make research design more than a passing fad.

If we do not have simple prescriptions for deciding what is ethical and what is not, we can at least begin to ask the questions necessary to forge a consensus about our values as archaeologists. Among these, two questions seem particularly crucial:

1. What constitutes useful archaeological work? It is easy to parody archaeologists with intense commitments to abstract philosophical, methodological, and theoretical issues because these topics play on the tensions arising from recent changes in the discipline. The discipline is currently attempting to strike a balance between "doing" archaeology and being properly reflective on the conceptual basis of the discipline. We want to be careful not to give way to a reactionary impulse to return to some more innocent time instead of taking on the more arduous task of figuring out how the field can assimilate changes that are already upon us.

2. How can we nurture creativity in research? The fact that the rugged individualist is going out of style causes concern because it represented the traditional locus of intellectual independence and energy. Increasingly, research is carried out in a collective setting because of the scope and complexity of the work and the nature of funding. If research designs are to be the blueprints of this new functional mode, they must

be effective, which means that they must be powered by innovative thinking and somehow connected to research that matters. It is for this reason that we must undertake serious scrutiny of research design methods in archaeology. At present they are too embedded in polemics, money-making schemes and specific research problems to allow a ready analytical overview. One hopes that attempts to reach judgments about values and ethics in connection with research design will follow from such efforts rather than the other way round.

There are a great many questions about research design outstanding in archaeology. Answering those questions calls for an understanding of the forces that have called forth research design and the uses to which designed research should be put. Such an understanding is a prerequisite for any theory of ethics connected with research behavior.

11

The Ethics of Excavation: Site Selection

Fred Plog

A primary tenet of the conservation ethic, set forth by William Lipe in 1974, is that a resource should not be used until there is justifiable reason to do so. Use, in this case, means excavation.

How does one operationalize that tenet? Working within the conservation ethic, how does one determine if excavation at a particular site is justified? This is the question addressed in the following essay.

The guidelines Plog proposes take into account the characteristics of the resource base and the proposed archaeological operations. These guidelines can, and perhaps will, become the standard test in the discipline of whether a proposal to excavate a site will be approved. They also could be an important part of agencies' plans for the management of cultural resources on public lands.

As with the majority of topics discussed in this volume, there is nothing approximating a developed literature in archaeology concerning the circumstances under which it is or is not justifiable to undertake an excavation project at a particular site. Given this void, this author has decided to take one of a number of possible approaches to writing an ethical statement concerning site selection. Basically that approach involves attempting to write a difficult test for justifying excavation: supposing that sites are as rare as some of our more extreme discussions claim, what are the most difficult standards that one might ask an investigator to meet before agreeing to the use of a particular site for an excavation project? The aim of this essay is to delineate a set of standards that might be used by a panel of archaeologists or land managers in reaching such a decision.

Clearly, this essay might have addressed a different question: What sort of justification is, on the average, acceptable? But, focusing on the issue of a genuinely rare resource sets a clear limit to what a decision maker might demand of the resource's user. The standards identified herein underwrite a far more extreme test than is probably needed for successfully allocating the majority of resources.

Philosophical Concerns

One can identify a number of assumptions that underlie archaeologists' concern in selecting a site for excavation. This discussion will focus on those that seem most essential given the current practice of archaeology and cultural resource management. First, however great the increase in archaeologists' abilities to derive information from site survey, excavation will remain our premier technique. Despite disagreement among archaeologists as to the kinds of inferences that can be made on the basis of survey data, everyone understands that a far greater array of information concerning the prehistoric past can be obtained through excavation. Similarly, even the stoutest defenders of survey archaeology would agree that we are still evaluating the efficacy of most approaches to "surface archaeology." Therefore, it would not make sense to discuss the relative merits of survey and excavation, even though the former is clearly far less expensive and far less destructive than the latter.

A second assumption is that all archaeologists, not just those in cultural resource management, operate in the context of the preservation and conservation ethics (Lipe 1974). That is, we all agree that sites are a nonrenewable resource that should be used only with good justification and when alternative research strategies are not possible. While the definition of these concepts has been made far more explicit in recent years, they are not novel. Insistence that sites be excavated only with good justification and in the best way possible, and that the results be published, has always been a professional concern.

Third, excavation is a very costly activity. Someone is always in the position of having to allocate scarce financial resources among the members of the archaeological community. These resource allocation decisions implicitly involve conservation and preservation issues.

Finally, our understanding of the nature and quantities of archaeological resources in virtually every area of the U.S. has increased dramatically within the last decade. Perhaps more sites have been tested or excavated during the last decade than in any other period of archaeological research. The increase in the number of sites described on the basis of surface remains has been even more dramatic. In the Apache-Sitgreaves Forests of Arizona, for example, a few dozen sites had been recorded at the start of the 1970's. At this writing, the number of recorded sites is approaching 2000. While the magnitude of increase may be less dramatic elsewhere, we are dealing almost everywhere with a data base far greater than anyone would have conceived possible a few decades ago.

This enhanced information creates a powerful obligation. No longer is it justifiable to treat the allocation of a site to an excavation project as if such a decision could be made only in the abstract. The archaeological data base in many states is sufficient to make projections of the total number of sites likely to occur there and, in several instances, of the total number of sites of particular time periods, cultural affiliations, or types. The impact that use of a particular site is likely to have on the aggregate data base is knowable. Given that we are no longer operating in a vacuum, if we expect to retain credibility among the politicians and managers to whom the conservation-preservation ethic has been "sold," no decision about excavation should be made without appropriate justification in relation to the existing data base.

Given the conservation-preservation ethic, the cost of excavation, our greatly increased understanding of the availability of archaeological resources, and the vital importance of excavation to the practice of archaeology, when is it justifiable to select a particular site for excavation? (Reference is made to single sites for the sake of simplicity, although more and more frequently decisions are made concerning groups of sites.) The following issues should be addressed in making such a decision.

1. *Has a research question been identified to which the site is especially pertinent?* While fieldwork always has involved and always will involve elements of chance, the likelihood of productive field investigation is greatest when that work is underlaid by a high-quality research design—a well-formulated problem, hypotheses, test implications, etc. This approach is now an integral part of the archaeological craft. A volume describing the bases of research design in different topical, theoretical, and methodological areas of archaeology is about to appear (Raab and Klinger in press). In addition, federal agencies, from the Forest Service and the Bureau of Land Management (cf. Cordell 1979; Tainter and Gillio 1980; Plog 1981; McGuire and Schiffer 1982) to the President's Advisory Council on Historic Preservation (King 1982), have invested enormous effort and substantial funding in creating literature that should enable any archaeologist to base any project on a meaningful research design. For most areas of the U.S., these discussions are sufficiently detailed that it is now reasonable not simply to ask whether a given research effort is well-conceived, but also whether the use of a particular site is essential for that effort.

2. *Does the research design specify the minimum amount of work at the site necessary for the successful completion of the research design?* Archaeologists rarely excavate 100 per cent of a site. Given the enormously increased understanding of sampling procedures within the profession, and the conservation-preservation ethic, any research effort ought to use the smallest portion of a site necessary for the successful completion of the research. Undoubtedly, such estimates will sometimes prove to be incorrect. But

the need to address the question of how much of a site genuinely needs to be used in a research effort is just as important as the question of whether that site needs to be used at all. In some instances, the planned research may simply prove too destructive of a unique resource to allow the project in question to proceed.

3. *Does the research design demonstrate that available archaeological methods and techniques are sufficient to address the problem or does it identify potential advances in the latter that will be addressed so as to minimize similar future impacts?* There are many research questions that archaeologists would like to resolve for which appropriate techniques are not available. To stipulate that a site cannot be used unless existing research techniques are adequate for the resolution of the problem that motivates the research would be too strong a test. Such a stipulation would have the effect of retarding the development of methods and techniques. But it is reasonable to insist that an investigator either demonstrate the efficacy of existing techniques for the resolution of the problem that motivates the research or explicitly identify the manner in which the proposed research will attempt to improve the state of the art in relation to the research question at hand.

4. *Does the research design demonstrate that no existing data base will suffice to address the research question?* It is very difficult to reconcile the aversion that most archaeologists appear to possess to the use of museum questions with the conservation-preservation ethic. That museum collections have weaknesses is clear. Provenience data are not always ideal. Excavation techniques used to recover the collections can be so poor in relation to existing standards that problems will arise if specific analyses are attempted. These problems are especially acute in relation to our current understanding of the manner in which the archaeological record is formed and transformed.

At the same time, the promulgation of the conservation-preservation ethic should have led to an enormous investment in the exploration of the kinds of pivotal research issues that could be addressed by museum collections. Little effort in this direction has been made. Until we demonstrate our commitment to minimizing the use of archaeological sites by insisting that the suitability of existing collections be explored, there is little reason that the public should treat our ethical commitments as meaningful ones.

5. *Does the research design demonstrate that it is not feasible to use a less well-protected site?* The legal protection of sites varies. In few areas of the U.S. is meaningful protection given to sites on private land. When it is possible to pursue a particular research effort on private land rather than federal land, one should do so to be consistent with the conservation-preservation ethic. Sites on private land are far more likely to disappear before archaeologists have an opportunity to explore them.

6. *Does the research design demonstrate that it is not feasible to use a partially disturbed site?* All of us instinctively prefer working at sites where there is

minimal to no evidence of surface disturbance. However, there are problems with insisting on the use of "pristine" sites. First, such an approach is not in accord with the conservation-preservation ethic. Second, there are increasingly fewer such sites in the U.S. Finally, our increased attention to site formation processes has resulted in evidence that apparently pristine sites are rarely so. Even when existing surfaces appear unmodified, they are likely to have been impacted by early episodes of pothunting, the evidence of which has simply been removed over time by natural processes (Plog 1981). The effect of later prehistoric peoples on earlier sites is now well known. For all of these reasons, there is little justification for rendering a genuinely pristine site less so if there are suitable alternatives for the research problem at hand. Similarly, it may be possible to incorporate disturbances into some aspects of a research effort. At Nuvaqwewtaka (Chavez Pass), for example, much of our early stratigraphic information was obtained by squaring and cleaning the sides of potholes.

7. *Does the research design demonstrate that the problem cannot be addressed at sites with greater interpretive potential?* Our obligation to the public is a substantial one. Were it not for inherent public interest in prehistory, cultural resource management would not exist and other public funding of archaeology would be far lower. In return, we should plan our work so as to maximize at least potential public access to sites. While the concern of land management agencies with interpretive uses of archaeological sites has not been great, it is growing. To the extent that it is possible, archaeologists should choose to work at sites where the cost of actually interpreting the site to the public will be least (e.g., at sites close to a highway, a district office, a ranger station, or a campground). Such a decision can sometimes be a difficult one. While logistically accessible sites reduce the costs of doing fieldwork, they are also the most likely to have been impacted by collectors and pothunters. Thus, while the question of interpretive use should be addressed, it will not always prove feasible to select the more interpretable of a set of available sites.

Excavations Based on Legal Requirements

Archaeologists are about to face an enormous ethical challenge over the question of the significance of sites. Collective experience with the legal procedures of cultural resource significance has demonstrated that virtually any site can be claimed as significant because of the information that it is likely to yield. Our ethical dilemma concerns our ability to establish standards that allow us to evaluate the relative importance of sites so that only those that are genuinely important are deemed legally significant.

Environmental and managerial officials in federal agencies and private firms are aware of this significance dilemma and have a very great interest in seeing the archaeological profession develop a superior set of standards so that their funds will be used to enhance knowledge of the past rather than employment of archaeologists. We cannot afford to continue recording and excavating sites whose ultimate yield of information is minimal. A number of standards would seem essential to remedy this increasingly difficult situation.

1. *The standards under which a site would be considered important must be identified at the outset of a particular project or planning effort.* After the fact, all of us are clever enough to find a means of arguing the importance of a particular site or set of sites. In fact, archaeologists as a group have become quite skilled in this enterprise. But such post hoc decision making is incompatible with good archaeology and good research.

In the first place, good research designs are not post hoc research designs. The reasons for making the research process explicit have been thoroughly described and argued in the existing literature. If sites are important because of their research potential, then it should be possible to describe the relative potential of different classes of sites before fieldwork or even initial inventory begins. In the second place, agencies and private companies alike have invested an enormous effort in the preparation of a data base that allows consideration of the relative importance of different classes of sites very early in the research or planning process.

An example is the Forest Service-BLM overview series for New Mexico and Arizona. Overviews also have been prepared for cities, counties, coal mines, electrical grids, etc. The best of these efforts prioritize the key research topics that need to be addressed for particular areas and time periods. If, as a profession, we do not begin to use these many studies in setting research priorities for particular projects and areas, then more than one individual will soon ask, quite justifiably, why the money was ever spent in the first place.

2. *The amount of previous investigation of the particular class of resource should be considered.* Some types of sites are truly unique and others are relatively common. Given the last ten years of cultural resource management, large quantities of sites have been recorded and excavated. If one cannot demonstrate that archaeologists working in a particular area still lack the excavated data base necessary to address the research questions that are said to make a site important, there is little justification for work at that site. Certainly, sites will continue to contain unanticipated information of considerable consequence. But the public trust must not be robbed by archaeologists who continue to argue for the growth of an already redundant data base for a particular site type.

3. *Investigate the quantity of the resource in question that is under high-quality protection on nearby lands.* The concerns that arise in respect to this issue are similar to those just discussed. Even if sites of a particular type may potentially yield important information, a question arises as to whether

sufficient quantities of those sites are under high-quality protection on nearby lands. Publically financed archaeology should give first consideration to resources that are both rare and in danger of disappearing.

Regardless of the informational potential of sites, justification for public underwriting of their excavation is minimal if they are abundantly available and not threatened in any way. For example, the most abundant site type on the Apache-Sitgreaves National Forests in Arizona is an artifact scatter between 100 and 999 square meters. Projecting from the current forest inventory, there are likely to be 3894 such sites in the forests. There have been 5 excavation projects done at such sites in the last 20 years. If archaeologists continue to use these sites at the rate of one every four years, the resource would not be spent until the year 17,555. Even if the sites were used at the rate of one per year, the resource would not be spent until nearly 6000. Given all of the changes in the practice of archaeology, as well as in the skill of managers, that are likely to occur during either of these time intervals, it is simply difficult to discuss the resource base as if it were threatened. Some artifact scatters will prove to have unique characteristics that do require mitigation, but the need for that mitigation should not simply be assumed.

Teaching and Interpretation

The use of archaeological sites for teaching purposes is as important as the use for interpretive purposes. If we really expect to stop illicit collection and excavation at archaeological sites, we must show as many students as possible what good archaeology is about. There is also the need to train the next generation of professionals.

The circumstances under which a site is to be excavated are not greatly changed simply because teaching or interpretation is at issue. For example, if the issues identified earlier in respect to research design and the availability of alternative resources are not addressed and identified to a class, then we are doing less than a complete job of teaching. If the excavation of a site for interpretation is not based on a high-quality research design, a high-quality job of intepreting that site is an impossibility. Certainly, teaching and interpretation interject unique logistical concerns into the selection of a site for excavation. But these logistical concerns are additions to, not substitutions for, the obligation to address basic scientific and ethical issues.

Conclusion

The development of any set of ethical standards raises the question of how those statements will be operationalized. How will they be applied to real situations? Who will decide how they apply to real situations?

Neither of these questions is an easy one to answer. Clearly, each of the standards proposed herein can be carried to an extreme that will result in poor archaeology. Black-and-white statements cannot easily be applied to an always grey world save by individuals and groups who are using those statements intelligently. Another pitfall is hollow claims to the acceptance of such standards. Too many research reports that claim to have been done in full accord with the Airlie House reports show little, if any, cognizance of the latter. Similarly, and quite unfortunately, membership in the Society of Professional Archaeologists is often used as a guarantee that the individual in question does high-quality and ethical work. Hollow citations and hollow memberships guarantee neither high-quality work nor ethical behavior.

Unfortunately, the claim that archaeology is a profession is only a hypothesis, the test of which is going poorly at the moment. Neither state nor national organizations have been quick to address ethical issues, even when these have been raised and a consensus reached among members that a given behavior was unethical.

The results of such failures are clear. Poor archaeology will be done, public monies will be wasted, and our failures will be used by public and private agencies to justify spending less and less on poorer and poorer work. Individually and collectively, we must bite the bullet and draw a clear boundary between those archaeologists motivated by a desire to understand the past and those motivated by greed. There is no *single* locus of activity for these ethical issues. Professional organizations at the national and state levels must be involved. Equally important are state and national efforts to plan for the wise use of cultural resources.

12

Ethical Dilemmas in Federal Cultural Resource Management

Dee F. Green

Since the majority of archaeological activity undertaken annually in the United States is funded by governmental bodies, any professional concern with ethics must take account of problems encountered by and within these agency cultural resource management programs. Ethical problems can arise both within the agency (e.g., differences in objectives between the specialist and the manager) and between agency and nonagency archaeologists. One much-discussed area of potential in-service ethical conflict is concern that the resource will be impacted without adequate consideration. An example would be the use of inadequately trained and supervised nonprofessionals for site inventory. Another classic ethical concern is that circumstances within the agency will force the specialist to compromise professional standards (e.g., by misrepresenting the significance of the resource or taking shortcuts in conducting the survey).

The education of managers has gone far toward reducing such conflicts. Apparent ethical problems in the federal sector often turn out to be the result of outsiders' misunderstanding of the agency's decision-making process. The organizational structure and methods of influencing decisions characteristic of academia may not be effective in the governmental sector. Indeed, they may produce the opposite of the desired result. Archaeologists are beginning to discover that in order to achieve resource conservation, they must learn the "foreign" (i.e., nonacademic) system. Dee F. Green has been very successful in working within one agency's system, having built an outstanding cultural resource management program in the Southwestern Region of the Forest Service.

THE PURSUIT OF ARCHAEOLOGY in the federal establishment has existed under a cloud of suspicion for many years. Archaeologists in the federal system have long complained about treatment by their academic colleagues (Weakly 1977). The Society of Professional Archaeologists (SOPA) (Davis 1982) and the American Society for Conservation Archaeology (ASCA) (Mayer-Oakes 1974) were formed in response to the explosion of federal archaeology in the 1970's. During the same decade, academic and federal archaeologists gathered on a number of occasions to discuss the how's and why's of cultural resource management (Lipe and Lindsay 1974; Matheny and Berge 1976; McGimsey and Davis 1977; Dickens and Hill 1978). Professional ethics, then, is a concern of the 1980's. This essay will focus on the ethical dilemmas faced by archaeologists in the federal sector during the 1970's. These will be used as a springboard for discussing what should be done in the present decade to help resolve some ethical concerns of the profession.

With the exception of the National Park Service, the National Trust for Historic Preservation, and the Smithsonian Institution, federal agencies do not usually have cultural resource management as a primary focus of their missions. Agencies such as the Bureau of Land Management, Bureau of Reclamation, Corps of Engineers, Federal Highway Administration, Forest Service, Housing and Urban Development, Tennessee Valley Authority, and Soil Conservation Service have been viewed with concern by the professional archaeological community. Archaeologists employed by federal agencies are thought by some to face severe ethical dilemmas because the agencies do not put cultural resource sites first in their considerations. These ethical dilemmas, which are the subject of this essay, are not necessarily any severer among federal archaeologists than among those in the private contracting or academic worlds (Lipe 1974; King 1977; U.S. General Accounting Office 1979, 1981; Plog 1980).

This discussion of ethical dilemmas in the federal sector deals with the issues in five areas: (1) agency policies; (2) agency decisions; (3) archaeological permittees; (4) management and development agencies; and (5) vandalism. In each area the dilemma is illustrated by an anonymous case.

Agency Policies

Agency policy regarding its activities should be based on statutes, regulations, Executive Orders, and direction from the Secretary of the Department under which the agency operates. To the extent that it is not, ethical dilemmas for the archaeologist can arise. The phrase "should be based on" is used to reflect the fact that agency policy is sometimes out of tune due to time lag between passage of the law or executive direction and policy formulation, conflict between law and executive direction (especially when administrations change), and court action.

The best example of the time lag between passage of law and policy formation, with regard to cultural resource matters, is the Historic Sites

Act of 1935. Except for the National Park Service, the act essentially was ignored by the federal government. In fact, it took the Historic Preservation Act of 1966 to focus attention on cultural resources, and most agencies did not make the provisions of either act part of their policy statements until the 1970's. As late as 1980, a federal court still found it necessary to order the Secretary of the Interior to "promulgate regulations setting out substantive criteria and procedural guidelines for landmark designation under the Historic Sites Act of 1935" (*Historic Green Springs Inc. v. Bob Bergland* 1980). Fairfax (1980) summarizes other time lag problems an agency can have between enactment of law and policy formulation.

Differences in interpretation of law sometimes result in different policies. For example, the 1974 Public Law 93-291, which extends the Reservoir Salvage Act to all federal projects, states in Section 7(a): "To carry out the purposes of this Act, and Federal agency responsible for a construction project may assist the Secretary and/or it may transfer to him such funds as may be agreed upon, but not more than 1 per cent of the total amount authorized to be appropriated for such project."

Some agencies have interpreted this to mean that no more than 1 per cent of any project budget can be spent on cultural resources regardless of who spends it. Other agencies interpret it to mean that no more than 1 per cent can be transferred to the Secretary of the Interior, but the agency can spend more than 1 per cent if it chooses to do so.

There is a problem for archaeologists in an agency that restricts cultural resources dollars to the 1 per cent interpretation. Cases will arise in which 1 per cent of the money is not sufficient to deal adequately with the cultural resources involved. For archaeologists in agencies using either interpretation, a dilemma may arise in dealing with archaeological contractors who want to spend more money on a project area than is necessary, even if it is less than 1 per cent.

The following example highlights this. A federal agency (with the policy that the 1 per cent rule applied to transfer of funds to the Department of Interior and not to total spent) was exchanging land with a large mining company. The mining company had spent several hundred thousand dollars on a cultural resource survey and testing program. The survey and testing had been done by a respected state university whose costs were known to be high compared to other contractors.

Mitigation was the next phase and the university had presented a budget of nearly 1 million dollars to the mining company. A federal archaeologist had inspected the area and met with university and mining company officials on numerous occasions. He had reviewed the pertinent documentation and had suggested to the mining company that less expensive contractors were available. The mining company for its own reasons had kept the university as its contractor. The federal archaeologist suspected that the final reports would show that the archaeological results were not worth spending over 1 million dollars, which amounted to about 25 per cent of the land value. He also suspected that someone might use the figures to embarass the archaeological profession and/or call for the deregulation of cultural resources. As a federal agency archaeologist, he had no right to interfere with the financial dealings between a corporation and its contractor. The dilemma was an ethical problem. Should he have raised the issue of exorbitant costs and pointed out the potential for damage to the profession or should he have kept quiet? The archaeologist in this example chose not to interfere. He used the rationale that his fears about the final reports and the misconstruing of the case might be unfounded and probably could not be proved in advance. Raising the issue through formal channels (SOPA, the state council) could put the agency in an awkward position and subject the individual to lawsuit or other sanctions.

Agency policies do lead to ethical dilemmas for archaeologists. Their resolution may involve adherence to either the professional code or one's individual standard, should these be different. In the above example, the dilemma was resolved on the basis of the archaeologist's individual standard rather than the professional code.

Agency Decisions

Agency policy may support cultural resources, but it does not follow that agency decisions will always conform to that policy. This has caused ethical dilemmas for archaeologists in agencies but, as explained below, the situation is more complex than appears at first glance.

Agencies differ in their decision-making processes, including the levels at which decisions are made and who has the authority to make different kinds of decisions. Decisions about the use or disposition of cultural resources are not usually in the hands of agency archaeologists. Ethical dilemmas may arise if the latter assume that they have such decision-making powers. Ironically, an agency archaeologist may be viewed as unethical by his academic colleagues when something goes wrong with a site because they assume he has the authority to make decisions about its use.

Cultural resources on federal land are owned by the people of the United States. Agencies administering the land are the custodians of those resources and are empowered by Congress to manage them. Until the 1970's and with the exception of the National Park Service, most federal agencies either ignored the cultural resources or abdicated their responsibilities toward them. The archaeological community traditionally has exploited the resource (Green n.d.). It was not until Lipe's voicing of the "conservation ethic" (1974) that archaeologists began to think seriously in terms of resource management. After years of ignoring or exploiting cultural resources, agencies have found that they have to deal with a nonrenewable resource. Articulating this new responsibility within traditional modes of management has caused dilemmas, ethical and otherwise, for many agency decision makers.

To illustrate the point, consider a large project-oriented agency that hired a private archaeological contractor to mitigate an important site by excavation. During the course of excavation, the site was visited by several professional archaeologists who questioned the techniques being employed. The agency noted the objections but failed to take prompt action. The agency's cultural resource specialist was not sufficiently trained to deal with the site in question.

After several months, the agency called in a consultant who examined the site and performed some tests. Before the report was completed, another archaeologist examined the site and questioned not only the techniques employed in the excavation but also whether a large portion of the location was actually an archaeological site at all. The case went before the state archaeological council, the state archaeologist, and the State Historic Preservation Officer (SHPO). Local newspapers picked up the story. Suddenly the agency, which was spending a great deal of money trying to cope with its archaeological problems and felt it was doing a good job, found itself in the middle of a professional controversy that it could neither control nor understand.

During the next few months, a flurry of activity began as impounded waters rose toward the site. The agency's consulting archaeologist filed a report that was generally supportive of the archaeological contractor. The state archaeological council appointed a committee to investigate the matter. The SHPO recruited several archaeologists to do additional validity testing. More newspaper stories appeared and more archaeologists and other specialists became involved. Paranoia began to manifest itself on all sides with numerous lawsuits threatened.

As the water level neared the site, the agency administrator found himself in this situation:

1. The agency lacked credibility with the local archaeological community.
2. The contract archaeologist was highly agitated because his professional credibility had been questioned.
3. Some archaeologists questioned the validity of the site.
4. Others believed that any problems were minor.
5. Another group urged neutrality until more investigations could take place at the site.
6. The press smelled a scandal and demanded more information.
7. The agency cited the 1 per cent rule and argued that the limitation only left funds for analysis and writeup.

Which sector of the professional community should the administrator have believed? Should the analysis and writeup funds have been diverted to an investigation of the site? Should a cofferdam have been built to protect the site until the professional community could resolve its concerns? Should a downstream flow have been allowed to prevent water from inundating the site, even though it might mean insufficient water later in the season for irrigation of crops already planted? Did the value of the site, some portions of which might not actually be a site, outweigh the public good to be derived from the recreational and agricultural values attached to the full flood pool? These were the dilemmas he faced.

The decision reached by the administrator was to continue to use the funding for analysis and writeup. No cofferdam was built. Water was allowed to inundate the site. He stipulated that any qualified professional or group of professionals who wished to investigate the site prior to inundation could do so within reason, but no funds would be provided. In this case, the agency decision contributed neither to the resolution of the individual standard nor to the professional code.

Unsystematic testing did not resolve the problem of the site's validity; some tests were positive and others negative. Some questions may be answered by the final report, but portions of the site will remain suspect in the minds of some archaeologists. Not only are there doubts about the site, but a cloud hangs over the archaeological contractor. It may never be dispelled.

Failure of the agency to resolve the issue in terms acceptable to the archaeological community leaves that community with ethical dilemmas of its own. Can the issue regarding the validity of the site be resolved with the available data? What should the position of the archaeological community be when an agency appears to be resolving a conflict situation on the basis of its own, or the greater public, need rather than the best interests of the archaeological community? What social mechanisms need to be developed or refined for dealing with these situations?

Archaeological Permittees

Holders of permits to excavate cultural resource sites on federal lands sometimes create ethical dilemmas for their colleagues in federal agencies. Any federal archaeologist can tell stories about academic colleagues who fail to produce reports. Most also can tell stories of poor-quality field procedures. Some can tell stories about sending the FBI after a permittee to recover artifacts he tried to keep in his personal possession. Sometimes the situations are not so straightforward. The issuance of a permit may be contraindicated even for legitimate research. For example, a permit was denied a researcher who wanted to excavate a Native American shrine. In another case, it was denied because a decision for long-term preservation of the site had already been made.

The site was in a right-of-way, scheduled to be part of a mitigation package for comment by the SHPO and the Advisory Council. Authorizing excavation could have undercut the archaeological contractor already hired for the job. None of this information was provided by the individual when he made his requests, although it was all known to him. In addition, the research design for the existing permit was not suitable for that site. Allowing excavation without the comments of the SHPO and the Advisory Council would have put the agency in a position of noncompliance with cultural resources laws.

The dilemma involved a decision about whether to prosecute the individual for violation of the Antiquities Act and probably destroy his career as an archaeologist, or to simply reprimand him. The administrating archaeologist felt that the professional code overrode any personal considerations and recommended prosecution, but his role was only advisory. The decision rested with the land manager, who decided to reprimand rather than prosecute.

Management and Development Agencies

Within the federal government one can distinguish between agencies that primarily manage land and those that are primarily oriented toward development. Activities of these agencies may affect cultural resources, although the development agencies tend to have much larger projects in terms of budgets and the land surface impacted. Private organizations and state agencies, such as power and gas companies and highway departments, also use federal land and have projects that might impact cultural sites. Dilemmas often arise when a development-oriented agency proposes a project on lands administered by a management-oriented agency. Policies, goals, decision-making processes, and attitudes toward cultural resources can be very different in such agencies. When combined with differing viewpoints among archaeologists about the nature of sites and the methods of doing archaeology, these differences may result in explosive dilemmas (U.S. General Accounting Office 1979).

Variations on this theme are as numerous as the cases that could be cited. The following case illustrates one variation. A development agency, in finalizing plans for a corridor over lands administered by a management agency, contracted with a major university for cultural resources expertise to handle both survey and mitigation. While the survey portion of the work was still in progress, an archaeologist who had a primary research interest in the area of the corridor discovered that some sites had been damaged by preconstruction activity. He also felt that sites had been missed in the survey of a section of the corridor. This information was reported to the land management agency, which directed its own archaeologists to assess the situation. They inspected the damaged sites and did a small sample check of a portion of the corridor that had already been surveyed but in which no sites had been recorded. They found sites that had been missed, and a meeting was called to discuss the situation and determine what should be done.

At the meeting, the contract institution admitted that there was a problem with the initial survey and agreed to resurvey the corridor. It was also discovered that the damage at one site had occurred when a member of the contractor's survey crew had directed the development agency to move a construction site to a new location away from a recorded site. In doing so, an unrecorded site on the new location had been impacted. The land management agency instructed, and the contractor agreed, that such decisions were agency prerogatives not to be preempted by an archaeologist on a survey crew.

The contractor put a new survey crew in the field, promising to give them more supervision, and the problem seemed to have been solved. In less than a month, agency personnel who were coordinating other aspects of the project reported that spurious areas were being identified as sites and that the new crew was not staying within the corridor boundaries. The agency personnel were not trained archaeologists but they did have some skills in site recognition. The agency archaeologists inspected several locations and found that some of the areas recorded as sites were either not sites or not the kind of sites specified on the contractor's site forms.

Agency archaeologists requested that the contractor send a senior archaeologist to examine the areas and give an opinion. The senior archaeologist examined several areas with the agency archaeologist but kept his own counsel about the matter. A call by the agency to the contractor's senior archaeologist confirmed the opinion that all sites were as represented on the site forms. The issue of the nature of sites had to be resolved since the project was under Advisory Council compliance procedures. The agency then invited the SHPO to inspect the sites. Representatives of the development agency, its contractor, and other local archaeologists, including the individual who had primary research interest in the area, were invited to a meeting with the SHPO in the field.

All the archaeologists except the contractor agreed that the localities were either not sites at all or not the kind of site listed on the site forms. The SHPO refused to make a judgment. This left the agency with an ethical dilemma. If the areas in question were not sites, should the development company be made to pay for their excavation, analysis, and writeup, with costs being passed along to the public? To do so would certainly foster the image of archaeologists as money-grubbing exploiters. If the agency refused to allow more work, including subsurface testing which might confirm that the areas in question were sites, what risk would it incur? After a history of allowing sites to be damaged, the agency was concerned about changing its behavior and its image with the professional community.

The agency archaeologist noted that the lithic objects being defined as artifacts could have acquired their characteristics as a result of past logging activity, fire spalling, and freeze-thawing. It was also noted that there was a lack of debris usually associated with lithic workshops. Despite these observations, he recommended that the areas be treated as if they were sites. In making this recommendation, the agency archaeologist was explicit in stating that the reputation of the agency came first. However, since the agency did not consider the areas to be sites, all ethical responsibility was shifted from the agency to the contracting institution. This advice was accepted by the land manager and the contracting institution, and the project proceeded.

Vandalism

With the passage of the Archaeological Resources Protection Act (ARPA) of 1979, federal agencies acquired a powerful new weapon to fight vandals, pothunters, and others bent on exploitation of the nation's heritage resources. Problems exist with the implementation of the act due (at this writing) to the lack of published regulations. The Act has been and is being used. At least three individuals have gone to jail under provisions of the act. (See Green and LeBlanc 1979; Collins 1980; Green 1980; and Green and Davis 1981 for details.) Criminal sanctions are not the only mechanism available for dealing with those who damage sites. Civil procedures under the Federal Claims Act of 1966 are also available (Lear 1981).

A few archaeologists actually believe that no one should be put in jail for damaging an archaeological site. Perhaps they have never seen a favorite pueblo site systematically bulldozed, room by room, into oblivion. The other extreme seems to be the more prevalent sentiment. That is, put them all in jail regardless of the damage done. The emotional attachment that archaeologists have for the resources with which they work tends to cloud judgment about rendering justice and often affects court testimony. Wisely, the judicial system leaves such decisions in the hands of a judge and jury.

The example for this section concerns a precedent-setting case that was resolved outside of the judicial system. A timber sale contract, with a protective clause for cultural resources, was awarded to a logger. He was furnished a map showing site locations. The importance of cultural resource sites was discussed at the prework conference, and the "woods boss" was shown site locations on the ground before beginning operations. Each site had boundaries marked with flagging tape. The contract made it clear that the agency's responsibility was location and identification, and the logger's responsibility was protection.

During the logging, five sites were damaged by heavy equipment. Upon discovery of this damage the land management agency archaeologist was directed to assess the situation and provide damage estimates. The logger was billed for damages and his performance bond was frozen. The logger hired a senior archaeologist from a major university to make his own assessment of the damages. This archaeologist reported that no damage had been done and that only one of the areas he had inspected was a site.

In his role as advisor to the manager, the agency archaeologist was faced with a dilemma. Failure on the part of a colleague to recognize small archaeological sites could be partially excused on the basis of the individual's having worked in another part of the world for most of his career. Yet the areas contained rubble mounds with shaped stone blocks and artifacts, both lithic and ceramic, readily visible on the ground surfaces. Should he push for resolution of the issue, possibly embarrassing the senior archaeologist in front of professional colleagues and the company that hired him? Should the operator be excused with the hope that he would be more conscientious about protection on the next sale? Should opinions be sought from archaeologists who could not be accused of bias in favor of either the agency or the operator? Should the opinion of the senior archaeologist be confronted by the agency?

The agency archaeologist recommended that additional opinions be sought. The reasons for this decision were to reassure the land manager about the nature of the sites and to have witnesses in the event the case went to court. Potential embarrassment to a senior colleague was unfortunate but did not outweigh obligation to the resource. Since a contract was involved, the dispute had to be handled under the Contract Disputes Act of 1978. This act stipulates that the contracting officer must render a "final decision" in any dispute. That decision is appealable to either the Court of Claims or the Agricultural Disputes Board.

The land manager agreed with the recommendation to seek additional opinions. The state archaeologist, SHPO, and president of the state archaeological council were invited to visit the areas. They agreed with the agency archaeologist that all the loci were cultural resource sites and that damage had been done. When confronted with these additional opinions, the logger agreed to settle the matter with the contracting officer. The contracting officer accepted payment of about 20 per cent of the estimated damages.

Conclusion

Resolution of ethical dilemmas in the years ahead will depend on our ability as individuals and as a profession to address the issues raised in this essay. If the dollars available to do archaeology diminish, ethical dilemmas will increase. Archaeologists already face difficult decisions regarding the management of the remaining resource base, and the number of sites available for research will continue to diminish. During the next decade, our reponse to this challenge will determine whether the future will see us embroiled in continuing ethical problems.

13

Ethics in Contract Archaeology

Don D. Fowler

The increase in contracting for archaeological services by agencies and private companies has resulted in more ethical problems than any other single change in archaeology in the past two decades. Problems are especially likely to arise when: (1) the contracting institution lacks archaeological expertise or considers the work to be outside its "mission"; or (2) the archaeological firm doing the work lacks business experience.

Don Fowler's essay identifies several basic conflicts in the total contracting milieu which lead to ethical dilemmas for the archaeologist. Fowler uses the MX missile episode as a case study to illustrate the issues he identifies. Drawing upon his personal knowledge of the situation, he leads the reader through the ethically perplexing and often personally wrenching decisions that archaeologists connected with the project were forced to make.

A common problem in contracting is differences between the legitimate objectives of the organization (agency or development company) and the discipline, which spring from differences in their perceived needs and interpretation of the laws. Since the organization's need for archaeological services is the result of legal requirements and regulations, its objective may be to minimally satisfy those legal strictures. However, current archaeological standards might call for certain analyses or data collection not specified in the legal regulations. In some cases such differences can be resolved by clear communication between archaeologist and agency. Another complicating factor is the difference in interpretation of the legal requirements by the nonarchaeologist land manager and the archaeologist.

One of the central issues facing the archaeological profession today is ethics in contract archaeology. While ethical issues have always existed in the discipline, they have become exacerbated over the past decade by a series of federal laws designed to protect and conserve cultural resources.

The ethical dilemmas faced by contract archaeologists are generally the same as those faced by other researchers who undertake contract "environmental" studies. The dilemmas exist for the same basic reason: the studies are undertaken solely because they are mandated by federal law, not because development companies choose to conduct archaeological studies. The companies would get out of the business of contract archaeology as quickly as laws requiring it were repealed. The situation is one in which an unwilling client contracts for undesired work to a company that owes its continued existence to pleasing that client. This creates a clear case of conflict of interest when dealing with a public trust.

The purpose of this essay is to examine some of the ethical implications for contract archaeology. The viewpoint taken herein is a highly personal one, growing out of 25 years of participation in grant and contract research, principally in academic and research institute settings, but with frequent formal and informal contacts and working arrangements with federal and state agencies and a wide variety of corporations.

To begin, some definitions are needed: "Ethics . . . 1. the study of standards of conduct and moral judgment; . . . Ethical . . . 2. conforming to the standards of conduct of a given profession" (Webster's New World Dictionary 1966: 499). Herein "contract archaeology" is taken to mean archaeological researches carried out under the mandates of federal or state laws requiring the inventory, preservation, or management of historic or prehistoric cultural resources, and the assessment of potential "impacts" on such resources by construction or land-altering projects (U.S. Code 1980a–g). Excluded from consideration is "grant archaeology"—research projects carried out using grant funds from public or private foundations such as the National Science Foundation or the National Geographic Society.

In addition to requiring archaeological and other environmental studies, the federal legislation cited above created a "federal preservation system," the mechanics of which are described by King et al. (1977) and D. Fowler (1982). The principal purpose of the system is the implementation of the "compliance process." Here certain federal and quasi-federal agencies, especially the State Historic Preservation Offices, the National Register of Historic Places, and the Advisory Council on Historic Preservation, act as watchdogs over other federal agencies or corporate entities receiving federal funding, licensing, or other assistance. The watchdog role is designed to insure that the legal mandates of the federal cultural resources legislation are met. Contract archaeology thus operates in what may, and often does, become an adversarial atmosphere. Many ethical issues in contract archaeology arise from the fact that the compliance process is an adversarial process necessary to enforce the federal mandates.

A second factor that bears heavily on ethical problems in contract archaeology is the notion that prehistoric and historic cultural resources on public lands and (arguably) on private lands form a part of the public trust. The concept of cultural resources as a part of the public trust was first established legally by the U.S. Supreme Court (1896); it has been reinforced by all subsequent federal legislation relating to cultural resources (U.S. Code 1980a–g; see also J. Fowler 1974; Nurkin 1982). This concept relates directly to the "conservation ethic" in archaeology (Lipe 1974), which holds that, if at all possible, extant cultural resources should be conserved and protected for potential future use. Behind the ethic lies the recognition that cultural resources are finite, nonrenewable, and unique "containers of information or potential information about past human activities" (D. Fowler 1982: 19). As many cultural resources as possible should be preserved intact for the benefit of future generations. Such a stewardship is motivated in part by the hope that future excavation and analytical techniques will permit the extraction of better and more meaningful data from the "containers of information" than is presently possible.

A third factor that bears on ethical problems in contract archaeology relates to variations in interpretation and implementation of federal legislation. As Meiszner (1982) has recently shown, each federal agency with cultural resource responsibilities has interpreted those responsibilities in a somewhat different manner. What may be legally acceptable to one agency may not be so to another.

While the three factors listed above are related and may all operate in a single contractual situation, for discussion purposes we will consider the public trust aspect first, the compliance aspect second, and the variable interpretation aspect third.

Public Trust, Proprietary Data, and the Client

The basic suppositions of federal cultural resource legislation are: (1) Knowledge of the prehistoric and historic cultural and social legacy of the nation is a public good; and (2) Such knowledge exists in history books, archives, and tangible phenomena (i.e., "significant" sites, buildings, objects, and structures). Knowledge about cultural resources is and ought to be public knowledge. Put another way, data about cultural resources are not proprietary but public. Contract research in, say, hydrology and geophysics undertaken for a corporation generates data used by the corporation to develop land or mineral resources and, it is hoped, to make a profit. Such data are usually held as proprietary by both parties to the contract. Although cultural resource data may be collected under a contract with a corporation, they are not proprietary because their end is to advance human knowledge. They have no other purpose. It follows that the ultimate client is the public. But the archaeologist may be caught between the public's right to know, the conservation ethic, and the priorities and goals of the archaeological profession and related disciplines.

One example of the conflict between the "right to know" and the conservation ethic is whether or not primary site records, especially site location, should be publicly accessible. Because public access to such data could lead to site vandalism, site records are held as proprietary by research organizations and federal agencies. Here the conservation ethic is served at the expense of public knowledge. The facts about cultural affiliation, artifact inventory, ecological setting of sites, etc., should be made available sans site location information.

There are other views on clientship within the archaeological profession. Fitting (1978) holds that if the archaeologist enters into a contractual relationship with a client, he or she is obliged to serve the interests of the client. Keel (1979) states that most contract archaeological research collects data basically for management and compliance purposes. If the data so gathered are useful to other archaeologists or to the public that is a serendipitous extra. In a sense, Keel is arguing that cultural resource data are proprietary. This view does not have the interests of the archaeological profession or the general public in mind. It ignores the reason cultural resource preservation legislation was enacted in the first place.

Agency or corporate clients who regard data collected under contract as proprietary, or who take the position that the laws require collection of data for management or mitigation purposes but not the dissemination of those data to the public, create an ethical bind for the contract archaeologist. Within the archaeological profession, it is held to be unethical to collect but not disseminate data. On the other hand, to hold that it is unethical not to make all data available is naive, given the volume of data generated by contract archaeology. As one example, there are nearly four thousand cultural resource reports (ranging in length from one to several hundred pages) in the Bureau of Land Management archives on deposit in the University of Nevada Reno Library. Technically, deposit of the reports in the archive constitutes a form of dissemination since they are available to qualified persons in a public institution. (Larger reports of more general interest are made available through a standard publication series.)

The ethical problem of information dissemination occurs when reports or data are held in agency or corporate files and not made available to other qualified researchers. Here the ethical action is to insist that the contract specify that data collected will be made available to qualified persons and can be used in summary reports of general interest.

The important point of the foregoing is that the ultimate "client" for cultural resource data is the public. Put another way, the basic purposes of federal cultural resource legislation are the generation and dissemination of knowledge about the past, and the preservation and protection of tangible sources of that knowledge. The primary ethical responsibility of the contract archaeologist is to act in a manner consistent with the intent of the federal legislation.

Compliance, Variation, and Mutual Expectations

The compliance process and the exigencies of contracting per se lead contract archaeologists into many ethical dilemmas. To repeat, cultural resource studies are contracted for because they are legally required, not because federal agencies or corporations have an interest in culture history. Federal "mission" agencies (except the National Park Service) and corporations contract for cultural resources and other environmental studies because they have to do so. But such studies are usually viewed as impediments to the real mission(s) of the agencies or corporations—impediments to be ignored or subverted if possible.

A few federal agencies appear to lean over backwards to circumvent or subvert the compliance process. A good example is the 1979–1981 MX Missile Project in Utah and Nevada. As initially proposed by the U.S. Air Force, the project was to consist of a series of missile shelters connected by roadways and "race tracks" covering nearly 20,000 square miles in Utah and Nevada. The Air Force grudgingly funded minimal environmental studies, as required under the National Environmental Policy Act of 1969 (U.S. Code 1980e), including cultural resource studies. Large sums of money were spent by subcontractors carrying out field studies designed by a subsidiary of a major Air Force contractor. However, the field data were never used in the Draft Environmental Impact Statement (DEIS) (U.S. Air Force 1981). State review panels appointed by the Governors of Nevada and Utah were presented by the Air Force with a "Tier I" DEIS. None of the collected field data necessary to make adequate judgments as to how the Air Force intended to mitigate adverse impacts on cultural or natural resources was included. Requests to the Air Force for the data elicited the reply that those data would be supplied in "Tier II" (which never appeared). The general consensus of the citizens of the two states was that the whole EIS process was being "sandbagged" by the Air Force. The cancellation of the MX Project in 1981 rendered the matter moot. At this writing, the environmental data (including the cultural resource data) remain unpublished and generally unavailable, despite the efforts of numerous individuals to have them made available.

From an ethical viewpoint, the MX Project was instructive on several levels. It should be understood that this author was one of the subcontractors and was also placed, informally, in a mediating and consulting position in relation to the Air Force, the Bureau of Land Management, the corporation responsible for production of the DEIS, and various other entities carrying out portions of the cultural resource studies.

A major ethical issue faced by the subcontractors, and especially the archaeologists working for the firm responsible for the DEIS, became whether to continue to participate in the project. There were major disagreements between the firm and the subcontractors over the sampling design for the first phase of the project. These were partially resolved by negotiation, with the expectation that additional modifications would emerge from Phase I fieldwork and be incorporated in Phase II plans.

The fieldwork proceeded and a skeleton outline of an overall research design was produced (D. Fowler et al. 1980). Meanwhile, the Nevada and Utah State Historic Preservation Officers, cultural resource specialists from the Utah and Nevada Bureaus of Land Management, and representatives from the Advisory Council on Historic Preservation were struggling mightily with the Air Force to develop a Programmatic Memorandum of Agreement (PMOA) to serve as the overall framework for the design and implementation of "adequate" inventory and mitigation studies for the project—assuming the project would be built as planned. The project was extremely controversial and, as time went on, increasingly unwanted by the citizens of the two states. One way the State of Nevada expressed its opinion was to refuse to sign the PMOA, thus putting the negotiation of a "proper compliance" with the Air Force in limbo. Although the cancellation of the project in 1981 rendered the matter moot, certain ethical considerations relating to the contract cultural resource studies remain relevant.

One is that participation in the project was viewed by many, including the present author, as a matter of "situational ethics." The view was, even though the Air Force seems to be mishandling the project, if we don't become involved in it, we won't have any real chance of influencing it to the benefit of the resource.

The contractors felt they were acting ethically and for the good of the resource base. Their purpose was to try to change the perceived direction of the Air Force and force the latter to comply with the mandated legislation. The Bureau of Land Management archaeologists, the staff of the State Historic Preservation Offices, and the staff of the Advisory Council on Historic Preservation had similar goals. Cynics might say the contractors' position was simply a rationalization of the old saw, "If you can't lick 'em, join 'em." Perhaps, but in retrospect there seems to have been no other effective way for the contractors to influence the conduct of the studies. The actual effectiveness of their action remained undemonstrated because of the project's termination. The archaeologists working for the prime environmental contractor faced even more difficult ethical dilemmas. As the "sandbagging" of the DEIS process by the Air Force continued, the archaeologists felt they were being badly compromised and they resigned from the company.

In terms of ethics, the following seems to have emerged from the MX project: (1) recognition by many persons, including archaeologists, that the Air Force seemed to be subverting the environmental impact process; (2) an attempt to try to resolve apparent ethical problems created by the apparent subversion by working from within the system, while at the same time pushing for Congressional actions to force the Air Force to comply with the law; (3) a clear ethical decision on the part of the corporate archaeologists to resign from the prime contracting company rather than be ethically and possibly professionally compromised.

Another example of ethical dilemmas in contract archaeology is the New Melones project in east-central California. Fitting (1982) has recently provided a succinct summary of the manifold scientific, ethical, managerial, and political issues and problems related to the project. Of the many lessons learned from New Melones, many were quite painful to archaeologists, environmentalists, and everyone else involved.

One ethical issue was whether to bid on the scope of work, given the apparent amount of funds available: $2.8 million. The response was the submission of two proposals, one for $5.2 million, the other for $4.2 million; the latter was awarded. In other words, both teams of respondents felt the budgeted funds were inadequate for the scope of work and bid much higher figures. Even those bids were felt to be minimal, at best.

Although the magnitude of the bids and the uniqueness of the New Melones situation skew matters, the general question is whether it is ethical to overbid, rather than not bid at all. If the scope of work appears inadequate and the funds available appear fixed, is it ethical to overbid, hoping to force the agency to up the ante so that the work can be "properly" done?

From a contractual standpoint, overbidding would appear unethical. But from a conservation-ethic viewpoint, an inadequate scope of work may well lead to a loss of resources. The recourse would seem to be outside political pressure on the agency to upgrade the scope of work.

A major lesson, learned elsewhere as well, relates to the archaeologist's ethical responsibilities when a large-scale construction project becomes a "political football." The New Melones project included construction of a large dam backing up a reservoir that was flooding many very significant cultural and natural resources. The proper treatment of the threatened cultural resources within the project area became a tool through which opponents of the project hoped to stop it. Further, there was serious disagreement within the archaeological community as to what needed doing and who should do it. There was, and will remain, considerable animosity over the entire question of how the impacted cultural resources were to be studied.

Archaeologists must consider the personal ethics of becoming witting or unwitting pawns in a larger game. Even more difficult are situations in which their professional conservation ethic becomes currency in the game. Both situations occurred at New Melones. In retrospect, Fitting's assessment (1982: 18) seems correct: "Everyone within the profession is a loser as a result of the circumstances surrounding the New Melones project."

Variation in Interpretation and Implementation of Federal Legislation

The final factor to be noted in relation to ethical dilemmas is the variation in the interpretation and implementation of federal legislation by different federal agencies (Meiszner 1982). There are numerous possibilities for ethical and other problems in this regard. One agency's interpretation may lead to the issuing of requests for proposals or scopes of work that are clearly inadequate on scientific and/or management grounds. The ethical decision then is whether to bid on such a project.

There are many "gray areas." For example, what percentage constitutes "appropriate" sample inventory within a given area? Is a policy of recording but not collecting artifacts proper? Such a practice would appear to be in accord with the conservation ethic and costs less than collecting (less laboratory processing and cataloguing), but it often results in loss of resources to vandalism or bulldozer treads and blades. This occurs despite assurances from construction operators that flagged sites will be avoided. In such situations, artifacts, if not the sites, are best conserved by collection.

The adequacy of a sample inventory depends upon professional judgment of statistical validity, and on the reason for the survey. If the agency wants to "get a feel for what's out there" as the first step in a more comprehensive inventory program, a small percentage survey may be adequate. If the agency intends to use the minimal inventory to "write off" the area, however, such a survey will not be adequate. The archaeologist's ethical responsibility is to ascertain how the survey will be used before making a decision to bid.

There are many other obvious ambiguities and ethical dilemmas. The entire area of contract relationships poses many potential ethical problems. One agency's definition of "allowable" charges may not agree with that of another. Again, the area of contract relationships is one deserving volumes of separate treatment, simply because most ethical dilemmas will arise there.

Conclusion

In sum, several factors may generate ethical problems in contract archaeology. First, inventory, evaluation, and, in certain instances, mitigation studies of cultural resources are required by law; without those requirements, the studies would not be funded by governmental or corporate entities A compliance process exists to enforce the law. The enforcement often involves contract archaeology in an adversarial process. Second, cultural resources are legally defined as a part of the public trust. Public trust implies stewardship—the conservation and wise use of resources for public benefit. If cultural resources are a part of the public trust, then it follows that the ultimate client in contract archaeology is the public. The contract archaeologist thus has responsibilities not only to the funding agency but also to the archaeological profession and, through the profession, to the public, which foots the bills for research through taxes or increased utilities' rates. Third, there are signification variations as to how different federal agencies interpret and implement cultural resources legislation. These variations may lead to ethical problems in certain contract situations.

The Society of Professional Archaeologists (1980) has a written Code of Ethics that covers a number of general issues. But most often ethical decisions must be made in "gray areas" not covered by the written Code. As the dictionary definition of ethics says, to be ethical is to conform to the standards of conduct of a given profession. Such standards can never be fully encapsulated in written form. They must emerge from the training archaeologists receive.

14

Economics and Archaeology

James E. Fitting

When archaeology entered the business world, in which monetary renumeration is dependent upon services performed to the satisfaction of the client, it had to deal with a whole new set of potential ethical conflicts specifically relating to the need to be profitable while maintaining professional standards.

Compared with many other businesses, an archaeological contract often has a fairly high degree of risk because it is impossible to know in advance what will be found and, therefore, exactly what will be necessary for a competent job and/or to satisfy the legal requirements. The following essay describes some ethical dilemmas particular to each stage of a project and alerts professionals to ethical decisions they must make on an individual basis.

THE MAJOR ETHICAL ISSUE in archaeology today, in this author's opinion, is not resource protection, adequacy of survey and mitigation models, or standards for practitioners, but rather *cost*, with all of its attendant institutional and personal traumas. All other issues revolve around the professional's need to perform a virtually limitless task—the identification, preservation, and interpretation of cultural resources—with a finite pool of dollars.

Clients, who are in a buyer's market, are free to use, and abuse, the confusion of the archaeological community to their own ends. Witness the example of the geotechnical engineer who recently dissolved his internal archaeological capability with the comment, "If I want archaeology done, I can subcontract; if I get three bids, inevitably one will be half the price of the others and far less than we could afford ourselves."

This author has long been an advocate of client interests in archaeological contract work. When one takes a contract, one is morally and ethically obligated to serve the interests of the client. On the other hand, most clients are out to get the contractor and do everything in their power to put the contractor out of business. This is a fact of the marketplace. Clients are also in business and are faced with their own ethical problems.

Even with work standardization, costs for the same work can vary greatly and still be legitimate. Each cost accounting system is different in its specifics, and results in a different "bottom line" cost for the same work. The ethical dilemma of the archaeologist is often to be found in the professional and human impacts of these variations, even though they are operating within a single economic system.

Cost Accounting Elements in Archaeology

The basic elements within any cost accounting system for archaeological projects are direct labor costs, labor burden, other direct costs, overhead, general and administrative costs, and fee or profit. There are many ways in which these costs can be articulated in reaching a bottom line, and all need to be considered in their ethical context.

Direct labor is likely to be the major cost within any archaeological budget. This is the raw salary paid to the people who participate in a project. It is the first source of the archaeological dilemma. The ideal project team will consist of seasoned specialists, people who have both academic qualifications and experience. This is often listed as a significant award factor. Every client wants a team composed of Ph.D.'s with 20 years of professional experience, but almost no client is willing to pay for such a team. The Contracting Officer's Representative, who earns $15,000 to $25,000 per year, commonly becomes upset at the very suggestion that a member of the archaeological team with equivalent qualifications might be paid the same salary.

In archaeology, the major distortions occur at both the upper and lower ends of the job scale. Managerial archaeologists are vastly underpaid, considering their responsibilities, in comparison with upper-level professionals in other fields. While *The Wall Street Journal* lists the average executive salary at $120,000 per year, very few archaeologists in universities, government, or the private sector earn much more than $50,000 per year. There is a major temptation among top professionals to get out of the field entirely or to transfer to other fields (e.g., more and more physical anthropologists seek appointments in medical schools, where their professional worth is better recognized in their paychecks).

An even greater tragedy occurs at the bottom end of the scale, where B.A., M.A., and even Ph.D. technicians work at $5 and $6 per hour, salaries far below the poverty level for someone with a family, in temporary and dead-end jobs with no job security in the current, highly competitive buyer's market. These underpaid professionals are hired on a project-by-project basis, with no guarantee of ongoing employment.

This leads us to the area of labor burden, or fringe benefits. According to the Service Contract Act of 1965, employees on federal contracts are required to get a certain number of paid holidays each year, a sick-leave plan, and premium wages for overtime work. The purpose of the act was to keep the contracts out of "sweat shops" that could bid low by exploiting their employees. However, it is doubtful that any archaeological contractor in the country could stay in business if he or she gave all of these benefits to all employees.

In order to be cost-competitive, archaeological contractors go to great lengths to keep their labor burden cost down. They can do this by hiring temporary or short-term employees who are exempt from benefit provisions, hiring through body shops where temporary employees sign away their rights to unemployment compensation, or by classifying their employees as "exempt" from the Contract Service Act. Some bids from academic institutions even avoid minimal workmen's compensation benefits for job-incurred injuries since their projects are classified as "training" programs. This may be survival, but is it ethical? Who can afford to take the first step to change it?

Other direct costs can vary considerably. They may include travel, transportation, housing, subsistence, and specialty services. Most archaeological travel, other than that for very specialized consulting, is still by motor vehicle. There can be a great deal of legitimate variation in mileage charges, depending on age and type of vehicle, insurance coverage, stage of amortization, and lease or rental cost. In a buyer's market, one can lower these costs by using old and cheap vehicles, keeping them in a state of ill repair, and providing minimal insurance.

What of housing and subsistence? The concept of the "crew house" has great currency in American archaeology. Other professions regard being away from "home" as a hardship, but the field ethic of archaeology has turned this into a positive value. Archaeologists have convinced themselves that it is part of the profession to live under conditions inferior to those at most prison camps.

Overhead and general and administrative costs—the costs of doing business and holding a program together when one is not direct charging—are yet another part of the pricing dilemma. These are the administrative, marketing, plant, postage, and telephone costs. Overhead is an actual and auditable cost. It is not "something that we can negotiate" (even on a dedicated contract, the forward bid rate that is negotiated is subject to a postperformance audit to determine the actual rate). It is not, as some academic archaeologists state, university profit at the expense of archaeological work.

Marketing is likely to be the single largest overhead cost; and most of marketing costs go into proposal preparation, particularly for marketing the federal sector. Most agencies simply do not realize the economic burden that this places on their contractors. Preparing a creditable proposal necessitates thorough research of the subject, study of the natural environment and past work in the area, and formulation of research problems and a concrete plan of work. If possible, project sites should be visited as a part of proposal preparation. This takes a great deal of time and money.

Other factors impact overhead, such as attending meetings, writing and publishing, visiting clients, subscribing to an array of national and regional journals, and actively participating in professional organizations. Even if these are not all directly paid for by a firm, they take time and dollars away from chargeable activities.

All of these activities increase the cost of archaeology. It is ironic that being a responsible professional is likely to make one less cost-effective and can actually drive one out of business entirely. One of the most successful contracting firms in the United States actually has a policy of discouraging employees from any type of professional participation, even on their own time and money, since they feel that it is not only not cost-effective but has the potential to expose their in-house secrets (jobs, bid rates, marketing strategy, etc.).

The matter of fee or profit also deserves some ethical consideration. Some archaeologists actually become irate at the idea of "making a profit out of archaeology." Nor is it easy to do so, despite tales to the contrary. A good gross does not necessarily mean a satisfactory net, and a good year can be followed by a series of very bad ones. The nature of business is cyclical. Many small firms have not been able to survive, especially those in government contracting, where one's audit cannot account for commercial marketing or interest costs as overhead. (The latter must come out of one's fee.)

The average fee or profit for most archaeological projects is around 10 per cent of the cost. Institutions have often pointed to the fact that they submit no fee proposals, which does make them more competitive in terms of price. For government projects, a 10 per cent fee is really marginal, since interest charges, overruns, and other unallowable costs in government accounting systems must come out of the fee. With the best of luck, a 10 per cent fee is likely to net a 3 per cent profit. Corporate profits are taxed at a rate of nearly 50 per cent; when state and local taxes are added, the real rate of return is closer to 1 per cent. If this is returned to investors, it is taxed again as personal income. If it is held as retained earnings, it is taxed a second time as capital gains at the time of disposal of assets.

When one looks at the price rates in other professional fields, one finds a great deal of uniformity in the rates charged by lawyers, engineers, and even plumbers. All of them view themselves as being worth $50 to $75 per hour when all elements of cost and pricing are considered. Archaeologists, by comparison, seem to view their own worth as being more comparable to dishwashers and cabdrivers. There are some who even point to low prices with pride, not realizing that such prices also indicate what they feel they are worth. Archaeologists tend to do grave injustice to themselves because they are not familiar with the real costs of carrying out large-scale projects and are not ready or are unable to seek help from accountants and purchasing agents—and sometimes even view them as enemies. Unfortunately, the mistakes made among the higher echelons within the profession tend to be passed down through the ranks. It is not the Principal Investigator who underestimated the cost of the job, or the person responsible for underpricing it, who is laid off or asked to work on the project without pay.

Actually, it is possible to be profitable; but the methods of doing so often pose an ethical dilemma. One can become very profitable by curtailing business development, particularly proposal, costs. In doing so, one cuts the actual overhead below the bid rate and adds to the profit. This tactic is used in the consulting field to make the profit-and-loss statement look attractive in anticipation of the firm's sale. Cutting inventory is an equivalent tactic in the retail trade. A prospect can look very attractive to a potential buyer; but, if one bites, he or she gets a burned-out backlog and must build the entire business base anew.

For the most part, the current system of training archaeologists does very little to prepare them for either the ethical or economic confrontations of the real world. Training in the greenhouse of university contracting is not real. This environment is based on a perfectionist ethic and emphasizes knowledge over performance. Projects are subsidized in one way or another, and there is no worry over such things as "receivable days" (the time between spending the money and being paid by the client).

The almost inevitable cycle that applies to institutions, firms, and individuals is as follows: one starts out in the real world by underestimating the real costs of doing business since one never had to pay the real costs in the greenhouse. Since one has a perfectionist goal and a bargain rate, one is immediately successful and shows a nice gross but actually is losing money. Increases in overhead rates and fees can cover actual costs but hurt the competitive edge. There is a tendency to panic as gross sales decline. This can lead to "dumping"—doing work at less-than-production cost to stay in business until something better comes along—or to a lowering of work standards. Finding the lowest common denominator and living with it is probably the best solution for staying in business.

Conclusion

There probably has never been a mitigation project in the United States where all of the costs of the project have actually been compensated as a part of that project. The real costs have been hidden by using field school students, who pay tuition to learn, as project laborers; by utilizing students on a seasonal basis with low salaries and few or no fringe benefits; by the degree-debt peonage of graduate students, who are viewed as a labor pool to clean up past mistakes; and by the long hours that mid- and senior-level project managers put in long after others have gone home at night. This has often been a "free lunch" for the agencies contracting for mitigation. Offering the "free lunch" has wiped out many small contractors, eliminated some institutional programs, and "burned out" countless archaeologists, particularly at the lower levels. In effect, the "free lunch" has been paid for in social costs to the field of archaeology.

As things stand, archaeologists have probably gotten just what they ask for and deserve. When they ask for more, when they learn to make accurate estimates of cost, when they realize what needs to be considered in pricing, and when they recognize their own worth, the days of the "free lunch" will be over.

15

Archaeology Abroad: Ethical Considerations of Fieldwork in Foreign Countries

Paul F. Healy

Archaeologists who work in other countries are sometimes so focused on their research that they give little attention to the political and social milieu of the foreign nation. Probably the most common reason is that the archaeologist feels pressed to accomplish a large amount of research in a limited time.

There are, however, distinct benefits to a sensitivity to one's responsibilities in the foreign country, especially regarding local interests and government requirements and customs. An obvious practical benefit is the possibility of further projects in that country. The other side of the coin is the foreign government's responsibilities to the researchers (e.g., facilitating the research and factual interpretation of the data).

The following essay identifies and discusses specific kinds of ethical responsibilities between the archaeological investigator and the foreign government and its people.

THE LAYMAN OFTEN PICTURES archaeology in foreign countries as exotic, exciting, and alluring. In reality, however, fieldwork abroad can be more difficult, involved, and problematic than work in the United States. The seemingly simple procedures of securing legal permits, finding suitable transportation and labor, and obtaining appropriate supplies and lodging take on new dimensions abroad. Each process can be

This essay was prepared on sabbatical leave from Trent University, with the assistance of a Leave Fellowship (1981–1982) from the Social Sciences and Humanities Research Council of Canada. The author gratefully acknowledges the contributions of many Old World and New World researchers; experiences working abroad were gleaned from more than twenty countries over two decades. Special thanks to Payson Sheets, to academic colleagues L. J. Hubbell, R. B. Johnston, M. J. Tamplin, and T. Topic for their helpful advice and copious editorial comments, and to archaeologists Jaime Awe, David Freidel, Fred Lange, Karen Vitelli, and Richard Wilk.

greatly complicated by the necessity of making long-distance arrangements, by adverse climates, or by cultural and socioeconomic differences. This point was driven home by one young Canadian conservator working in Central America who lamented that he had just bought the last tube of Duco cement in the tiny republic, with no prospects for reorders for at least a year!

To be sure, archaeology in foreign countries has its romantic lure and mystique, a heritage from the days of Schliemann, Uhle, and Morley. But the projects usually entail difficulties, and sometimes risks, which seriously test the endurance and diligence of many workers.

This essay briefly examines some of the ethical responsibilities and concerns inherent in conducting fieldwork in foreign lands. It is not a comprehensive guide to the special problems of working abroad. It is hoped that it will help to initiate greater dialogue on these matters within the profession, and between archaeologists who work abroad and the host governments that license them.

Responsibilities to the Host Government

Probably the most fundamental obligation an archaeologist has while conducting fieldwork in a foreign country is to comply faithfully with all of the local laws and, in particular, to conform to the legal statutes of his or her archaeological permit. This may seem simple enough, but it requires the archaeologist to be well versed with local legislation. For example, most countries today have established laws regarding matters such as minimum wages, employee taxes, health insurance, labor safety conditions, social security, and pension deductions, all of which affect the professional archaeologist as a legal employer of laborers. Other common areas touching upon foreign archaeology and the law are importation of equipment, vehicle and equipment insurance, and artifact collection export regulations. It means enlightening imported staff and students regarding local laws and even unspoken taboos (e.g., drug use, sexual relations, language), and supervising their public behavior so as to avoid blatant conflicts with local community standards. Familiarity and compliance with the laws can usually be facilitated by the host country's Department of Archaeology, Institute of Anthropology, or other governmental permit-granting agency. Indeed, introduction to these pertinent items of legislation ought to be one of the early points of discussion between government representatives and the archaeologist. Nevertheless, the onus remains upon the foreign archaeologist to seek out such information and comply with both the letter and spirit of these laws.

Working in a foreign country in the 1980's invariably means conducting research under a government license, which is usually a legal contract. Rules and regulations regarding archaeological permits are different in each country. Obtaining and maintaining a permit can be a major hurdle for the success of a project, as most archaeologists who have worked abroad will testify. Once the guidelines and statutes of an archaeological permit have been agreed upon by the host agency and the archaeologist, it is incumbent upon the archaeologist to adhere strictly to the regulations and to abide fully by any restrictions. Problems can frequently develop in this area since permit statutes occasionally act to restrict, sometimes severely, the flexibility of an archaeological program and research design. For this reason it is crucial for field archaeologists to have sufficient input into the drafting of the parameters of their license; they must be fully cognizant of the limitations imposed in their permits before accepting them. If an archaeologist working in another country cannot, on ethical grounds, accept all of the requirements set out in the proposed license because they are too restrictive to permit the fulfillment of professional obligations or agency requirements, then the agreement should not be signed.

From a practical point of view, this can be a very difficult (even traumatic) situation since many foreign governments simply will not negotiate or issue permits in advance of the applicant's physical presence in the country. Futhermore, many North American funding agencies will not release support monies or, in a few cases, even accept proposals without a permit in hand from the host government. Thus, there can be occasional undue pressure placed upon the archaeologist to enter into less than satisfactory legal agreements rather than face the prospect of a return home empty-handed, minus the cost of airfare or any results for a project long in planning.

Generally speaking, officials of government agencies abroad work to their fullest capacity to complete satisfactory arrangements for both the visiting archaeologist and their own nation. Nevertheless, some fairly perplexing situations have arisen in recent years with the introduction by some governments of restrictions on where archaeologists may work (e.g., this side of a river valley but not the other side), restrictions on sites of particular time periods (e.g., early sites but not later settlements), or limitations on the breadth of the study (e.g., site survey but no excavation).

In many instances, the reasoning behind such restrictions is both legitimate and understandable. For example, the host government may have preexisting agreements with local archaeologists or other foreign archaeologists for work in a particular region or at a special site, resulting in unpublicized restrictions on where others can work. In all cases, however, the nature of, and reasons for, the permit restrictions ought to be made apparent to visiting professionals so that they may objectively decide whether to accept the limitations, negotiate further, or reject the permit offer.

In some cases, the reasons behind license restrictions are questionable. As a not uncommon example, a government may encourage foreign investigation into archaeological sites of the extraordinarily remote prehistoric periods, but virtually prohibit research into the sites and regions sure to produce archaeological evidence of significant (more recent) aboriginal cultural achievements. The reverse also holds; archaeology may be viewed as a political tool for emerging nations seeking to "create" a glorious past. Both cases raise the question of complicity through cooperation. If the archaeological information produced will lead to suppression of any racial or ethnic groups, then the morality of the work has to be called into question. (See Tamplin [1981a] for a different perspective on this.)

Furthermore, most of us today are aware of the ill-conceived uses of archaeology by the leaders of National Socialist Germany, where the interpretation of data was made to fit Nazi dogma of Pangermanism and Aryanism (Clark 1957: 259–260). In some parts of the world today, professional archaeologists are still faced with restrictions on the interpretation of artifactual remains. The strong political persuasions in such countries require that interpretations (and their generators) adhere rigidly to what might be termed the "party line." For foreign archaeologists, divergence from the accepted dogma may result in the nonrenewal of their permits or may make trouble for host scholars who collaborated on the project.

It has also become increasingly common for countries to prohibit the export of study collections, or even samples of such, for analysis. From a political and nationalistic view, however, this position is understandable. In some undeveloped nations that lack facilities for adequate analytical investigation, however, such restrictions mean that an archaeologist is faced with a virtual loss of data. Is it ethical for a professional archaeologist to enter into such agreements knowing in advance that inherent restrictions will inhibit complete reporting of evidence?

Some visiting archaeologists accept permit restrictions, but take the attitude that the host country will never be able to monitor their fieldwork adequately or supervise export of "their" samples successfully. A few international archaeologists seem to enter into such agreements with the expectation that the statutes will be broken. To do otherwise, they theorize, would be to do less than a thorough job and therefore to be professionally unethical. Underlying such an attitude is the implication that foreign laws are somehow less binding or significant than their own. This attitude appears to be derived from a perspective of these foreign lands as remote extensions of North America in which there is an almost "inalienable" right to conduct research. It is a type of archaeological "imperialism" (Evans and Meggers 1973: 257).

Archaeology departments in Third World nations are often grossly understaffed and must rely to a large extent upon the integrity of visiting scholars. Aside from the immorality of such flagrant lawbreaking, a professional archaeologist who deliberately ignores the statutes of a permit obviously endangers the likelihood of any future fieldwork opportunities. This is a clear breach of professional ethics.

Responsibilities to Foreign Scholars

A major area of dual responsibility for archaeologists working abroad is in consultation and contact with foreign scholars. In addition to dissemination of information and findings to colleagues back home, there is an accepted obligation to communicate with appropriate interested foreign scholars residing in the host country. The degree and level of contact will vary from one researcher to another, but at the very minimum should involve informing appropriate host-nation archaeologists of research plans and any prospects or opportunities for collaboration.

At first appearance, such action would seem to have obvious benefits to all involved. Local researchers can lend scholarly assistance, wise counsel, and practical advice that will aid visiting researchers and their studies. Not uncommonly, their familiarity with local conditions can save visiting archaeologists time and money. Foreign archaeologists, on the other hand, often have access to research grants, resources, skilled technical personnel, and support equipment that are well beyond local means. Therefore, cooperation can and should be mutually advantageous. Finally, it would seem only proper professional etiquette to keep interested local scholars reasonably well posted of investigations of mutual interest being carried out in their own homeland.

Clearly such contact and cooperation are desirable and ideally should be actively pursued. One must remember, however, that foreign archaeology involves a surprising level of diplomacy. Archaeological research, like most complicated pursuits, is not carried out in a sociopolitical vacuum. At times, well-intentioned courtesy visits to a local university or museum archaeologist are met with hostility and resentment, or result in prolonged delays in permit release. In other words, attempts at such wide-based cooperation have all too often embroiled a naive archaeologist in internecine political and/or personal conflicts at the local level. It is not uncommon to find competing host factions trying to manipulate a prestigious foreign archaeologist to enhance their own local status.

This is an age-old social predicament, and one must be aware of and sensitive to such political gamesmanship. One response to such problems is to try to deal with all parties involved. As professionals, we should be capable of rising above local personality conflicts for the advancement of our discipline. In one instance, the visit of a foreign archaeologist of considerable repute actually assuaged the differences of local quarrelling professionals and brought about a temporary rapprochement.

Such situations clearly pose delicate ethical problems for the visiting archaeologist. To shun a foreign colleague or local faction is irresponsible and unprofessional. Yet this responsibility must also be weighed against the risk of possible ostracism by those in political control, and therefore of total project loss. Visiting archaeologists are rather vulnerable targets in this sense. It is unfortunate that some international archaeologists have been forced to take sides or place their research projects in jeopardy. As outsiders, we can only hope that local authorities will have the integrity to divorce their own sentiments from scholarly decisions, to realize the value of interscholastic communication, and not to succumb to the temptation to use foreign colleagues as unwitting political pawns. But we should be prepared to deal with such manipulations tactfully and in such a way as to not be injurious to either the parties involved or the objectives of the fieldwork.

Directly related to all this is the basic professional responsibility to convey the results and conclusions of fieldwork to the host government and its regional scholars. Quite simply, this obligation means providing (free, if possible) copies of professional papers, article reprints, reports, books, etc., on the work done in their country. The archaeological licenses of some governments (Belize, for instance) require that reports be sent to specific educational institutions and libraries in the country. Other governments (such as Honduras) request a specific quantity of published reports or reprints, which their institute authorities redistribute to appropriate local researchers.

Whenever possible, this obligation should be taken to include publishing some accounts of work in the official (or predominant) language of the host country. This not only makes the results more broadly available to nationals, it enhances the investigator's status. In certain countries, such as Peru, local publication has recently become a requirement of licensing. Similarly, a number of republics today maintain their own journals of anthropology and archaeology. Sometimes these are not as slick or prestigious as more established North American journals, and in the past there seems to have been a blatant disinterest in publishing in these magazines. Although this avoidance may stem partly from the feeling that to publish in *American Antiquity* fulfills all publishing obligations in one effort, it also bears something of an impolitic air of snobbery. The fact is that these local publications and their readers are deserving of cooperation and support. Furthermore, such local journals are invariably more widely read in the host country than any North American professional journal.

Finally, we have a professional obligation to make ourselves fully aware of the research and publications of foreign scholars. Some years ago, in a biting *American Antiquity* editorial, Evans and Meggers (1973) commented upon the tendency toward an "imperialistic" attitude by some North American archaeologists. Although the responsibility or fault is partly shared by the local archaeologists, who often fail to supply copies of their publications for review or exchange abroad, those working abroad have a scholarly duty to be aware of such foreign works and to cite them where appropriate. Rhetoric aside, such cooperative exchanges and collaborative efforts will in the end benefit the whole discipline and its practitioners.

Responsibilities to the Foreign Public

The people of the host nation, who are perhaps the group closest to the actual archaeological remains, are the most commonly neglected in regard to archaeological research and results. For decades, professional archaeologists have made poor excuses for avoiding communications with local populations when conducting fieldwork. Thus, thousands of North Americans have access to information on the prehistory of some countries, while the same information is denied the inhabitants of the archaeological sites!

Although it may take some extra effort, it is essential to take time out from normal project operations to organize a controlled (if small) exhibition of findings or to deliver a public presentation to the community in which the project is based. This common courtesy is simple enough to arrange in most cases and need not—indeed, should not—be a professional-level presentation. The best approach is a straightforward statement to the local people about what and why research is occurring and its significance and relation to their cultural heritage. We have to keep in mind that many people in Third World nations find it surprising to see foreigners coming to their homeland to spend large sums of money on equipment, supplies, and labor just for the sake of "research." There is a natural tendency to be just a little suspicious that there is a "profit" being made, and probably at their expense.

For more than one fieldworker, such a small accounting has quelled hostile local suspicions about smuggling, drug running, and undercover intelligence activities, and has improved local relations so as to considerably facilitate daily activities. Several archaeologists have noted that such "talks" to local groups invariably brought forth site data, volunteer guides, artifacts, and a genuine wealth of archaeological interest. They might even make the labors of local graverobbers more difficult. By and large, local suspicions grow out of a lack of information and communication.

We have already noted the need for foreign archaeologists to make their findings available to the government, local scholars, and national journals. Virtually all countries today have newspapers and/or news-oriented national magazines which are widely read and appropriate for dissemination of news on archaeological research. Whether or not we like to think of our research as popular, archaeology is virtually always "newsworthy" and we may further our obligation to distribute this information by means of news reports. When the task of "enlightening the public" seems burdensome, it is helpful to consider how we would feel if, year after year, foreign researchers came to our homeland, conducted research, and never let us know what was transpiring or being learned from this work. Such accounting is not only good public relations, but a legitimate ethical concern.

Culture Resource Management and the Foreign Archaeologist

An area of increasing concern for archaeologists working in foreign lands is that of culture resource management. To what, if any, extent are foreign archaeologists responsible for the protection, restoration, and preservation of sites with which they are associated? Some foreign governments have raised the issue of serious site damage due to short-term research projects. The problem is well known: a small project brings publicity to a previously unknown site, facilitating access of unsupervised traffic to the locale after the departure of crew members. Do archaeologists have a responsibility to prevent disproportionate loss of information by financing site protection for those localities which they have opened up and are investigating?

Similarly, to what extent are foreign archaeologists responsible for the consolidation, restoration, and preservation of architectural structures and artifactual remains revealed in excavation? In a recent incident in Italy, a Canadian archaeologist with research funds for structural excavations hit a spectacular mosaic floor. The need for, and desirability of, preservation was obvious, but the question of financial responsibility arose immediately. Not surprisingly, the archaeologist contended that his limited funds were for research rather than restoration; the host government argued that the individual in question had a professional duty to preserve what he had uncovered, and threatened revocation of his license if the restoration work was not undertaken.

In this case, the archaeologist was successful in obtaining additional funds from the Canadian government Social Sciences and Humanities Research Council (SSHRC) to complete the work, but the vexatious nature of the problem and the contentious areas of responsibility were evident to all. Clearly this is an issue of growing concern for archaeologists and funding institutions alike, since granting agencies may soon be faced with proposals requiring a type of "blank check" support in order to carry out their investigations.

If, as some international archaeologists argue, the protection of sites and the restoration of monuments are the domain of the host governments, then we may soon be faced with financially strapped foreign nations simply putting the lid on new research, particularly small-scale projects. There is an unmistakable need for clarification of responsibilities *before* such problems arise, and a need for acknowledgment by developed nations of their moral responsibilities to assist in the culture resource management of underdeveloped nations.

Another ethical concern of archaeologists working outside the country is dealing with private collectors of antiquities. In Latin America and other places, it is often perfectly legal for the citizenry to possess local archaeological artifacts. Most countries today require that these pieces be registered with the national government branch dealing with archaeology, but this is difficult to enforce. Local laws often prohibit export of these antiquities, but they do allow private ownership. The professional archaeologist faced with an opportunity to examine such collections has an ethical dilemma. In some small, Third World countries without national museums, or with official collections that pale by comparison to local, private holdings, the archaeologist is confronted with a choice of suppressing a natural curiosity and professional interest or, by viewing the pieces, of flattering the collectors' egos and condoning the sacking of sites to obtain these artifacts. Some archaeologists view private holdings from the vantage point that they may find significant data that they can bring to the attention of scholars through publication. Clearly one does not wish to be a hypocrite, simultaneously deploring the looting and destruction of sites by vandals seeking artifacts for sale, and fawning over private collections whose owners invariably have financed this destruction for their own personal aggrandizement.

It has been suggested that through dealings with collectors one can educate them and introduce a different "ethic." Others have noted that such collecting is a "time honored, elite tradition" in some parts of the world and that the practitioners are virtually impervious to enlightenment. The obvious solutions include tighter policing of archaeological sites and strengthening of antiquities legislation regarding artifact ownership, but neither is likely to be politically or economically feasible for many countries. Some nations simply lack the trained personnel to protect and care for their cultural heritage on anything but the most minimal scale. Indeed, this is an argument often put forward by collectors to validate their own activities.

This brings us back to the area of culture resource management. There has been an increasing interest in providing aid for the development of programs to improve the training of local professionals (Miller 1980). Most archaeologists familiar with work in foreign nations would accept the position that it is a professional responsibility to assist and advise foreign agencies when it is possible and such guidance is requested. Many countries have attempted to improve their personnel expertise through license regulations that require the inclusion of local students on foreign archaeological projects. Mexico is a good example of the successful application of this policy. In this way, nationals can obtain firsthand, professional training which may be lacking in local educational institutions. There are obvious limitations to this sporadic, uneven, smörgasbord approach to archaeological training, however.

As the world economy has slowed down this decade, foreign archaeologists have become more cognizant of the severe crisis facing poor Third World nations regarding their often spectacular cultural resources and the management of them (cf. Keatinge 1980 on Peru; Miller 1980 on the Solomon Islands; Tamplin 1980b; White 1982 on Angkor). To what degree are international archaeologists responsible for aiding the agencies of the host countries in which they conduct their investigations? Most would agree that a more professional corps of local archaeologists should be cultivated, but how can this be most successfully achieved?

A recent example of intergovernmental cooperation involves Belize and Canada. Canada has had a long-standing tradition of archaeological research in Belize, largely through the activities of the Royal Ontario Museum (Pendergast 1981). In 1978, Trent University in Ontario, the Royal Ontario Museum, and the Belize Department of Archaeology signed a novel, six-year agreement for wide-range training of department employees in archaeology, museology, and culture resource management. The uniqueness of the program, which was funded by the Canadian government through the Canadian International Development Agency (CIDA) and by the other three parties, was in its holistic nature (Healy 1981). It included funds and provisions for the education and training of Belize employees in archaeology at all levels of the department, from the site caretakers to the Archaeological Commissioner. It involved "field" training in Belize and university/museum training in Canada. This program has been successful, with positive results for all, and could be effectively introduced elsewhere. In Belize there is now a larger, better-trained and better-equipped staff in archaeology, which can only improve research effectiveness for visiting archaeologists. For our profession, there is the advantage of having a trained staff who is better able to protect and preserve Belize's rich archaeological resources than in the past. Similar programs could, and should, be instituted in other countries. Almost certainly, such a course would lead to a reduction in, or an amiable resolution of, the concerns raised regarding site protection, looting, and problems of preservation.

This essay has attempted to focus attention on some of the problems encountered in working outside the United States. Their resolution extends beyond the resources and capabilities of individual archaeologists, however. Wider discussion by the entire profession is essential to motivate greater responsibility and to help avoid the ethical pitfalls that await.

16

Ethics and the Museum Archaeologist

Richard I. Ford

Management of the collections from archaeological field investigations can be as critical to science as the original fieldwork. Indeed, the day may come when most of the data are in museums rather than in the ground.

Richard I. Ford, who is curator of one of the major museums of anthropology in this country, discusses a number of current ethical issues in the management of archaeological collections. His advice and guidelines apply to *any* institution that curates materials, including university departments, research units, laboratories, and governmental agencies that house collections.

"To dig is to destroy" is an adage as old as archaeology. Its validity has survived methodological revolutions and paradigmatic changes. The negative consequences of digging for an archaeological site fostered scientific excavation techniques and repositories to house the remains from the past. The American public has acknowledged the inherent value of the cultural relics and their interpretation by legitimate archaeologists by sanctioning legislation at federal, state, and local levels of government to salvage the nation's history, preserve its cultural heritage, and punish vandalism (cf. McGimsey 1972). Despite public faith in the professional archaeologist, an ethical question remains. If even the application of modern excavation procedures by archaeologists destroys a site, are the collections from now-extinct sites preserved adequately for future generations of professionals as well as for enlightened citizens?

The answer is unknown, but there are many ominous signs. Indeed, in 1978 the Interagency Archaeological Service contracted the American Anthropological Association and Alexander Lindsay to survey the storage condition of federally owned antiquities housed in museums and research institutes across the United States. The results revealed that conditions were far from adequate (Lindsay and Williams-Dean 1980). Further recognition was accorded this problem at the 1979 Society for American Archaeology meeting in Vancouver in a special symposium. Again, its participants revealed that uniform standards for archaeological curation, storage, and conservation of artifacts were lacking (Novick 1980). Most recently, public attention has been drawn to improper storage of skeletal remains in several museums in California. Archaeologists must recognize that their responsibilities to the past do not end when excavation and analysis cease. In the not-too-distant future, most of America's archaeological resources will be in museums, not in the ground. With the sites gone, it is imperative that the collections survive.

The ethical actions of archaeologists and museum professionals must be harmonized to satisfy mutually acceptable desires and interests (Toulmin 1970: 222). Immediate experience and self-interest are not compatible with long-term actions required to fulfill community goals in an impartial manner. To function effectively museum archaeologists must have ethically sound reasons for choosing a particular course. If we acknowledge that archaeological sites are a nonrenewable resource, then any forces—social, political, or natural—that adversely affect the archaeological record must be assiduously avoided or thwarted. The necessary efforts include site protection, up-to-date excavation procedures, and perpetual care for the objects once they are recovered. For the museum, this ethical principle must guide collection management, the "editing" of collections, the handling of human osteological collections, publication practices, exhibition procedures, and the authentication and monetary evaluation of artifacts. If these areas of museum practice are dictated by political expediency, personal whim, or limited experience, the consequence is an accelerated and detrimental assault on the archaeological record in the ground as well as in storage.

Ethics of Archaeological Collection Management

A museum is a permanent, public educational institution that selectively acquires, curates, and interprets collections of cultural or scientific significance (a composite definition; see Burcaw 1975: 9–13). Such an institution need not have the name "museum" attached to it. Research institutes, departments of anthropology, herbaria, and rare book libraries all qualify as long as they curate collections. A "museum" then, is legitimatized by the public as a national repository for the cultural or biological evidence of the changing present and selectively forgotten past. No other institution is charged by all national constituencies with this responsibility.

Archaeologists often forget that the basis of the museum is its collections. Whether particular museums' primary purposes are exhibition, research, or storage, maintenance of collections unites them. Unfortunately, difficulties arise when archaeologists assume that collections are only the physical objects themselves. They are not. A collection consists of the physical objects *and* their documentation. An archaeological collection may be from an individual site, a region, or the same cultural period, or may be a type collection of projectile points, etc., but each collection shares several linking attributes. Museums have many collections and, depending upon the classification employed, a single object can belong to more than one collection. What permits this is the documentation for each collection. Archaeologists who do not regard field notes, maps, photographs, and research descriptions of the objects as part of the collection are violating the ethics of collection management. Without their documentation, objects are rendered useless, and the archaeological record is impoverished.

Archaeologists have regarded artifacts as *public property*, and disposition in a public respository as a professional responsibility; but for too long, their documentation has been viewed as *private property* to be kept by the archaeologist who excavated a site or surveyed an area. As long as the notes are in the archaeologist's possession, it signifies an intention to write up the site or survey, even if a score of years has elapsed. Often the notes are not returned to the museum even after the report is completed or abandoned.

In archaeology, one can distinguish two types of collections. Primary collections, which are derived from direct field observation and scientific collection, usually consist of excavated material and surface-sampled objects, although photographs of sites qualify as well. Secondary collections consist of primary objects grouped around common themes. They may be built in the museum from the latter's primary collection. For example, comparative collections of objects made of similar raw materials (e.g., ceramics, crypto-crystalline stone) are frequently maintained by museums. Secondary collections may also consist of "life collections" assembled by avocational archaeologists or private collectors who purchase objects from dealers. If the number of items in a life collection is substantial, the donor's name remains associated with it in the annals of the museum. The documentation for each type of collection is obviously different.

Documentation describes the spatial derivation and attributes of physical objects. It is most detailed for primary collections. Field notes, site plans, photographs, and daily logs all qualify as documents of the work. Regional surveys require descriptions of individual sites (which may be augmented by aerial photographs and/or topographic maps locating the sites), inventories of artifacts collected and those left in the field, and preliminary observations and assessments of material found. Donated material in secondary collections necessitates a history of the objects, details about collecting methods, records of ownership, and legal documents or affidavits confirming legal possession. The last has the highest priority for objects from foreign lands. It has also become very important in the United States since the passage of the Archaeological Resource Protection Act, which made the acquisition of illegally collected material from federal lands a felony. These detailed descriptions of the provenance of the artifacts exceed what is required in a catalogue and should be maintained in a secure location with the accession records of the collection.

Photocopy technology now makes it possible for all documents to be duplicated at a reasonable cost. If an archaeologist must have a set of the field records, it should be a copy, with the original safely stored in the museum curating the physical objects. If the objects are moved to another public institution (e.g., to the state where the site is located), their documentation must accompany them as part of the collection. By means of duplication, the profession maintains its unwritten rule that fieldworkers have the first right to publish a primary collection; but the integrity of the collection remains intact for the future.

A museum has as its first responsibility the curation of collections and, while the number of objects in a single collection may not change, the documentation should increase over time. It is assumed that the institution will employ the latest museum practices and that posterity will benefit from the effort. By this standard, thee artifacts of primary collections may not increase (unless additional donations are made to the collection), but neither will they decrease through loss or deterioration. The documentation is expected to grow through time. This is an area of collection management that archaeologists frequently ignore. Every collection can be studied for different ends. Each time it is examined, a report of the observations should be added to the documentation. If a visitor who uses a museum collection makes new measurements or reaches new conclusions about it, copies of the results should be sent to the museum for inclusion with the records of the collection. This practice is not only a courtesy, but a logical extension of ethical behavior based upon the definition of a collection and the responsibility a museum has for interpretation of its collections.

"Editing" of Museum Collections

Many museums are becoming saturated with archaeological remains. The spread of cultural resource management programs in response to state and federal laws has produced more material than most museums can accommodate. A few administrators have succeeded in implementing a policy of deaccessioning artifacts through dispersal or even destruction. It is unimaginable that objects once saved from the ravages of the bulldozer at great public expense confront a second threat in the one institution expected to preserve a nation's cultural heritage for the future—the museum.

The consolidation of collections is a reasonable solution to the curatorial problem if it improves accessibility and facilitates research. Except for purposes of comparison and teaching, which really do not require many items, there is little basis for objects from one site to be housed in several museums. If such a scattered collection could be consolidated at the museum closest to the site of origin, archaeological interpretation would be enhanced. The American archaeological profession is long past the era where museums must fill empty shelves and exhibit cases with exotic artifacts from around the world. The field has matured to a point where avarice is a professional disservice that impedes research, forcing investigators to criss-cross the country examining portions of the same collection in multiple museums. The reconstitution of collections from the same site in one museum close to the place of origin would expedite research and further archaeological interpretation.

The proper storage of archaeological collections requires the internal reorganization of collections. Every item need not be stored as a unit within the museum; certainly, with the ready availability of electronic data processing equipment, collections can be divided among several locations in the same institution (Wilcox 1980). One possible solution described in detail elsewhere (Ford 1980) is to have on-premises collection storage for easy accessibility during active research, with transfer of analyzed and catalogued material to other locations while they await future reinvestigation. This second- or third-order storage may include use of a prefabricated building and industrial storage equipment. Such a system demands careful inventory of the collections but will open valuable laboratory space for the study of collections. Internal editing of collections which disperses material objects from the same collection does not imply destruction of a collection. It simply recognizes research priorities of immediate concern without ignoring the future potential of all collections. Failure to discriminate these differences in emphases by storing everything together within already crammed laboratory space impedes efficient research and can result in senseless and unfounded calls for the destruction of previously investigated objects, especially less spectacular ones such as bulky body sherds, debitage, and fire-cracked rock. Granted, there is an initial expense to edit collections properly; but when amortized over the long run, the cost is actually cheaper than the status quo and, more important, archaeological collections are better preserved for future investigators. The transfer of collections can be accomplished by exchanging collections (including the documentation) with another institution, with each absorbing part of the cost. The cost of internally reorganizing collections can be absorbed by allocating curatorial time over a period of years once proper storage space becomes available. Because climate control and security needs are much less than for some other museum collections, the storage of nonperishable archaeological materials need not be expensive—old warehouses, basements, or unused Butler buildings may be ideal. The museum archaeologist is obligated to undertake these efforts as part of an ethical commitment to the future authenticity and availability of archaeological remains.

Human Osteological Collections

The area of museum practice that has created the most public controversy is the possession and curation of human skeletons, particularly those of Native Americans. Many Indian groups have expressed outrage over the removal of skeletons from the ground and their storage in museums. Their partisans claim that only their ancestors are treated so crassly, while failing to acknowledge that some museums contain more skeletons of other ethnic and racial groups. Rosen (1980) reviewed the legal questions as they pertain to Native American skeletons and determined that the vagueness of laws increased with the antiquity of the skeletons. This does not mean that they should not be treated sensitively. In fact, many Americans of all ethnic backgrounds and religious persuasions are sensitive to the handling of skeletons. It behooves the museum curator to treat all human osteological remains with dignity and to determine on valid scientific bases which skeletons will be maintained in the museum for research purposes.

Museums are beginning to follow general guidelines with respect to all human bones. First, all skeletal parts should be stored in protective containers, out of sight, and guarded against physical deterioration, theft, and malicious use. Second, skeletal elements should be exhibited only when furthering human understanding; and, whenever possible, the use of casts should replace the actual object. Most important, no ethnic identification should be affixed if it is demeaning (e.g., if only Indian burials are displayed) or if no useful purpose is served. Third, historical burials with known, living relatives should be disturbed only if they are endangered and then should be handled according to the wishes of the relatives, even if reburial in a safe location is their desire. Fourth, historical burials with *probable* living descendants should be left buried unless their security is threatened. If they must be removed, study should be preceded by negotiation with a legal corporation, such as a state Indian commission, that will ultimately determine their fate. Fifth, depending upon the locality, late (post-A.D. 1000) skeletons should be handled as in the previous example, if archaeologists can demonstrate, or descendants can substantiate, connection to known tribal groups. Finally, human bones of greater antiquity with no demonstrated connections to the present can be exhumed for study and long-term curation as long as they are accorded respect. Naturally, local circumstances will necessitate different policies.

Many museums have become sensitive to the problems mishandled skeletons have created and the disrespect Native Americans have experienced when viewing the remains of their ancestors. Unfortunately, in several recent cases, the museums have attempted to rectify their past malpractices, only to discover that once the political issue had abated, state and local Indian groups were unwilling to assume responsibility for repatriated human skeletons. Under such circumstances, the museum curator must take the initiative to remain in contact with the group while at the same time providing a proper environment for the curation of this recognizably significant part of the archaeological record.

Human skeletons are indispensable for archaeological research. Ancient diets, disease pathologies, genetic patterns, and environmental adaptations are but a few research areas that osteological remains can illuminate. However, the archaeologist should be prepared to justify these ends when the excavation of skeletons is questioned. Archaeologists are one of several constituencies with legal claims to these remains. The state and federal government, private landowners, and ethnic groups all have legal rights. Museums with skeletons must be prepared to demonstrate their legal claim, their ethical responsibility for providing appropriate curation, *and* the public benefit of maintaining them for scientific investigation. Failure to do these tasks will result in the loss of an important aspect of the archaeological record under the force of new legislation.

Publication of Archaeological Information

A professionally excavated site is no better than a looted one if the notes documenting it are separated from the artifacts while the excavator postpones publication. Also, publication by professionals should emphasize the interpretation of the site or region rather than the artifacts as objects. When archaeologists publish descriptions of objects at the expense of the integration of all the data, the public and, more particularly, collectors, feel that this is what archaeologists look for. The difficulties involved in protecting the archaeological record are compounded when archaeology is reduced to uninformed object gathering, and the personal collections of antiquities are regarded as the equivalent of a museum.

Professional publications should establish a standard. This does not require an arcane vocabulary or incomprehensible writing style. The results of our labors can be written for both a professional reader and the lay public. The former audience demands timely publication and the full disclosure of research data. The latter demands a readable book and insight, a commodity that only a professional archaeologist is equipped to contribute. (Additional comments on publication for the lay audience are in the essay by Fagan in this volume—ed.)

The publication of museum exhibition catalogues and popular books are sought by the public precisely because they picture artifacts. Photographs of privately owned antiquities in reputable books is another sanction of private collecting, another assault on as-yet unexcavated artifacts. Antiquity dealers love it when an established archaeologist publishes any artifact from a private collection. The object is automatically authenticated and, with its pedigree thus established, the resale price skyrockets. Archaeological artifacts belong in research institutes and museums for study; their use for visual education further enhances these institutions and can discourage private acquisition of prehistoric relics. In this author's opinion, *no* museum should publish any book that depicts artifacts belonging to private collectors. This practice undermines the purpose of museums and encourages the acquisition of antiquities through theft or looting by private individuals.

Exhibition of Artifacts

Museum curators are often pressured to display objects donated by patrons, benefactors, or alumni of a university with which the museum is affiliated. How a museum responds to such demands should be defined in a policy manual. No curator should be required to make a decision that might be at variance with that of other colleagues or with general policy. Defined procedures protect the curators from political retaliations when negative responses are given to these requests.

It is this author's opinion that, even if such demands are honored, the name of a private citizen who donates archaeological artifacts should not be placed on exhibition labels. To do so simply conveys to the rest of the public that the museum condones the private acquisition of archaeological objects. The inference is that, despite the irreparable damage done to the site by the original collector and the destruction others could do if the example were followed, the museum will publicize such donors as charitable citizens. Of course, the tax deduction is yet another inducement. There are ample negative impacts on sites without museums fostering another by encouraging collecting for the sake of the personal enhancement of a benefactor. If it is necessary to acknowledge publicly all charitable donations to a museum, then a listing of all individual and corporate donors can be maintained separate from the actual objects and without reference to the actual pieces.

The same restriction should apply to special exhibits as well. Museums are recognized as public repositories of cultural items. No archaeological objects held by private collectors are so unique that similar examples cannot be found in some public museum or research institute. With a little effort, these artifacts can be located and borrowed. To do otherwise is simply to honor private collectors and to encourage others to invest in these collectibles. The result is further looting and site destruction, and the loss of information and research data to the public and to professional scholars.

Artifact Authentication and Evaluation

Some museums, though fortunately not the majority, require their archaeologists to authenticate artifacts and provide monetary estimates of their worth as a public service. Such practices are potentially deleterious to the integrity of the archaeological record. A museum curator who dates and values an object encourages further collection and an elevation of the price of antiquities for investment purposes. There is also the problem of mistaken authentication, which reflects badly on the museum.

Authentication of privately owned antiquities from foreign countries is particularly worrisome. Most pieces in private hands left their country of origin without documentation and sometimes without an export permit; they were derived through clandestine excavation encouraged by an international network of dealers. While reputable museums do not engage in these import practices because they violate the laws of the country of origin and pillage sites, to assist those who do is just as devastating to the context of the objects. Even if only one surreptitiously looted object is brought to the museum for validation, its discovery and recovery probably was preceded by hundreds of shovelfuls of broken vessels, midden fill, burials, and architectural debris. If museum curators and academic archaeologists would cease this practice, the cautious small-time buyer who accounts for the purchase of the bulk of these imports might be more skeptical when archaeologists explain their refusal and desist in this practice.

It is sad that museum archaeologists must become the public's villain in the international effort to thwart the illicit antiquities trade. Individuals are willing to gamble on an expensive relic if they know that museums will validate their investment. When notified that this is not a curatorial responsibility, they may become irate because they will have to pay a professional appraiser to perform this task. The more detached museums are from importers, dealers, and collectors of archaeological objects, the better the prospect of regulating this trade, of protecting the remaining sites, and of maintaining the respect of the public. Moreover, it is wise to explain to the public why illegally exported objects will not be authenticated.

The most difficult aspect of this policy is confronting an innocent child who has found his first arrowpoint. The last thing on his mind is to sell it, but he does want to know what it is. Actually, educating the child with a discussion about what archaeology is and why collecting is discouraged may be very beneficial. One can teach a child about America's prehistoric past without encouraging further collecting. This should be the primary objective of exhibition museums, and the child's artifact may be the perfect pedagogic item to reinforce teaching about the nature of archaeology.

Dealing with adult collectors is another matter. Again, giving monetary appraisals is reprehensible. However, the number of avocational archaeologists scouring the countryside is many times larger than the number of professionals engaged in surveying. These amateurs are the sources of our knowledge about most sites and their cooperation is essential. The solution to the problem of unscientific excavation and overzealous collecting is education. State programs to certify amateurs are not designed to create a third column of archaeologists. On the contrary, they are teaching proper recording techniques to surface collectors, communicating the details of local archaeology as a cultural pattern rather than as discrete artifacts, and channelling excavation energy into useful scientific projects. By this means, more can be learned about the archaeological record. Once public interest is directed away from discrete artifacts, the demands for dollar values and authentication will be greatly reduced. The museum that can marshal this interest and energy in a responsible way will benefit our knowledge of the archaeological record. Trouble begins with the collectors who refuse to contact professional archaeologists.

Conclusion

King (1980) has discussed the ethical obligations curators have to the museum and has encouraged museum archaeologists to recognize that their concerns and obligations are shared by other professionals in all museums. The American Association of Museums has a code of ethics which is a useful guide because of its universal applicability. By refusing to recognize the common concerns of all museums and the ways other museums have solved their problems, archaeological curators are missing an opportunity to spare themselves needless grief.

At the same time, archaeological curators do have professional responsibilities to a nonrenewable cultural resource whose full dimensions are only now surfacing. Many practices common in art museums, such as working closely with dealers and even curating private collections, would be absolutely disastrous to the prehistoric record. Guided by the concern for a dwindling and fragile data base, the archaeological museum curator must be vigilant not to engage in activities that might have any negative repercussions for either the artifacts still buried or those in a public institution. We are accountable to many constituencies—ethnic groups, legislators, administrators, the general public. Ultimately, however, our ethical conduct will be judged by the professional community of the future.

17

The International Traffic in Antiquities: Archaeological Ethics and the Archaeologist's Responsibility

Karen D. Vitelli

Theft and destruction of resources is of critical concern to archaeologists. Professional ethics in the area of antiquities law enforcement extend beyond the obvious sanction against the purchase or sale by archaeologists of illegally acquired cultural materials to the prevention of all such trafficking. This includes assisting law enforcement officials and educating the public to discourage those activities.

The antiquities market today is different in many ways from that of 15 years ago. It has grown from a relatively small-scale "Sunday afternoon" search for arrowheads and potsherds to a big—and dangerous—business. Felons, narcotic dealers, and other criminal elements participate in the antiquities black market. A recent law in this country, the Archaeological Resource Protection Act, provides stiff fines (up to $100,000) and jail sentences (up to 10 years) for certain activities. When there is the potential for big bucks balanced by the threat of large fines and jail sentences, antiquity traffickers may not hesitate to harm an unprepared archaeologist. Indeed, antiquity thieves have threatened and attempted to murder archaeologists in the United States and other countries. A word of caution is appropriate here. Although cultural resources are priceless for their scientific value,

Eric C. Schneider of the University of Baltimore School of Law provided valuable assistance in explaining the compexities of the relevant laws. Ellen Herscher offered information on current activities in Washington. Sebastian Payne, Oscar Muscarella, Michalis Fotiades, Tracey Cullen, and DeeDee Green read early drafts of this paper and contributed valued criticisms. Warm thanks are also due to Clemency Coggins, Jim Wiseman, and Al Wesolowsky for their support, encouragement, and hard work on behalf of the antiquities market problems.

they are not as valuable as a person's life. If you discover looting in progress and have reason to suspect that the vandals are more than casual pothunters, do not approach them. If the site is on public land, contact a law officer or a representative of the land-managing agency.

Karen D. Vitelli's essay deals with the international antiquities trade and the archaeologist's responsibilities therein.

THE BEGINNING OF THE POSTWAR art boom may be dated to a specific auction in Paris in 1952. That auction saw a record price of nearly $100,000 paid for an Impressionist painting. Over the next twenty years, the prices paid at public auctions for all categories of art objects multiplied 10 to 20 times, while average industrial stocks increased by a multiple of 5 (Meyer 1973: 4). U.S. Customs now estimates that, in the category of illegal trafficking, the dollar value of the traffic in smuggled artifacts is second only to that of the traffic in drugs (Nagin 1981: 61). A number of Christmas 1981 mail-order catalogues included antiquities among their luxury gift items, and a new investment company, Intercontinental Antiquities, Inc., specializing exclusively in "antiquity assets," apparently intends to exploit this thriving market. A wholly owned subsidiary of International Diamond Incorporated, IAC, states in its advertising brochure that "antiquities have appreciated over the last 25 years at rates that surpass most investments, including both hard and tangible assets." This author knows of no reason to question this claim. All the evidence suggests that the market in antiquities thrives.[1]

Many collectors of antiquities collect for the "thrill," and "uplifting experience" of living closely with beautiful ancient objects. Many justify their collecting with a passionate love for the objects and try to learn about the cultures which produced them. Some collectors, including a number of museum curators and directors (T. Hoving, J. Carter Brown, Jr.: see Glueck 1981), seem to be indulging a passion for the adventure and intrigue of the process of collecting as much as, if not more than, for the objects themselves. Underwater treasure divers probably belong in this category (Cockrell 1980). Increasingly, a new kind of collector is emerging—one who looks at ancient objects as a good financial investment, a hedge against inflation. Whatever the motivation for collecting, a great many people are doing it, and the impact in all cases is the same.

The Market and Archaeology

The connection between the booming market in antiquities and the looting and destruction of archaeological sites is direct and well doc-

[1] IAC has now gone out of business, for reasons unconnected to the quality of the market.

umented. A particularly stunning recent example is the site at Ban Chiang in Northeast Thailand. Antiquities from Ban Chiang first attracted international attention in 1970 when the University Museum Labs at the University of Pennsylvania released thermoluminescence dates of 5th and 4th millennia B.C. derived from some potsherds found at Ban Chiang. The sherds had arrived for analysis in a rather unusual way. An American undergraduate in Thailand visited the modern village of Ban Chiang in 1966 and took some of the antiquities he saw there back to his Thai hostess in Bangkok. She, recognizing that the sherds were unique in her collection of Thai antiquities, showed them to a friend, who eventually arranged for samples to be sent to Philadelphia for analysis. The dates (since recognized as erroneous: see Gorman 1981: 11) were considered surprisingly early. They served to focus the attention of the National Museum in Thailand on the site. Test excavations were conducted in 1967 and 1972 by the Thai Department of Fine Arts, and, from 1973–1976, more extensive excavations were carried out jointly with the University of Pennsylvania, under the direction of Chester Gorman.

The careful archaeological excavations at Ban Chiang produced a variety of cultural and environmental evidence which "has supported and greatly enhanced the view that Southeast Asia was an early and innovative center of cultural development. . . . Southeast Asia is now contributing data of fundamental importance to the study of the origins of domestication and the origins of metallurgy as they occurred throughout the world. We suggest that rice was domesticated in Southeast Asia, and the metallurgy in this area may also have been of indigenous origin" (Gorman 1981: 10).

Archaeologists were not the only ones who turned their attention to Ban Chiang. The site provided a whole new area of interest for collectors. Gorman has documented the results:

> After living on the mound for over 200 years, and after digging latrines and thousands of substantial postholes to support their houses . . . [the villagers] most certainly knew what lay under the mound's surface. Yet they never systematically dug for remains. The Thai test excavations of 1967 provided interesting if inconclusive results. Still, there was no major looting. . . . By 1970, the results of the TL dates had been reported to Thailand . . . as word of this passed to the Bangkok circle of collectors and dealers, many of them immediately organized Ban Chiang pottery market trips. . . . the wealthy hostess of the young university student [made her first reported trip to Ban Chiang in 1970 and] returned to Bangkok with over 100 vessels in her own car, and contracts to local villagers to dig and sell more. Other wealthy Thais joined the fashionable trek. . . . For the poor subsistence farmers of Ban Chiang, all this attention was a blessing . . . children went to better schools . . . real doctors were consulted for illnesses and funds were put aside for . . . the days when their supplies of pots would be exhausted [Gorman 1981: 12].

In 1972, various Thai laws forbade excavations by villagers and made it illegal to sell Ban Chiang material. Several government excavations were opened.

> Faced with an official presence and a rapidly dwindling supply of pots, the Ban Chiang villagers had two options; first to fan out and prospect for antiquities under other mound villages nearby; or, two, to manufacture fakes and sell them as the real thing. They, of course, chose both . . . dealers and collectors scoured practically every village within a 100 km. radius of Ban Chiang. . . . *In the last five years of survey no unlooted site has been located.* The *market* for Ban Chiang material set in motion the systematic plundering of the sites, and it continues [Gorman 1981: 13, emphasis added].

That it continues, in spite of the strict Thai laws, it only too clear: the August/September catalogue for the Horchow Collection offered "Museum quality Bronze Age pottery, 5000–3000 B.C. from Ban Chiang in Northeast Thailand." The pieces, ranging in price from $700–2,900, were sold out by mid-September[2]—even though such red-on-buff painted pieces are known to date to the Late Iron Age of Ban Chiang, much later than the advertised dates, and even though many experts in the field believe that the bulk of the "Ban Chiang" pottery in the U.S. is fake. We shall return to the Ban Chiang example later. It is but one particularly well documented and exceedingly unfortunate case.

Closer to home, similar destruction has recently been documented for many areas, including Belize (Pendergast and Graham 1981), Guatemala (Stuart and Garrett 1981), and the U.S. (Rippeteau 1979). Sometimes the looters supplying the market don't even bother to do their own digging: witness the theft of 243 ceramic vessels from the Moundville excavation storerooms (Oakley 1981). Excavation and museum storerooms frequently have minimal security and little or no record of individual pieces in their collections, making them easy pickings that are essentially untraceable once removed.

Whether the saleable objects are looted from sites or stolen from the unstudied collections of archaeological excavations, the loss is severe and unrecoverable. Individual objects on the market often cannot be assigned a precise country of origin, much less a site or stratigraphic context with accompanying information. Dealers will often supply "information" about reputed origins; history and logic show the inaccuracy of these purported provenances (Muscarella 1977b: 200, 209, and *passim*).

The context, and everything that this implies to an archaeologist, is lost for the discrete object sold on the market. Furthermore, objects that

[2] Several archaeologists responded to this ad by writing to Roger Horchow to explain their distress and concern that the sale of Ban Chiang pottery was contributing to the destruction of Thai sites. In response, Horchow promised not to deal in antiquities in the future. See Vitelli (1982b) for a discussion and examples of these successful protest letters, and Bard (1982) for an interview with Horchow on the subject.

strike the looters as less marketable are lost and even destroyed in the interest of finding the "important" objects for sale. Every archaeologist can probably think of finds of major significance which would have been considered to have little market value at first glance. An example is the unimpressive-looking bits of obsidian found at Franchthi Cave in Greece, which, because of their secure paleolithic context, stand as the world's earliest evidence for seafaring.

Large objects may be cut up and mutilated for easier transport. Mayan stelae and Egyptian tomb paintings cut out of the walls of tombs come to mind. Objects found in groups are dispersed; or new, false groupings are created to heighten interest and raise the price. We will never know if the Dorak treasure existed as a real archaeological group (Mellaart 1959). Structures and features are obliterated by looters. All environmental evidence is hopelessly lost. In fact, all studies on health and nutrition and on developments in agricultural practices or other areas that depend on careful statistical analyses of stratified evidence are impossible once a site has been disturbed. Even art historical studies, which depend primarily on stylistic or iconographic analyses, are affected by the loss of reliably dated, sourced information and by the increased potential for forged objects and forged provenances. Forgeries are easier to produce from a looted site—from aftercasts of the original objects, or by combinations of ancient and modern pieces and practices (Muscarella 1977a: 165, 178; Rieth 1970: 108, 113, 129)—and easy to pass off as genuine on a market that heightens interest through secrecy. The loss of information about the single object is but the tip of the iceberg of lost information about the site and the culture that produced it.

Laws Affecting International Trade in Antiquities

Most nations have recognized the direct connection between the destruction of our archaeological heritage and the international market in antiquities by enacting laws to control both the excavation and the export of antiquities. Typically, these laws claim ultimate ownership by the *state* of all antiquities originating within its borders. *All* excavation requires a license or permit issued by the state. Private individuals usually may possess and collect antiquities, but ownership rests in the state; hence, the export of the objects is strictly limited and requires a permit from the state. Some states grant export permits more freely than others. Any antiquity exported without an official permit is considered stolen. Obviously, the details of the laws vary from state to state. Bonnie Burnham's *The Protection of Cultural Property* (1974) provides a handy summary of the different laws, country by country. Antiquities deriving from contexts under water have a particularly precarious legal status, as they are subject to questions of jurisdiction over territorial waters.

U.S. laws concerning the international traffic in antiquities are significantly different from those of most other nations. They regulate the excavation of antiquities on publicly owned lands, although there is currently no protection for sites in federally owned waters (Cockrell 1980).[3] Antiquities from privately owned lands, however, are the property of the individual landholder, who has the right to dispose of the objects as he or she chooses, including export abroad. The export of antiquities stolen or illicitly excavated from public lands could fall under the National Stolen Property Act (see below), but once an object has been removed from its buried context, it can be extremely difficult to determine whether that context was on public or private land. Additionally, U.S. Customs officials do not routinely search shipments going abroad, so they are not likely to intercept antiquities unless they have been alerted to check a particular shipment. At the moment, then, there is essentially no control over the *export* of American antiquities. The U.S. is one of the few nations that place no restrictions on the export of antiquities. This suggests interesting implications for our perceptions of the value and relevance of our Native American heritage.

There are some restrictions, however, on *importing* antiquities into the U.S. A single law currently addresses the issue directly and it is extremely limited in scope. PL 92–581 Title II, Regulation of Importation of Pre-Columbian Monumental or Architectural Sculpture or Murals, effective June 1, 1973, forbids the importation of some Pre-Columbian architectural sculpture and wall painting from any country in the Western Hemisphere without an appropriate permit. Only some monumental pieces of outstanding importance are covered by the law; smaller, moveable objects are not.

In March 1971, the U.S. and Mexico signed a Treaty of Cooperation Providing for the Recovery and Return of Stolen Archaeological, Historical and Cultural Properties. The key word here, as in most antiquities cases, is "stolen." We have already noted that most nations— and, since 1972 Mexico is one— claim state ownership of all antiquities; hence, objects exported without a permit from the owner (e.g., the state) are stolen from the state, even if they were excavated from privately owned land or acquired from a private citizen. Private citizens in Mexico may possess, but not own, antiquities. Since U.S. residents may, and do, own antiquities, a legal conflict occurs when a U.S. resident (living in the U.S.) claims ownership of an artifact that came from Mexico since 1972 and, hence, is claimed by Mexico as well. This issue was addressed in one of the most important antiquities cases in recent U.S. history, *U.S.* v. *McClain* (545 F.2d, 988 [5th Cir. 1977]).

In this case, four individuals were convicted under the National Stolen Property Act (18 U.S.C. 2314 and 2315) of receiving and selling

[3] Legislation that would provide protection for historic shipwrecks located underwater was considered at the 97th Congress as H.R. 132. It will be revised and reintroduced by Congressman Charles E. Bennett of Florida in 1983. See Vitelli (1982b).

stolen property in the form of antiquities exported from Mexico without a permit. The National Stolen Property Act "prohibits the transportation 'in interstate or foreign commerce [of] any goods . . . of the value of $5,000 or more' with knowledge that such goods were 'stolen', converted or taken by fraud. . . . The Act also subjects to criminal liability 'whoever receives, conceals, stores, barters, sells, or disposes of any goods . . . *knowing* the same to have been stolen, unlawfully converted, or taken' " [Wisdom 992 F.2d (5th Cir. 1977), emphasis added].

In the McClain case it was established that the objects had been exported from Mexico after the 1972 Mexican law clearly declared ownership by the State of Mexico of all antiquities from her lands. Therefore the case turned on whether the antiquities in question were knowingly stolen within the meaning of the NSPA. Testimony suggested that the defendants were aware of the Mexican law, thus meeting the "knowledge" requirement of the NSPA. Judge Minor Wisdom found the defendants guilty of trafficking in stolen property under the NSPA. Judge Wisdom's decision suggests that, to meet the conditions of the NSPA, the foreign state must have declared national ownership of the antiquities in question and broadcast the ownership claim sufficiently for violators to know they are dealing in stolen property, and the export must have taken place after the declaration of ownership went into effect. In the McClain case, the Treaty with Mexico supported the argument that the Mexican law was widely known. The extent to which the *McClain* precedent may be effectively applied in other cases involving antiquities from other countries remains to be tested. U.S. archaeologists can help by explaining the NSPA requirements to officials in host countries. For example, officials can be encouraged to see that English-language signs explaining the local antiquities laws are prominently displayed in airports and at customs checkpoints. Generally, the more frequently we mention the laws of specific countries, the more likely it is that collectors will "have knowledge" of them.

On September 17, 1981, the U.S. and Peru signed an Executive Agreement for the Recovery and Return of Stolen Archaeological, Historical and Cultural Properties. The content of this agreement is practically identical to that of the Treaty with Mexico. However, unlike a treaty, an executive agreement is not ratified by the Senate and carries no legal force. It still may be a powerful and influential statement of policy. It serves to broadcast in the U.S. Peru's claim to ownership of all her antiquities. Peru has begun to post signs in Peruvian airports explaining the prohibition on exporting antiquities. This makes it more likely that any prosecution for trafficking in antiquities stolen from Peru under the NSPA could result in a conviction.

The Pre-Columbian monuments law, the treaty with Mexico, the agreement with Peru, and the decision in *U.S.* v. *McClain* combine to provide some limits on the free movement to the U.S. of some antiquities from some New World countries. The Cultural Property Implementation Act, which would provide protection for additional kinds of objects from more countries, has been under consideration by Congressional committees since 1976. The origins of this act go back to the 16th General Conference of the United Nations Educational, Scientific and Cultural Organization, which met in Paris in October and November 1970.

At that conference the UNESCO delegates proposed and adopted the Convention on the Means of Prohibiting and Preventing the Illicit Import, Export, and Transfer of Ownership of Cultural Property. The preamble to the Convention states that "cultural property constitutes one of the basic elements of civilization and national culture, and . . . its true value can be appreciated only in relation to the fullest possible information regarding its origin, history, and traditional setting" and that the illicit traffic in cultural property "is an obstacle to . . . understanding between nations." The protection of cultural property "can be effective only if organized both nationally and internationally among states working in close cooperation." (The full text of the Convention is published in *Journal of Field Archaeology* 3 [1976] 217–220). The last statement, emphasizing the need for close international cooperation, is utterly crucial and very difficult to bring about. No nation and, indeed, no international body can legislate for the international community. The Convention is an important statement of principles and guidelines, devised and endorsed by representatives of many nations. It is not legally binding until and unless it is implemented by law in the individual countries. The Convention calls for individual states to protect their own cultural heritage, to develop legal means for the exchange of cultural property, and to provide legal protection for the cultural heritage of other nations. No nation in the world has the resources to police all archaeological sites, all borders, all shipments leaving the country. International cooperation is the only hope for controlling the market, for bringing it within reasonable bounds.

The Convention was submitted to the U.S. Senate in February 1972. On August 11, 1972, the Senate gave its advice and consent to ratification by a vote of 79–0. Before a country can deposit its instruments of ratification to the Convention, thus becoming a State Party, it must enact its own implementing legislation. At least 50 other states have done so. On December 21, 1982, the 97th U.S. Congress finally passed S. 1723, The Cultural Property Implementation Act, as a rider to H. R. 4566, a general tariff bill. The Act was passed without major amendments. (Opposition to the bill was withdrawn and redirected toward amending the National Stolen Property Act so that it would not apply to cases involving antiquities. If this attempt is successful, we will have acquired legal protection for a few critically endangered sites while removing that protection from most other sites.)

This bill represents years of work by the State Department, the Department of the Treasury (U.S. Customs), Congressional committee staff, art dealers, museum representatives, private collectors, archaeologists and anthropologists to address the legitimate concerns of all involved. A great many compromises, which reflect political realities as well as cultural concerns, were made. Far from banning the importation into the U.S. of all antiquities, the bill defines several very limited conditions under which the importation of specific antiquities might be banned. Sections 2 and 3 of the bill define a set of complicated conditions whereby another State Party to the Convention must initiate action through a request that the U.S. embargo a certain category of artifacts because (1) that category comes from pillaged sites, (2) there is reason to believe that market demand in the U.S. is contributing to the pillaging, and (3) the government in question has already done everything possible within its own borders to stop the pillage. Then, subject to several other conditions, the U.S. may embargo that category of artifacts for five years, with the option to extend the embargo for several more years.

The bill also prevents legal entry of "stolen" items, defined as "items of cultural property appertaining to the inventory of a museum or religious or secular public monument or similar institution" (Section 7). Ban Chiang might have been saved had we had this legislation 15 years ago.

Real changes in the antiquities market are not going to come about through legislation alone, however. For real change to take place, archaeologists must take greater responsibility and show more concern for the public perception of their discipline and the ways in which archaeologists themselves appear to contribute to and condone the market. Here we return to Gorman's description of the looting of Ban Chiang. The looting there began in earnest after the archaeometric determination of early dates for the pottery, which the archaeologists then associated with some of the world's earliest developments in metallurgy. Gorman makes it clear that the villagers who carried out the looting did not initiate it. (Nor does he blame them for taking advantage of the economic benefits it brought them.) He says that the market demand for Ban Chiang pots started the looting and destruction and falsification of information. But the archaeological studies created the market interest in the pottery. Until the archaeologists excavated the site and began to develop the cultural and environmental context of the pots, there was no market for them.

This seldom-acknowledged responsibility should be very much in our minds whenever we present our work to the public. If we do our work well and produce interesting results, we will generate interest in the cultures and ideas that we are studying. We have a responsibility to see that the interest we generate is not in objects per se, that we do not convey the impression that objects themselves are the end of archaeology.

Presenting Archaeology to the Public

Museums legitimate the collection and presentation of objects as objects. Many museums use public funds to buy objects without provenance and often show little concern for the source of the pieces. They compete for the donations of objects from private collectors, who take a tax deduction for their donated treasure and receive public acclaim for their generosity. The objects are displayed in cases and glossy catalogues and posters, with a two- or three-line label. The clear message proclaimed to the public is that the object is a beautiful or curious treasure to be admired, even coveted. Museums might, and a few do, redirect their limited budgets from acquiring and driving up the prices of objects to acquiring and exhibiting information. Archaeologists are in a good position to make persuasive arguments to this effect, and to provide the kind of information that could make for lively and exciting exhibits.

To the extent that archaeologists give professional advice on the value of objects for the museum collection, authenticate pieces, write descriptions for catalogues, and give public lectures on the collections without reference to the way the objects got to the museums, they are advancing the collection and view of objects simply as objects.

Collectors complain that archaeological reports are so dry, so full of minutiae and jargon, that they kill any interest a layman might have. They conclude that archaeologists "can't see the forest for the trees" and really "don't know as much as dealers and collectors." This is, in part, a misunderstanding of scientific process and scholarly endeavor. Few nonspecialists would get very far with a scholarly treatise on mathematics or a detailed study on a specific branch of cancer research. But the complaint suggests that we have a popular audience that is not getting the information it wants from us and that is getting a distorted impression of our discipline. In this respect, *Early Man* and *Archaeology* magazines are more important journals than many professional archaeologists recognize. Have we left too much of the popular writing to nonarchaeologists?

When we do write a popular account or give a public lecture we tend to emphasize results. We present illustrations of objects, highlighting the best preserved, the most decorative or spectacular pieces. Perhaps there are a few scenes of trenches, a survey team, a sieve. Rarely is there discussion of the process of archaeological thought and study, the long, hard, often boring process of making the steps from data recovery to meaning. Our presentations may note in passing that, for six weeks in the field collecting data, we had to spend six months or six years studying and interpreting that data. To other archaeologists that statement conjures up a world of activities; to the layman it tends to mean "mending pots." Perhaps we think that the public isn't interested in the hows, but books such as June Goodfield's *An Imagined World: A Story of Scientific Discovery,* which details the process of one woman's life in medical laboratory research—complete with the demands and limitations imposed by funding agencies, the many dead ends of her research, the wear and tear on her family life—find an appreciative audience, and one that ultimately has a greater understanding of her discipline.

Students in general archaeology and ancient culture classes always groan at the great lists of characteristic objects and dates that they have to memorize. For many, this is their sole formal encounter with archaeology. Many learn little about the archaeological process. They may be given no way to distinguish an archaeologist's trench from a looter's trench. They may hear nothing about looting, fakes and forgeries, or antiquities laws and the reasons they exist. They may feel a thrill when objects are passed around the room and they get to "actually touch something that was made by a person 5000 years ago" or enjoy an assignment in a museum looking at objects "said to be from ______" with no explanation of how they got here from there. They probably hear something about surface surveys, which may easily leave the impression that all the information one needs to know is in the object one finds sitting there, right on the surface. They may come for an appointment and find the archaeologist's office decorated with antiquities and, not realizing they are replicas or on temporary loan for study, may receive the mental image of the archaeologist comfortably living with artifacts. Should we be surprised, then, if they become dealers and collectors and credit us, their teachers, with providing the initial interest and inspiration?

Most archaeologists have more direct encounters with the antiquities market, although they may not see them as such. An example is that call out of the blue, from a stranger or friend who has found an "artifact" in his uncle's attic, while digging in the garden, or on a trip to Mexico, Arizona, or Turkey, and who wants to know something about it. It is tempting to show off one's expertise, especially when the object turns out to be something reasonably familiar or potentially important; another tendency is to dismiss the object and its owner quickly, to get on with an already overloaded schedule. But that encounter will convey a great deal about archaeology to that individual and to everyone who hears of his or her visit. It can say the the *object* is important and worth lots of money; or it can say that the object out of context reveals very little, that the archaeologist cannot assume that it is genuine, and why not.

The actual response will, of course, depend on the particular circumstances, and the innocent caller should not be made to feel like a thief. The point is that the archaeologist has a responsibility to explain archaeology, to be professionally responsible in giving professional advice.

A more difficult encounter, at least for some archaeologists, comes with the opportunity to publish unprovenanced objects in museums or private collections, or to cite them in reference to one's own work with excavated materials. The decision to publish or not will depend on the individual archaeologist's questions and goals. The objects exist. Some are certainly genuine and possibly relevant for limited archaeological inquiries. Some lost their context so long ago, under conditions very different from those of today, that moral stances about their means of acquisition are relatively meaningless. Still, any scholarly publication should differentiate between reputed stories of origins and secure archaeological facts, and only use the objects to draw conclusions that are justifiable by applying rigorous archaeological standards. Archaeologists should also be aware that dealers cite scholarly publications of unprovenanced objects to "prove" authenticity and to justify high prices. Thus, archaeologists who publish materials that go on the market may contribute to the desirability of the pieces, and may find themselves in the awkward position of being quoted in the marketplace or involved in a legal case (Bruhns 1977: 462).

Finally, archaeologists should be sensitive to two arguments frequently made by dealers and collectors. First, they remind us that, since all excavation entails destruction, an archaeological excavation that ignores available stratigraphic, cultural, or environmental information is just as destructive as the uncontrolled excavation of looters. This is true, with the exception of certain salvage operations, although it does not justify the looting of sites. Second, they point to the large numbers of unpublished archaeological excavations and argue that our claim to making all our results public is false; that an unpublished excavation is the equivalent of a looted site, with all information lost except for the discrete objects extracted from the site. This is not entirely true, for field notes and records usually still exist from unpublished excavations and might yet be made public. Nevertheless, to the extent that we are unprofessional and incomplete in our mission as archaeologists, we appear to be "just like the collectors and dealers," and our condemnation of their activities translates, in their eyes, into a greedy desire to keep all the action for ourselves.

Conclusion

We have seen that the international market for antiquities is a booming market. We recognize that the looting of sites and the manufacture of forgeries to meet the growing demands of the market are destroying and distorting the evidence that our discipline requires to make its contributions to human knowledge and understanding. International laws provide limited protection for selected sites and materials, but to be effective the laws require international cooperation and respect—respect for law, for the discipline, and for the goals of archaeology. Archaeologists have the responsibility to develop and deserve that respect.

18

Cultural Resource Law Enforcement in the United States

Martin E. McAllister,
J. Scott Wood,
and
Dorothy M. Goddard

In recent years, there has been a rapidly intensifying effort in the United States to enforce laws designed to protect archaeological sites from vandalism and looting. As cultural resource law enforcement has developed, some archaeologists have become active participants, even though such efforts are not a traditional component of the discipline. This raises a legitimate professional issue: To what extent should archaeologists be involved in cultural resource law enforcement?

This question is appropriate to a volume on archaeological ethics and values because a basic ethical tenet in the profession is that archaeologists never condone the wanton destruction of cultural resources. Thus, there is an obvious ethical requirement for some level of archaeological involvement in cultural resource law enforcement. Ignoring theft and vandalism of archaeological materials or simply being philosophically opposed to these destructive activities is not enough.

Destruction of both prehistoric and historic sites by looters and vandals has occurred throughout the history of the United States. Unfortunately, detailed historical research is lacking on the development of these activities and their effects over time on the cultural resources of this country. This is particularly true for the East, though it is known that burial mounds and other sites there have been targets for destruction since Colonial times.

More is known about the history of the problem in the Southwest, thanks to the recent work by Nickens et al. (1981: 37–52). The discovery of large, well-preserved sites there in the 1870's and 1880's created increased interest in Southwestern artifacts in other parts of the country. This gave rise to commercial looting activities, such as those of the Wetherills, and also to "recreational" digging and collecting by both local residents and many tourists. The problem was aggravated when more inhabitants of the area turned to looting as an alternative source of income during the depression of the early 1890's, and was only reduced by the drive for preservation which led to the enactment of the Federal Antiquities Act in 1906. This reversal was also caused by the unfortunate depletion of many of the more spectacular sites.

For both the Southwest and other parts of the country, we know less about destruction of sites by looting and vandalism between 1906 and the late 1960's. It is difficult to assess the effect of the Antiquities Act on illegal digging in the years after its passage because of a lack of documentation during that period. There must have been some convictions under the 1906 Act prior to the 1970's, but they are not widely reported. There is some indication of an upswing in illicit destruction of sites during the depression years of the 1930's (Nickens et al. 1981: 46–47). The only early Antiquities Act investigation we are aware of was carried out by the FBI in the Tonto National Forest in Arizona in 1936. Although brought to the attention of J. Edgar Hoover, it did not result in prosecution. Reclamation and development activities became an increasingly significant threat to the nation's cultural resources from the late 1930's onward. It may be that the expanding federal commitment to archaeological salvage reduced looting and vandalism, but undoubtedly not to the point of hiatus. A complete picture of events between 1906 and 1970 requires additional historical research.

If, in fact, illegal destruction declined prior to 1970, a significant reversal occurred shortly thereafter. In 1972, Hester Davis (1972: 269) was warning that "digging by relic collectors has reached alarming proportions" and, further, that it had become "a close second as a cause of destruction," exceeded only by the loss of sites to development activities. In his anecdotal history of illicit art acquisition, *The Plundered Past,* journalist and avocational archaeologist Karl Meyer (1973: 8–10) attributed the new wave of looting to "the growing interest in American Indians" and the "growing market" and "new record price levels for Indian art." While, in his view, these developments stemmed from a single auction, that of the Green Collection of Indian Art in New York in 1971, the widespread rekindled passion for Native American culture and the past seems to have begun as early as the late 1960's, at least in the Southwest. The resurgence in commercially motivated destruction may be related not only to new markets but also to gradually worsening economic conditions in the 1970's, a trend that has continued into the 1980's.

For whatever reasons, the limited information available indicates a drastic increase in illegal looting and vandalism of cultural resources in the United States during the last 10 to 12 years. During this period, nearly 30 cases involving federal or Indian lands were recorded in the West; as a result, formal criminal charges were filed against more than 40 people (Green and Davis 1981: 75–79). In addition, cases have occurred on state and private property in Arizona, New Mexico, Utah, and probably other states as well. Finally, there is also evidence of new activity farther east, in Arkansas and the Mississippi River Valley (Green and Davis 1981: 77; Davis 1972: 269). Given the documented level of looting and vandalism incidents since 1970, the actual frequency of occurrence must be frighteningly higher.

The magnitude and scope of the problem as it exists today can best be illustrated by a brief look at the sophisticated techniques employed by commercial looters and the levels of destruction they have brought about. The term "commercial looting" is used here to identify the "systematic looting of sites for commercial purposes by individuals who are fully aware of the impacts and illegality of their acts" (McAllister 1979: 32). Casual or noncommercial looters and vandals can also do considerable damage to archaeological sites but, relative to the large-scale destruction brought about by commercial activities, this is a lesser concern.

Commercial thieves who use heavy earth-moving equipment have the capability to completely destroy even the largest sites in surprisingly short periods of time. We recently observed the mechanized destruction of a large prehistoric masonry site on private property. The primary structures encompassed at least two acres and probably contained several hundred rooms arranged around an earth-filled masonry platform mound about 10 feet high. Despite 100 years of casual exploration and minor pothunting, the site remained relatively intact until 1980. The property was sold that year, and the new owner arranged for two commercial looters to remove the artifacts in exchange for half of the material, which ultimately included more than 1000 pots. Using a bulldozer and front-end loader, the site was levelled and pushed over the edge of its river terrace, where the loose fill was searched for pots and jewelry. It took only a few days of machine time. All that remains now is a scraped surface and a small portion of the architecture.

Although heavy equipment is the ultimate weapon of destruction in their arsenal, it is not the only sophisticated technique employed by commercial looters to obtain artifacts or avoid detection. Others (McAllister 1979: 32) include:

1. Use of probes to locate burials and artifact deposits quickly, followed by the use of "sharpshooter" shovels to determine rapidly if the deposit is rich enough to merit digging with conventional hand tools.
2. Use of camouflage devices, such as bottomless tents, to conceal digging activities.

3. Work at night using lights in exposed, nonremote areas.
4. Use of aircraft to locate sites, coordinate access by radio-equipped, four-wheel drive vehicles on the ground, and provide surveillance to avoid detection.
5. Use of helicopters to locate, access, and transport artifacts from sites.
6. Use of boats for access and transport in lakeshore areas with looters posing as fishermen.
7. Use of two-way radios for communication purposes and to provide an early warning from lookouts and local informants to avoid apprehension.
8. Use of multichannel radio scanners to monitor the location and activities of law enforcement personnel.

As an indication of the level of destruction occurring in the Southwest, at least 27 per cent of the known sites in the Tonto National Forest have been affected (Woodward et al. 1981: 2–3). Other public land jurisdictions in the Southwest evidence similar and higher levels of documented disturbance. If our own records are any indication, all of these percentages are undoubtedly low due to small samples, inadequate recording, and outdated site records, some of which are 50 years old. When applied to a projected total of 60,000 sites in the Tonto National Forest, the potential amount of destruction and loss of irreplaceable data is staggering. It is even severer for those types of sites most frequently selected for looting (e.g., more than 90 per cent of the large sites in the Tonto sample have been seriously disturbed).

The Legislative and Judicial Response

A number of federal laws and regulations have been established over the last 80 years to stop the theft and vandalism of cultural materials. Briefly, their provisions are as follows:

1. American Antiquities Act of 1906 (PL 59–209)—fine of up to $500 and/or imprisonment for up to 90 days (misdemeanor).
2. Code of Federal Regulations: Department of Interior (43 CFR), U.S.D.I., National Park Service (36 CFR), and U.S.D.A. Forest Service (36 CFR)—fine of up to $500 and/or imprisonment for up to six months (misdemeanor). The Department of Interior regulations (Bureau of Land Management, National Park Service) are based on the authority of the Antiquities Act. Forest Service regulations are based on enabling legislation and property jurisdiction statutes.
3. Embezzlement and Theft of Government Property (18 U.S.C. 641) and Malicious Mischief (18 U.S.C. 1361)—fine of up to $10,000 and/or imprisonment for up to 10 years, if the value

of the property stolen or destroyed exceeds $100 (felony), and up to $1000 and/or one year if the value of the property is less (misdemeanor).

4. Archaeological Resources Protection Act (ARPA) of 1979 (PL 96-95)—fine of up to $20,000 and/or imprisonment for up to two years if damage exceeds $5000 (felony), or up to $10,000 and one year of imprisonment if it does not (misdemeanor). It also calls for a fine of up to $100,000 and/or five years of imprisonment for subsequent convictions and has provisions for assessment of civil penalties for damages.

In addition, several important court rulings have affected the federal laws and regulations. The 1974 Diaz decision of the Ninth Circuit Court of Appeals reversed lower court decisions by finding the term "object of antiquity" and other language in the Antiquities Act to be unconstitutionally vague. The effect of this decision was to render the criminal prohibitions of the Act unusable in the Ninth Circuit area, which includes Arizona, California, Idaho, Montana, Nevada, Oregon, and Washington. Department of Interior regulations deriving from these prohibitions were also negated in the states listed. Conversely, the 1979 Tenth Circuit Court of Appeals ruling in the Smyer-May case upheld the language of the Antiquities Act and therefore allowed prosecutions under its provisions. At this writing, the United States Supreme Court has not yet resolved the discrepancy between the Ninth and Tenth Circuit Court decisions.

In another Ninth Circuit ruling, the Jones, Jones, and Gevara case, the 1978 U.S. District Court held that looters of archaeological sites on federal lands could not be prosecuted under the theft and destruction of government property statutes, but had to be prosecuted under the Antiquities Act—but, of course, the latter could not be used because it had been declared unconstitutional in that circuit. Fortunately, this decision was reversed by the Ninth Circuit Court of Appeals in November of 1979. However, for most of 1978 and 1979, sites on federal lands in the Ninth Circuit area were virtually unprotected from thieves and vandals. These circumstances led members of the U.S. Congress from Arizona and New Mexico to introduce and work for enactment of the Archaeological Resources Protection Act, which became law on October 31, 1979. Detailed discussions of the cases mentioned above and copies of court documents pertaining to them have been compiled by Green and Davis (1981).

After the passage of the Federal Antiquities Act of 1906, many states enacted comparable legislation to protect sites on state lands and, in some cases, even those on private property. For example, the 1927 Arizona State Antiquities act was patterned very closely on the 1906 federal act. This process has since repeated itself in the form of a 1981 amendment to the Arizona act which provides for stiffer, felony penalties basedon those of the federal act of 1979.

Cultural Resources Law Enforcement Procedures

What are the procedures of cultural resource law enforcement? Since the mid-1970's, a basic set of procedures has become more or less standard. Much like those of any other area of law enforcement, these procedures involve the following activities: investigation, detection, and apprehension; evidence identification and collection; and case preparation and prosecution.

Investigation, Detection, and Apprehension

Investigation in the context of cultural resource law enforcement involves obtaining information about looting and trafficking activities. Law enforcement officers have developed a variety of techniques for gathering this information which may or may not require direct assistance from archaeologists. Two important areas in which such assistance is commonly requested can be termed "intelligence forwarding" and "evidence clarification."

Archaeologists are often the first to know about pothunting activities, either from their own observations in the field or because information about looting and vandalism is more likely to be given to an archaeologist than to a law enforcement officer. Once received, such information should be turned over to law enforcement officers as rapidly as possible. In one case in the Tonto National Forest in late 1979, an archaeological contractor reported a disturbance to law enforcement officers, who led an undercover operation that produced one of the first successful convictions under ARPA.

Archaeologists may be called upon to provide assistance when law enforcement officers feel they have evidence of illicit disturbance but are not certain of its validity or import. This need for clarification may occur at any phase of an investigation (e.g., before or after apprehension). It may be as simple as determining the evidential value, if any, of a recovered object or an area under investigation. Is the object they believe to be an artifact actually an artifact, is the tool a specialized looting implement, is the location they are watching a site? On the other hand, evidence clarification may require sophisticated site or feature evaluation and/or detailed artifact analysis.

A good example of this type of effort occurred in the 1979 Hancock, Brady, and Brady case. Four suspects were observed digging at a site in the Apache-Sitgreaves National Forest, but the distance was too great to allow positive identification and they left the site before they could be apprehended. They were stopped while attempting to depart from the area, and potsherds and digging tools were found in their vehicle. Though archaeologists identified these items for the law enforcement officers, it did not prove that the individuals were digging at the particular site. However, based on previous experience with the Smyer-May case in the Gila National Forest in New Mexico, the archaeologists decided to try to match sherds found in the vehicle with sherds left in the disturbed area at the site. After attempting reconstructions with hundreds of sherds, three matches were found, thus proving conclusively that the suspects were at the site. These efforts contributed significantly to a successful prosecution.

One other potential area of assistance by archaeologists in investigation should also be mentioned briefly. Behavioral research on archaeological looting and vandalism is still in its infancy, as indicated by the few in-depth studies that exist (L. Williams 1977; Wright and Reid 1979; Nickens et al. 1981; Woodward et al. 1981). However, the ability to reliably predict which sites are more likely to be pothunter targets would obviously be of tremendous benefit to investigators. This is especially true in the Western United States, where investigators are faced with a large number of sites spread over vast and often remote areas. Archaeologists should attempt to collect and analyze data on this behavior whenever possible.

Evidence Identification and Collection

As the Hancock, Brady, and Brady case example indicates, archaeologists can provide valuable assistance in detecting violations and making apprehensions, though such assistance is likely to be somewhat incidental. There are certain aspects of evidence identification and collection, however, which require specialized expertise, making the presence of a qualified archaeologist imperative. Proper identification of the nature and extent of the archaeological evidence at a site is the most important role of the archaeologist in culture resource law enforcement. Since forensic archaeology is dependent on an unbroken sequence of observations, it is likely to be more effective when the archaeologist is present from the beginning. If this is not possible, the site should be secured and left as is until archaeological assistance can be obtained.

In addition to archaeological evidence, other kinds of evidence are important in successful convictions. These may include equipment such as camping gear, firearms, vehicles, ordinary digging tools (shovels, picks, etc.), specialized pothunting tools (probes, sharpshooter shovels, screens, etc.), and even bulldozers, backhoes, and other types of earthmoving machinery. Other items commonly taken as evidence include beverage containers, cigarette butts and empty packs, and other types of litter. Unusual kinds of evidence may also be encountered. For example, in the Jones, Jones, and Gevara case in the Tonto National Forest, the suspects had taken Polaroid pictures of their activities at the site. In addition, archaeologists must be cognizant that some important elements of criminal evidence, such as fingerprints, tire tracks, and footprints, are fragile and can easily be destroyed. Law enforcement officers should assume responsibility for collection and/or impoundment of non-archaeological evidence.

Archaeological evidence in a looting case consists of the same types of artifactual material and contextual information which make up traditional archaeological data. As might be expected, evidence collection techniques are much the same as those used for archaeological data recovery. Artifactual evidence can usually be found in a variety of locations on or about a disturbed site: in spoil dirt in and around the excavation, on the person of a suspect, in vehicles, or off the site in such places as camps or caches. It may be concealed in luggage, packs, hidden vehicle compartments, or other containers such as boxes, bags, and even ice chests. It is critical that search and seizure occur according to strict legal procedures. Improperly obtained evidence may not be allowed in court. When archaeologists know or suspect the location of concealed evidence, they should always alert the officers present and not attempt to collect it except under their direction.

As important as locating and recovering the removed objects is the process of assessing physical damages to the site. This is especially critical when subsurface disturbance is involved, particularly when prior looting has taken place at the site. Archaeologists should never assume automatically that all disturbance at the site was caused by those apprehended. Instead, the disturbance linked with these particular individuals must be identified specifically, through observation and/or circumstantial and material evidence. If this is not done, a case can be seriously jeopardized, since it may be argued that the exact nature and source of the damage was not ascertained at the time of the alleged violation. The information necessary to make this distinction can be obtained in two ways: by direct observation of looting activities, and/or by examination of the site to identify fresh disturbance areas. Even circumstantial evidence may be inadequate without corroborating material evidence.

Eyewitness observation, coupled with on-site identification and confirmation of the activity areas as soon as possible after apprehension, is obviously the more definitive method and may be essential in cases involving only surface collection of artifacts. When archaeologists are not present initially, they should, upon arrival at the scene, ascertain what activities were observed and where they occurred. If archaeologists are present when violations are detected, they can provide valuable assistance by noting the particulars of what is being done to the site. This will aid law enforcement officers, because archaeologists are best qualified to assess what is occurring. Careful observation and good notes (at the time of detection or as soon as possible thereafter) are essential, as they can become the basis for later testimony. The ethical question of how much damage must be witnessed before an apprehension is made might become an issue, but we have found that officers generally want to move as quickly as possible after the initial observation of disturbance so that the opportunity is not lost. This may result in reduced penalties due to lower dollar values in property damage.

In cases involving subsurface disturbance at sites where prior activity has occurred, prompt on-site examination will allow freshly dug areas to be segregated from earlier ones, even when the activity was not witnessed or when observation was hindered by factors such as vegetation or distance. Proper assessment by the archaeologist of the age of disturbance is necessary regardless of previous site condition or the circumstances leading to the apprehension. Soil in the form of spoil dirt at disturbance areas is the critical phenomenon. Almost all archaeologists have the opportunity to participate in and observe excavation, so they should be able to distinguish freshly removed soil from that which has been exposed to the elements for any length of time. Surface texture, overall consistency, and moisture content will probably be important variables. Careful examination of soil conditions by the archaeologist, documented by notes and photographs, should be sufficient to allow the identification of fresh disturbance areas, especially when combined with other material evidence, including any suspect admissions as to the length of time present in the area. Documenting the condition of older disturbance areas can also be useful in identifying fresh ones.

It should be remembered that placing a monetary value on the extent of archaeological damage is a requirement of ARPA provisions, and may be a requirement under state law as well. This must be done by professional archaeologists experienced in determining the costs of data recovery, analysis, and curation. If those present do not have such expertise, there are two options. The area of damage can be recorded so that value estimates can be made without actual site inspection, or qualified archaeologists can be brought to the site as soon as possible. Experience in such instances indicates that the first approach is preferable when, as is usually the case, the necessary assistance cannot be obtained immediately. Also, it will provide equal access to the information by both prosecution and defense in any legal proceedings. Unfortunately, the best method for actually arriving at the monetary value figures from the data continues to be a subject of debate (e.g., Donaldson et al. 1981) and so will not be considered here.

As the preceding discussion indicates, inspection of the site is crucial in identifying suspect-related disturbance, artifactual evidence, and other material evidence before the collection process begins. At least one law enforcement officer and an archaeologist should be involved to insure that no evidence is overlooked or inadvertently destroyed. Again, when an archaeologist is not present initially or when there are delays while the apprehension process is completed and any necessary evidence collection is made at other locations, the site should be watched but left as is until the inspection can be conducted properly. In addition to identifying disturbance areas and collection loci, the inspection team should also determine the collection strategy, including collection assignments, evidence cataloguing, order of collection, and precautionary measures necessary to prevent loss of evidence.

The actual evidence collection procedures employed will vary according to the system preferred by the law enforcement officers involved and the circumstances of the case, such as site type and condition. Basic elements of the process include photographing each collection area (first, as is and then with a photo board or other visible designation), plotting the location of each on a site sketch map, measuring and recording dimensions and other pertinent information at all fresh disturbance areas, and, finally, working at each location separately, collecting and recording the item recovered (sherds, lithics, ground stone, human bone, etc.). An evidence tag or other comparable form of identification should be provided for every sealed container of evidence. To facilitate this task, we have developed a standardized set of procedures which involves the use of prepared evidence collection kits, streamlined mapping techniques, and specialized photograph and evidence recording forms. As the final step in the collection process, all evidence is transported to the location where it will be held and secured in evidence lockers.

Case Preparation and Prosecution

When looters or vandals are apprehended, information on the case must be readied for presentation to prosecutors and other authorities who will determine what legal action will be taken. This process is usually distinguished from the additional preparations necessary once it has been determined that the next stage, prosecution, will be undertaken. Basically this will consist of providing law enforcement officers and prosecutors with substantiation that a crime has been committed. The first step will be to prepare a detailed written statement on what was seen and done at the scene of the violation. Other duties will be expected of the archaeologist once the decision is made to go to trial. These can include artifact processing and analysis, production of site maps to display disturbance and evidence collection loci, and assistance in the preparation of a case report document, usually in the form of interpretation and evaluation of evidence and damages. In addition, there may be a need for specific analyses designed to link suspects with vandalized portions of sites. In the Jones, Jones, and Gevara case, over a thousand hours were invested in this process, much of it devoted to reconstructing 15 pottery vessels from the thousands of sherds collected as evidence from fresh disturbance areas at the site. Finally, both indictment and prosecution may require testimony by the archaeologist before grand juries, judges, and trial juries.

As a cautionary note, it must be emphasized that the potential range of results in these cases is no different than in any other legal proceeding. Despite heroic efforts, indictments may not be obtained, charges may be reduced or dismissed, suspects ultimately may be found not guilty, or plea bargaining may reduce the severity of sentences imposed. Archaeologists should remember that their job is to provide the assistance requested of them; other circumstances are beyond their control. Even after all the work in the Jones, Jones, and Gevara case, the original charges against the suspects were dismissed the day before the trial was to begin, and a successful prosecution involving plea bargaining resulted only after a lengthy appeal process.

Trials and pretrial preparations are both time consuming and arduous. The preparation of testimony for the pretrial hearings and the trial itself are of paramount importance. Days or weeks may be spent as prosecutors work with each witness, developing a strategy for testimony and attempting to anticipate the nature of examination by the defense. Since potential prosecution witnesses are usually excluded from trial proceedings except during their own testimony, the prosecution generally wants all witnesses to be present throughout the preparation process so that they become familiar with the testimony of their colleagues and the overall prosecution effort. Preparing, listing, and numbering all physical evidence and other exhibits to be introduced is also a time-consuming process.

The actual experience of testifying in a pretrial hearing or trial cannot be adequately described here. Suffice it to say that even veteran witnesses may find this to be nerve-racking and difficult, and for first-time witnesses the tension level is beyond comparison, especially under cross-examination by the defense. Potential witnesses should bear in mind that cases are seldom won or lost on the basis of one person's testimony and that the main requirement in responding to questioning is a clear and accurate account of the facts. Fortunately, the prosecutor is always present to assist the witness by rephrasing questions, reorienting the direction of testimony, or objecting to an approach taken by the defense. The witness should always pay close attention to the prosecutor and be ready for any verbal or visual signals. Depending on the complexity of the case, trials can last for several days or more, and witnesses may be asked to testify more than once. All archaeologists involved in the case may have to testify, and testimony from at least one expert witness on the damage value appraisal is definitely required when such an appraisal affects the severity of penalties, as it does under ARPA.

Finally, archaeologists may be requested or subpoenaed to testify as expert witnesses for the defense for the purpose of challenging prosecution appraisals of the extent and value of damage. Although we are not aware that this has yet occurred, the issue merits serious consideration. While it may be objectionable in principle, such a situation need not produce a serious ethical dilemma. Archaeologists faced with such a request should demand the right to consult with their prosecution counterparts who have had prior and better access to the evidence of the case, and should then assess the data, applying the most rigorous professional standards. As long as this approach is taken, it seems unlikely that prosecution and defense appraisals will vary greatly. Scientists from other disciplines have been testifying as expert witnesses for years, and the lesson from their experience seems to be that the potential for abuse by attorneys is directly related to the level of good judgment exhibted by the witness.

Conclusion

The purpose of this rather detailed discussion of cultural resource law enforcement procedures in the United States has been twofold. First, it indicated that their implementation can be a difficult and demanding task, due not only to the nature of the procedures themselves but also to the time and financial resources they can consume. The investigation process may take months and never produce positive results. When violations are detected and suspects apprehended, law enforcement and archaeological personnel may be at the scene for hours or even days until all evidence is identified, collected, transported, and secured. Finally, there are the legal proceedings and the attendant procedures of case preparation. Although not constant, the work required in this phase of a case will occur at regular intervals over a period of several months or longer, without any guarantee of a successful prosecution. To document the point, it should be sufficient to note that while investigation of the Jones, Jones, and Gevara case began on December 19,1977, the final sentencing did not occur until June 2, 1980. As can be imagined, the cost of such endeavors may be astronomical. The Hancock, Brady, and Brady prosecution cost the government approximately $50,000.

The second purpose of the preceding discussion was to reinforce the argument concerning commitment on the part of archaeologists. It is time to dispel the myth that cultural resource law enforcement is simply a matter of cops catching the bad guys and locking them up in jail. Archaeological expertise may be required even to establish that a crime has been committed, and successful prosecutions and resultant public awareness of the problems they represent will occur only when archaeologists are ready to participate fully in the exacting procedures involved. Therefore, a commitment to cultural resource law enforcement must be an integral and basic value in the professional ethics of archaeology. Without this support, the efforts of even the most dedicated law enforcement personnel will be ineffective. If the current level of looting and destruction of archaeological sites continues unabated in the years to come, ultimately—possibly within our own lifetimes—the archaeology of America will cease to exist except in museum collections and the black market art trade.

PART III

Responsibilities to the Public

19

The Value of Archaeology

Charles R. McGimsey III

When archaeologists talk among themselves, they rarely ask questions such as: Why spend considerable time and money studying a subject that doesn't produce food, shelter, or energy? Is it either worthwhile or morally acceptable to devote one's life to a pursuit that results in a qualitative, rather than quantitative, benefit? Is public education about past culture and societies worth the public and private resources and considerable professional talent expended to retrieve the information?

For several reasons, archaeologists don't like to wrestle with these kinds of questions: justification of one's professional existence is rarely pleasant; the fact that these questions are raised is sometimes seen as a threat; examination of our most basic values, particularly for an unsympathetic audience, is often unpleasant.

Yet, when archaeologists interact with those in business, politics, and the media, they are asked these things. The following essay gives some answers to these questions.

THE NEED TO CONVEY what archaeology is all about to the interested but unknowledgeable amateur, to the mildly interested editor-reporter, to the totally uninterested Colonel of the Corps of Engineers, or to the avowedly antagonistic mayor who thinks the archaeologist is holding up his project can be a real challenge to those who have gone through life assuming that *their* view of the importance of archaeology was shared by everyone else. The following is a brief and simplified outline that may help others to develop basic, direct methods of conveying that archaeology *is* important and can be meaningful to almost everyone.

Anyone who bends over to pick up a piece of worked stone or a fragment of pottery and turns it to see it better is likely to wonder when the object was made, what it was used for, and who made it. The discipline of archaeology has developed theories and techniques for answering these and many other questions about human activity in the past.

The Rationale for Archaeology

But why is considerable professional talent, as well as public and private resources, expended to determine this type of information? Why do we want and need to know about the past? First, there seems to be a deep-seated human need to know about our predecessors and an innate curiosity about the past. It has been said that those who do not know or understand the past are doomed to repeat the mistakes of the past.

Second, archaeology and archaeological research challenge our ability to think and to come up with answers. This challenge can range from the intellectual exercise of making all the bits of information into one coherent whole, to the physical exercise of trying to recreate the original form of a broken pottery vessel. In this sense, the archaeologist functions very much like a detective.

Third—and extremely important—archaeology increases the size and scope of the social scientist's laboratory. Every scientist develops and tests hypotheses against the real world. Many social scientists currently are in the fortunate position of obtaining a grant to travel and make direct observations. Nonetheless, despite this broad informational base, there are many questions about human behavior, interrelationships, and adaptations that simply are not adequately exemplified in current situations. The only recourse available to use is to look into the past. By doing so, we have increased the social scientist's laboratory from the present to one that encompasses thousands of years of human experience. The recognition and determination of the elements of this human experience over thousands of years provide an unparalleled data base for social science. As this information increases in volume and reliability, social scientists will better understand the nature and direction of current and future human activity.

The Rewards of Careful Analysis

Given this basic goal, it is astounding how few facts are actually available to the direct sense awareness of the archaeologist. In the simplest terms, only two classes of facts are available: (1) artifacts and features, (i.e., manmade or modified elements or entities that can readily be taken back to the lab [artifacts] or that normally are studied solely in the field [features]); and (2) the locations of these artifacts and features in the ground, both absolutely and relative to each other, and to natural and artificial soil strata. These are the facts. All else is hypothesis and theory, albeit often so well tested as to be accepted by the unwary as fact.

Nonetheless, careful field research followed by equally careful testing and analysis has enabled the archaeologist to develop well-documented and widely accepted ideas about an incredibly broad cross-section of the past.

Careful analysis of objects, with close attention to the exact context in which they were found, can lead to considerable evidence about the origin and use of the objects, and the technical knowledge and ability of their manufacturers. Studying an entire collection can yield information about what standards society set for the utilization of that knowledge and those abilities. One can gain some appreciation for the artistic tendencies of a given group at a particular point in time. It is also possible to get considerable insight into the communication network of the group concerned. With whom did they trade? From what distances and in what quantity were materials gathered?

By doing other forms of analysis, it is possible to determine with some degree of assurance from whom the group in question was descended, what type of social organization was practiced, settlement preferences, and economic orientations. All in all, a detailed study of the artifacts themselves and their specific context in the ground can yield a great deal of information about past cultures. While we cannot ever hope to construct a total ethnographic picture of a past way of life, we can come a great deal closer than initial inspection of the few facts available to the archaeologist might lead one to expect, as long as the data are recovered and recorded in an appropriate manner by a knowledgeable and discerning individual.

It is important to recognize that the end product of archaeological research is not restricted solely to the social sciences. The initial determination of the rate of decay of radiocarbon isotopes, a dating technique of value to many disciplines, was based to some degree on archaeological data. In addition to their theoretical value, the results of archaeological research can often have direct practical application to modern society. For example, careful analysis of prehistoric canals in Arizona and Peru has brought out information directly applicable to current attempts to provide these areas with adequate water resources.

Finally, it must be remembered that the analytical core that serves to identify and set archaeology apart from all other scientific disciplines is the study of material culture, individually and collectively, as a means for gaining a greater knowledge and understanding of human behavior and of humanity itself. No other social science is so dedicated to this approach. Thus, the popular—and, to a very large extent, the professional—view of archaeology as an analysis of the past is an unnecessarily limiting concept of the discipline. Archaeology is an analysis of the relationships of material culture and nonmaterial human activity which utilizes data from the former to determine and interpret the latter, with a view toward the fullest possible understanding of both. Only to the degree that the study of material culture leads us to an extended and more profound understanding of human behavior and patterns can archaeology be justified as the critically important link in the total study of human behavior.

This definition has ramifications only now being recognized. The practical and conceptual techniques used to understand data from the past often can be applied directly to the analysis of the material culture of the present, thereby yielding a greater understanding of present-day culture. The study of present cultures utilizing archaeological techniques and concepts is only just beginning, but this author predicts that it will become an increasingly important element in the total practice of archaeology in the future.

Summary and Conclusion

This essay offers a basic, direct approach to conveying to the public what archaeology is capable of doing, what its limitations are, and the theoretical and practical areas to which it can contribute, directly and indirectly. The points touched on here can be woven by nearly anyone with basic professional archaeological experience into a product that can be presented effectively to a wide variety of audiences.

20

Archaeology and the Wider Audience

Brian M. Fagan

When people see abandoned structures, prehistoric villages, or ancient artifacts, they ask, Who made these? Where did the people come from? Why did they disappear? How did they live? What was their life like? There is no doubt that a large segment of the American public is fascinated by the ancient and unknown. The attendance at National Parks that feature prehistoric and historic resources has risen at a greater rate than attendance at other National Parks (Green 1975). In response to growing public interest over the past 10 years, the entertainment media—movies, television, books, and newspapers—have produced more and more works on prehistory, archaeology, and archaeologists. How has the profession responded to this interest? Have we given the public answers in language that can be understood by the layman and in media that are easily accessible?

Few archaeologists would deny that the public is entitled to information about America's cultural heritage. Archaeology is the only discipline which can provide information about past cultures and peoples, about cultural responses to changes in the natural and social environment, about population dynamics, and so on. Valid projections of future trends and developments are dependent, in part, on information derived from the study of the past. How have archaeologists responded to their ethical responsibility to inform the public about the nature and development of human culture? What kinds of explanations of the past are readily available to the public? How could the profession be more responsive? The following essay examines these questions and suggests several approaches to improve public understanding of and support for archaeology, and to better fulfill our ethical responsibilities to this wider audience.

AMERICAN ARCHAEOLOGY has always had a public. Ever since the best-selling days of John Lloyd Stephens and Frederick Catherwood, the

American archaeologist has worked in front of a vast audience with lively expectations of the past. This is hardly surprising. Unlike many professionals whose research is of tantalizing obscurity, archaeologists deal with problems of fundamental concern to many people. We attempt to explain the human condition and the processes that have shaped our past and present, and perhaps will affect our future. Our search is a bold and challenging one conducted under the bright and remorseless spotlight of public scrutiny. American archaeology is a public discipline and therein lies the problem. Whether we like it or not—and many of us frankly do not—we archaeologists are dependent on our audience, an audience that often has romantic and simplistic notions of what we are attempting to explain. Others consider archaeology an expensive, useless luxury, while never pausing to question esoteric researches in medicine and other disciplines which are perceived to be more relevant to today's industrial world. One cannot entirely blame the average citizen for questioning our activities, for our best research efforts often remain outside the awareness of the public, whose taxes paid for them. In some respects an excavator is like a playwright: the most brilliant play does not really exist until it is performed (Cunliffe 1981). Archaeology is unlike many forms of science in that its researches are conducted, at least in part, in the open air. Our audience has readier access to our work than to chemical laboratories or medical research facilities. This gives us an unusual prominence and a primary responsibility to share our findings with the widest possible audience. Unfortunately, many of us have forgotten about this audience.

The archaeological world was simpler in the days of Stephens and Catherwood. Their books were bestsellers, for they described unexpected, mysterious discoveries from an almost unknown land. *Incidents of Travel* (Stephens 1841) appeared at a time when science was in its infancy. Myth and fantasy were still common articles of faith in rural America. Popular writers like Josiah Priest (1833) fed on these myths with their stories of ancient Mound Builder Civilizations in the Midwest. Today we live in a vastly more complex technological world of austere scientific research. Archaeology has become a science that feeds on detail, computers, and esoteric theoretical models. As scientific archaeologists we believe that the world of the past is explainable and devoid of mysteries and unfathomable conundrums. We are quite comfortable about this and assume everyone else is as well. How wrong we are! Even a cursory glance at the TV screen or the bestseller list reveals lost civilizations, Noah's Arks, and Ancient Astronauts, to say nothing of Vikings, Ancient Egyptian Americans, and the Seven Lost Tribes of Israel. Only rarely does a spectacular scientific discovery receive such rapt attention, and then only when accompanied by gold or ancient hominids. It is as if the scientist and the public were in two different worlds. What is one to make of this strange phenomenon?

The Public Image of American Archaeology

In some circles, the view of archaeologists has not changed much since the days of Heinrich Schliemann and Howard Carter. Cartoonists and novelists still rejoice in depicting us as eccentric, pith-helmeted diggers, perennially finding hieroglyphics and the tomb of Tutankhamun. This stereotype reached its most elegant expression in David Macaulay's bestselling *Motel of the Mysteries*, a rib-tickling spoof on archaeological research that appeared when the Tutankhamun exhibit was the sensation of the country in 1977. The romance of archaeology is always hovering in the back of the minds of any audience at an archaeological lecture. The speaker is often perceived as a talented treasure hunter whose goal is to find and sell gold-decked burials, papyrus scrolls, and fine artifacts for enormous sums. This stereotype appeals to another basic human urge, the desire to possess material objects. It is assumed that archaeologists act in cooperation with top antiquities dealers to make huge sums of money. The current boom in metal detectors and pothunting is a direct reflection of a popular desire to collect the past and, by implication, to share in the financial action.

Then there are those who regard archaeologists as an irrelevant nuisance, as people who are determined to hold up industrial development at all costs just to save "a few rubbish heaps." This school of thought resents the expenditure of some $200 million a year on cultural resource management, for which it sees little tangible return, and regards the whole exercise of archaeology as an irrelevant and useless luxury. It must be confessed that there is some justification for this viewpoint, given the poor standards of much field research conducted by well-meaning but badly trained professional archaeologists under the euphemistic rubric of cultural resource management. One can hardly blame a financially pressed administration for looking hard at the relevance of archaeological expenditures to the general scheme of things. But the people who are scrutinizing American archaeology often have little comprehension of why the taxpayer supports research into the past. We should not be surprised, since we have rarely bothered to justify our work to our wider constituency or to government. It is time we began.

American archaeology's public image is simply appalling, for our credibility has been sadly eroded in a basically materialist society that believes in profit and free enterprise and enjoys the fun of unsolved mysteries. The audience is fickle and accustomed to instant gratification in archaeology as in any other activity conducted under public scrutiny. Archaeologists dislike the spotlight of publicity, never espouse instant gratification, and regard all ancient drama with deep suspicion. There is almost no scholarly literature that addresses the problem of the archaeologist and the wider audience (but see Evans et al. 1981). In a world where the significance of archaeology is being questioned and budget cuts are lancing deep into established research programs, our public responsibilities can no longer be neglected. At stake is not only the fate of thousands of threatened sites, but the future of archaeology itself.

Another reason for the public's limited understanding of modern scientific archaeology is the latter's extreme complexity. The anthropological archaeology of the 1980's bears startlingly little resemblance to the archaeology of even 25 years ago. Many of the major developments in American archaeology of recent decades have passed by our wider constituency. While there is some public awareness that archaeology has become more scientific and is leading to many new discoveries, there is also a widespread feeling that archaeology has become too technical and scientific for the lay person to understand. Many feel that professional archaeologists have done little to communicate their findings to the general public. Undoubtedly, they are right.

Current Means of Communication with the Public

Why are archaeologists reluctant to communicate with a wider audience? One reason is the increasing specialization and complexity of research. Our technical jargon is extremely difficult to pass on to casually interested people in a meaningful way. The academic reward system and graduate curricula reinforce specialization and militate against the wider viewpoint, against the training of multidisciplinary archaeologists with well-developed anthropological and historical skills and a broad, synthetic perspective. Unfortunately, the demanding technical training now required of professional archaeologists leaves little time for absorbing broader training or learning how to communicate with a wider audience. Although most archaeologists give at least a few lectures for lay people every year, it is an uncomfortable fact that the major burden of communicating modern archaeology to the public has fallen on scientific writers and journalists.

Consider for a moment the available summaries of North American Indian archaeology. The most widely read popular books are *The First American* by C. W. Ceram (1971), Peter Farb's major synthesis (1968), and Alvin Josephy's often neglected *The Indian Heritage of America* (1968). *The American Heritage Book of Indians* (Josephy 1961) contains one essay on the subject, while Time-Life Books and the National Geographic Society have set admirable examples with lavishly illustrated works. All of these works come from the pens of popular writers. No archaeologist has undertaken such a venture. The closest endeavor is Jesse Jennings' recent edited volume, *Ancient Native Americans* (1978), a highly technical work designed for the major in anthropology and the professional scholar.

The general reader is somewhat better served by descriptions of local and regional archaeological work. Ruth Kirk's *Hunters of the Whale* (1975), although billed as a children's book, is a superb example of responsible writing about the Ozette site in Washington. Stuart Struever has collaborated with Felicia Holton on *Koster* (1979), a very popular account of this important excavation on the Illinois River. This book is one of the few on American archaeology to achieve the giddy heights of a Book-of-the-Month Alternate Selection, let alone purchase by one of the more specialist book clubs.

America lacks the rich literary tradition that is such an integral part of European archaeology; by contrast, the British market is saturated with archaeological books. There archaeology is a familiar topic to every schoolchild and is commonly featured on radio and television.

Why is archaeological literature so different in North America? One reason is that many people perceive archaeology as anthropology rather than history, as the study of prehistoric cultures that are not part of mainstream American life. Europeans regard prehistory as an integral part of their unbroken cultural traditions, as history rather than anthropology. Another curious phenomenon is the unspoken dichotomy between prehistoric anthropological archaeology and the history of the American Indian. Historians and archaeologists have only recently started to communicate with one another and to collaborate in research. There is a rich historical and archaeological literature on the American Indian, much of it widely read by the general public. Yet literature on American archaeology is thought of as an unspectacular stamping ground of limited appeal, certainly not the stuff of which epic history is made. A major cause of this view is the inability of most archaeologists to write anything but highly technical, jargon-laden prose. We can only blame our own graduate training, which often stresses jargon and highly technical dissertations at the expense of clear writing and exposition. How much longer can we afford this luxury?

No one knows how many Americans are interested, even casually, in archaeology. Many school districts mention the American Indian and archaeology in their curricula. Landowners are aware of sites on their property. A vastly expanded college audience has discovered archaeology through survey courses and as part of anthropology. Public awareness of archaeology can reach almost hysterical heights; witness the recent furor over the Tutankhamun exhibit. This growing *awareness* has not been matched by adequate public *education*, however; we archaeologists have left this job to the mass media. The mass marketplace is an arena of vast profits, audience ratings, and wheeling and dealing. With the notable exception of some National Geographic Society TV programs, archaeology rarely reaches the networks, for it is perceived, probably correctly, as a low-profit item, unless accompanied by a good, old fashioned "mystery" like Noah's Ark.

The Public Broadcasting System has given archaeology much more serious attention, through programs such as *Nova* and *Odyssey*. This latter is of particular importance, for it stresses the close marriage between archaeology and anthropology. Above all, *Odyssey* portrays archaeology as a serious, scientific activity, much of whose data comes not from spectacular discoveries, but from small objects and sophisticated analyses of food residues, environmental evidence, and other sources. The image of the archaeologist as a normal human being rather than an eccentric comes across clearly; archaeologists talk about their research in a low-key, natural way.

Much mass audience information on archaeology comes from newspaper articles distributed by the wire services, who in turn pick them up from university and college, as well as museum, press releases. It is astonishing how widely such stories are disseminated, for most public institutions are relentless in their pursuit of public relations coverage. Few archaeologists have bothered to make full use of this highly effective way of communicating their discoveries to a mass audience. Even fewer have used radio for the same purpose.

Very few archaeological discoveries, even really significant studies within the discipline itself, achieve national visibility and mass market attention. Fortunately, archaeology does figure prominently on the local scene from coast to coast, in hundreds of communities and neighborhoods. In the final analysis, the credibility of archaeology depends on effective communication with the *immediate* constituency of local people, who are basically sympathetic to an archaeologist with ties to their community. The audience may be local landowners, people who have taken college courses in archaeology or anthropology, or readers of *National Geographic* who are prompted to ask whether there are any sites in their local area. It is among this group that amateur archaeologists may be found and trained. These are the people who will lobby for site preservation before planning commissions and boards of supervisors, donate money, and report archaeological sites. Unfortunately, while many archaeologists agree on the desirability of catering to this audience on a day-by-day basis, relatively few efforts have been made to develop systematic strategies for doing so.

Few archaeologists would deny their basic responsibility to the public or the desirability of improving public understanding of what we do. The task of transforming Americans' social attitudes about archaeology is a monumental task, one that will never be achieved by national initiatives or lavishly financed public television series. It is a task that faces every archaeologist, whether he or she is a computer expert, theoretician, excavator, or Paleo-Indian specialist. Only our individual initiatives will change public perceptions. Fortunately, there are many effective strategies available to most of us.

Strategies for Change

One obvious place to start is the classroom. All too many introductory college and university courses portray archaeology as a specialist discipline bristling with local sites and esoteric jargon. How many courses approach archaeology as an integral part of our daily lives, as much a part of the modern world as astronomy, political science, and history? Such an approach enables one to discuss the ethics of archaeology, how archaeology works, and why it is important in a logical, enjoyable way. Sometimes we take archaeology too seriously for, after all, most casually interested students take courses in our discipline out of curiosity, a sense of discovery, or just for fun. The interested college student of today is the informed citizen of tomorrow.

Another obvious strategy for change is to encourage amateur archaeologists through volunteer participation in excavations and surveys, formal training programs, and museum exhibits. European experience has shown that, with proper training and encouragement, the amateur can play a full role in archaeological research. Amateurs are respected members of the archaeological community in Great Britain and elsewhere, but we tend to distrust them as potential pothunters and often treat even committed enthusiasts as minor pariahs. We have much to learn from our Old World colleagues in this regard. A few organizations have taken initiative in this direction. The Arkansas archaeological Survey and the Koster project in Illinois have both maximized the talents of the amateur to their great mutual advantage. Clearly the amateur archaeologist is a critical interface between the world of professional scholarship and the "real world" in which contemporary archaeology flourishes. In many cases, properly trained amateur archaeologists are the people who will bear the burden of changing popular social attitudes toward our discipline.

Perhaps the most effective strategy of all is good public relations on the local level. This can take every form, from working closely with local media and chambers of commerce to running entire community archaeology programs. The Alexandria Archaeology Project in Virginia is a superb example of a local program that has involved the general public at all levels, including the development of a modest museum that focuses on the heritage of city neighborhoods. Such efforts are still few and far between, but they offer hope for the future. Alexandria is one of the few U.S. cities to have an archaeologist actively involved in the urban planning process. In Alexandria, archaeology is in the mainstream of community activities; it is not considered an idle luxury. The pragmatic strategies that achieved this desirable state of affairs are clearly applicable elsewhere, even in times of budget stringency.

One of American archaeology's largest constituencies is the American Indian. Yet most of us seem reluctant to become involved in anything more than the anthropology of the American Indian in the past. Many of us seem unaware of alternative data sources, of ways in which American Indians look at their own history, and of the importance they attach to their traditional culture. With the notable exception of a handful of ventures like the Ozette project, relatively few archaeologists appear to be concerned with American Indian history on a day-by-day basis. By the same token, many American Indians have a deep distrust and suspicion of archaeologists and anthropologists. They suspect, often with good reason, that we will desecrate burial grounds and sacred places in the name of science, and ride roughshod over cultural sensitivities.

Only a handful of archaeologists have ever developed systematic programs for familiarizing American Indians with the results of archaeological research. For complex political, economic, and philosophical reasons, the Indian community has not yet pressed archaeologists into assisting them in their search for cultural and historical identity, a commonplace phenomenon in Africa and elsewhere for almost a generation. Current Indian concerns revolve around the revitalizing of traditional culture and the preservation of burial grounds and sacred places. However, it is possible that the impetus for archaeological involvement in American Indian history will come from the American Indians themselves.

The close involvement of archaeologists in the historiography of American Indian history will require entirely new directions in graduate training, as well as academic expertise. As Joseph Winter recently pointed out, archaeologists will have to become sensitive to the practical difficulties and limitations of working with American Indian communities, the factionalization of their society, and the ways in which they look at the world. "No matter what we do in our relations with the Indians, it is essential to realize that all of our actions (even our inaction) will have an effect on their heritage" (Winter 1980: 127). The development of strategies for communicating with a wider American Indian audience must be regarded as one of the most urgent problems facing contemporary archaeology. Recent controversies in California and elsewhere over the reburial of prehistoric finds symbolize decades of misunderstanding and misdirected archaeological endeavors.

Some archaeologists have worked systematically with radio and television, appeared on talk shows, educational programs, or even developed their own radio spots. Many have dabbled in instructional films and documentaries, but all too often these are amateur efforts, of extremely local application, designed for classroom use. Filmmaking and television production are enormously expensive, and the problems of packaging and fund-raising are beyond the cababilities and expertise of most archaeologists. Radio is another matter, and offers fascinating, unexploited opportunities to bring archaeology to the wider audience.

For most of us, though, the time-honored and immensely effective public lecture remains the primary way of reaching the taxpayer. The Archaeological Institute of America has taken the lead with its lecture program for many years. This program brings well-known archaeologists to AIA chapters throughout the nation and recent research to lay audiences far from museums and university communities. The lecturers are paid a nominal fee, and the travelling is hard work, but the intellectual rewards are enormous. Many of us give the occasional public lecture to schools, extension programs, and adult education courses, and tend to regard this as the limit of our responsibility. The enterprising archaeologist can find numerous outlets for getting the message across to lay people: service clubs, small conventions, and senior citizen homes all offer unique chances to educate, entertain, and learn of hitherto unreported sites and artifacts. Most scholars willing to lecture entertainingly about their research will soon receive more invitations than they can possibly accept, especially if they donate their services. As the Arkansas Archaeological Survey has found, a presentation accompanied by a film about local archaeology is enormously effective in making people aware of the importance of the past.

Conclusion

Many archaeologists argue that they have little time to spare from teaching, museum duties, or research to popularize their work. This may be true, be we have never trained qualified scholars to undertake this central objective of archaeology on our behalf, either. Basic research has traditionally been the pathway to academic recognition and success. In a frenzy to publish and excavate, we have forgotten that our discipline has a responsibility to the general public that is, today, almost as important as much of the research we publish in specialist journals and monographs. In training the archaeologists of the late 1980's and 1990's, it behooves us to develop graduate curricula that that combine a rigorous academic background with special training in popular writing, synthesis of varied data, and media and communications skills. Why such radical steps? If most of us are unwilling to communicate with the wider audience, we should train colleagues to do so, and *recognize them as academic equals* whose work is at least as demanding as work in the field or laboratory. It is not an exaggeration to predict that the future of archaeology may depend on radical changes in the graduate curricula. Nor is it an exaggeration to forecast that this may be the greatest challenge our discipline has ever faced.

21

Avocational Archaeology: Its Past, Present, and Future

George C. Frison

The estimated 50,000 avocational archaeologists in the United States can and do contribute to the profession in many ways. The responsibilities, however, are mutual. The following essay explores several ethical considerations in the mutual responsibilities between amateur and professional. In order to maintain interest and enthusiasm, the professional must encourage, reward, and educate the amateurs. They, in turn, can support the profession by helping to enforce the ethics of the discipline, reporting newly discovered sites, assisting with recovery and analysis, protecting sites from vandals and looters, lending political support at the local and national level, and occasionally providing financial support. While most professional archaeologists realize the positive benefits of working with avocationals, many fail to take time out from their day-to-day work to encourage and educate the avocational, even though this is part of their professional ethical responsibility. (See the essays by Healy and Fagan in this volume—ed.)

George C. Frison became interested in archaeology as an amateur, decided to become a professional, and is currently the President of the Society for American Archaeology. He maintains strong ties with avocational archaeological societies, especially in his home state of Wyoming.

ARCHAEOLOGY CAN TRACE its beginnings to a nonprofessional interest that gradually developed into more serious and dedicated inquiries into human origins. Avocational archaeology has continued and flourished through time; there are now dozens of formally organized amateur archaeological societies; ranging from small, locally active groups to those composed of many segments with ties to statewide organizations. Many avocational archaeologists are also active members of local, regional, and national professional societies.

The number of avocational archaeologists in the United States is not known, but some idea may be postulated. One state with a wealth of archaeological resources is Arkansas, which has an active state society of about 700 members. This is about .035% of the total state population. After a good deal of time and effort, the professionals have established a certification program in Arkansas which they view as successful. About 100 really active members are regarded as the actual core of the society. In Oklahoma, another state rich in archaeology, the society is slightly smaller, probably comprising about .025% of the total state population. In Wyoming, a much less populous state, the figure is about .055%. If we postulate that avocational society membership comprises .025% of the population of the United States, there could be over 50,000 amateur archaeologists in this country, or more than ten times as many as are presently members of the Society for American Archaeology.

State archaeological societies are usually divided into local chapters. They are nearly always formally organized, with by-laws and regular local and state meetings. Societies usually publish a regular journal and a newsletter, which serve to unify members. The publications vary in size and quality. Many have professional editors who try to upgrade the quality of articles accepted for publication. Most avocational societies are relatively sophisticated and knowledgeable; speakers at annual meetings tend to be the best professionals in many different areas and topics of research. As a result, many amateurs can intelligently discuss the issues of archaeology on the same level as the professionals.

Avocational groups usually flourish and diminish in direct relation to the quality of leadership. An active and resourceful local and/or state president can generate interest and maintain a productive group. Consequently, both state and local societies fluctuate in membership and productivity. It is inevitable that some members will develop new interests and leave as their enthusiasm for archaeology wanes. Continual change in the composition of societies is a major weakness, as is the occasional absence of interested younger members. The strong and healthy society recognizes the danger inherent in not encouraging younger members, who may inject new and sometimes disruptive thoughts and ideas. Archaeology is not a static profession; it thrives on changes in methodology.

Besides the organized societies, there are a few highly trained individuals who prefer to operate outside the framework of a formal organization. Every professional archaeologist who does the normal amount of fieldwork maintains a file on such individuals, who often operate in a very secretive, confidential manner and share their knowledge only with selected professionals.

Beyond these true avocational archaeologists is a large group of collectors, whose interests center on the finding and possession of objects. They range from those who confine their activities to surface hunting of artifacts on Sundays and holidays to the systematic looters who search out prehistoric burials, dig prehistoric ruins and cave sites, and follow behind the professional archaeologist in the hope of locating rich sites such as Paleo-Indian animal kills that have been left for future work. These looters can be highly efficient at their work and pose a real threat to the data base of archaeology.

The Philosophy of the Avocational Archaeologist

It is difficult, if not impossible, to evaluate and understand the interwoven influences of the amateur and professional archaeologist in the development of archaeology as an academic discipline and profession. Prehistoric archaeology had its beginnings in English antiquarianism during the last half of the 16th century and the 17th century (see, e.g., Daniel 1950). William Cunnington was digging barrows on Salisbury Plain in 1803 (Daniel 1950: 30) "in the hopes of meeting something which might supercede conjecture." His interest clearly was not mere collecting. The nonscientist collector is either not concerned about answers or is content to rely on conjecture for answers. It is the person who recognizes the inadequacy of conjecture and is prodded into efforts to explore alternatives to gain more knowledge who is the true avocational archaeologist. Once this basic philosophy is accepted, the acquisition of artifacts for their intrinsic value alone becomes secondary and the possibility to become a true archaeologist is greatly enhanced.

According to Daniel (1950: 13,14), there are four natural curiosities that have aroused interest in prehistory: curiosity about immediate ancestors; curiosity about cultural origins and change; curiosity about existing human groups living at lower levels of culture; and curiosity about prehistoric human artifacts. Unfortunately, another aspect, pure collecting, intruded upon the scene and became an unwanted and detrimental force in prehistory. Avocational archaeology developed out of a mixture of collecting and curiosity centered around prehistoric artifacts and peoples.

The New World provided a unique situation for the development of prehistoric interests. New World civilizations were regarded as heretical entities to be destroyed, exploited, or conquered, rather than studied. Europeans felt they were dealing with lower forms of life that in no way reflected their own ancestry. For example, human burials were treated with no more respect than any animal carcass. The looting of Mesa Verde, Pueblo Bonito, and other Pueblo sites in the late 19th century (see Judd 1954) presents a clear picture of the low regard given to our antiquities. It also set the stage for a collecting philosophy that still prevades archaeology to some extent.

Objects of past human origin have the potential to arouse great curiosity, but the interest may be fleeting and the object or artifact and its implications may be discarded and forgotten. On the other hand, the discovery of such an object can create a desire to acquire others and to learn something about them. It is the desire for true knowledge rather than possession alone that can best be channelled into activities that will benefit archaeology as a science. The desire to collect, not properly directed, has resulted in massive, irreparable damage to the systematic study of prehistory. Some of the more highly motivated collectors ignore all ethical and legal rules in their efforts to acquire rare and valuable objects, and the removal of archaeological materials from their site contexts is all too frequent.

Our archaeological resources are finite and nonrenewable, and the forces of nature have allowed us only biased samples, particularly when dealing with older manifestations. Contexts of cultural materials are often as important, or more important, than the materials themselves. Interpretive methodology continually changes, making the proper treatment of contexts absolutely necessary. Too many avowed collectors disregard context, a philosophy that must be fought at every turn.

Archaeological resources have relatively little general economic value, except for the few that promote tourism. Among interested parties, their value as objects for collection may be high. Since scientific values and collecting values are almost totally at variance, those involved in the two groups are usually adversaries. Since the resource involved is of little value in a true economic sense, the scientific or academic group has faced an uphill battle in enforcing legislation that protects cultural resources. The profession has been forced to rely on education and professional ethics, rather than punitive sanctions, to bring about a better attitude toward archaeological resources.

Between the profession of archaeology and the looters is a body of avocational archaeologists seeking the proper directions in archaeological studies. This group may very well constitute one of the strongest forces working for the best interests of cultural resources—provided that professional archaeologists are willing and able to devote enough time and effort to properly channel avocational efforts. This is not a commitment to be taken lightly by professional archaeologists. It requires large amounts of time and effort and can also be very frustrating. However, ignoring this professional responsibility may result in a quantum loss of our data base.

Free and unrestricted use of public lands in this country has for several generations been regarded as an inalienable right, even though laws against unauthorized collection and destruction of archaeological sites have been in existence for three-quarters of a century. Enforcement of these laws, however, has been lax. In fact, prosecution of cases involving the unlicensed removal of archaeological objects has been difficult and the permit process for legitimate research has operated to the detriment of professional archaeologists. The result has been essentially to allow anyone to pursue nonacademic archaeology in about any desired direction. This has undoubtedly resulted in a different feeling toward archaeological resources than in countries where objects of antiquity are regarded as belonging to the people as a whole.

Fortunately, there has been a strong tendency for most avocational archaeologists to band together in groups to share their interests. There are a few loners who collect in secret and, almost without exception, refuse to show their acquisitions or discuss proveniences, particularly with professional archaeologists. They express a fear that, if they do, they will be forced to turn over their collections and, by divulging the provenience, will be deprived of further collection. It is difficult for professionals or even other amateurs to gain the confidence of such individuals and convince them that the best interest of the archaeological resource is to subject it to proper study.

The Professional and the Avocational Archaeologist

Working Relationships

Avocational archaeologists can become involved in and contribute to the profession in many ways, but there must be something in return from the profession. Perhaps the greatest reward to the amateur is professional recognition of worthwhile contributions. Since very few true avocational archaeologists are seeking monetary compensation, the key to a viable and productive avocational archaeological program at any level depends largely upon the personal and professional relationships between the two groups. Failure to recognize and acknowledge worthwhile contributions of avocational archaeologists can quickly and effectively destroy the working relationships between the amateur and the professional.

The ways in which the amateur may participate are many and varied. Most want to share in some way in the process of data recovery. Lesser numbers want to continue into data analysis; even fewer wish to complete the process and properly compose and publish the results. Unless the amateurs involved are sufficiently trained, they will need professional help and direction at all three stages. There is a strong incentive to train amateurs and advance the qualified ones into analysis and publication; without such help, the professional can quickly become inundated with basic data at the final stages of analysis and dissemination of results.

It can be difficult to convince the amateur that data collection should occur only when justifiable through the formulation and presentation of specific research problems unless, of course, the data are in immediate danger of being lost and salvage operations are mandated. Amateurs are prone to select a site project because of its appearance or promise of artifact yield; professionals must educate them regarding selection based on a research design with stated research goals.

A small percentage of the amateur archaeologists have the necessary time and commitment to pursue the subject on more than a casual or part-time basis. Some get academic training to gain various levels of proficiency. Some amateur societies arrange with professionals for their members to acquire field and classroom expertise. Some develop enough expertise to accept the responsibilities of an entire project. And since the funds to conduct problem-oriented research and to salvage threatened sites are never sufficient, valuable data may be saved through efforts of the amateurs, with the complete support and blessings of the professionals. These contributions must be accorded the highest acknowledgment.

The average avocational archaeologist is not satisfied with the guided field trip, the visit to site excavations, and the speaker or the educational movie at a monthly society meeting. It is no wonder that many become frustrated and are sorely tempted to strike out on their own because personal gratification has not been realized. It is difficult to place the blame in this situation. Due to time restrictions imposed by academic institutions and other employers, the professional can only devote a certain amount of time toward extra activities. Unfortunately, it is the resource that suffers when the amateurs are neglected.

Political Activities

A good share of the advances made in archaeology during the past decade have resulted from political activity. Legislative action in the late 1960's and early 1970's marked the beginning of an era that resulted in massive inputs of money into archaeology from federal agencies. This change came about because of the tireless efforts of a small number of dedicated archaeologists. It was also a relatively new experience for those whose normal activities were in teaching and research.

The results have been both good and bad for archaeology. There was a great expansion in the number and kinds of jobs available. Public lands administrators were charged with management of their cultural resources and could no longer ignore their presence. All activities that affected cultural resources and received federal support were to be monitored in order to protect and manage archaeological resources. Cultural resource management became a major part of the jargon of the profession. Contract agencies formed and proliferated overnight to meet the demands of industrial expansion, particularly in energy-related projects. No longer could dams and highways be built or large surface areas be disturbed without archaeological surveys and subsequent mitigation of endangered cultural resources.

Avocational archaeologists were directly affected by this and they reacted in many ways. Unauthorized removal of cultural resources from public lands had been declared illegal since shortly after the turn of the century, but enforcement had been almost nonexistent except in certain National Parks and National Monuments. Many amateurs took these restrictions seriously and ceased gathering archaeological materials on federal lands. Certain archaeological societies even voluntarily agreed to cease all artifact collection. However, other individuals felt that there had to be a better definition by cultural resource managers of what constituted actual loss of archaeological data. As a result, there is an uneasy truce between federal regulators and many persons who still gather surface material but refrain from digging or otherwise removing materials from interpretive contexts. This action is justified by a philosophy that surface artifact material is in a poor context and has little,if any, interpretive value. Unfortunately, some refuse to respect antiquity laws. Because of the difficulties of enforcement, a discouraging amount of cultural resources is thereby lost. On the positive side, there is a continually greater awareness of the value of cultural resources and most avocational archaeologists are setting a good example for others to follow.

Enforcement of antiquities laws, although only minimally successful, has left little doubt as to who are the true avocational archaeologists and who are the looters. The former is a strong force that operates to help the profession while the latter engages in clandestine activities.

Since archaeology deals with resources that are noneconomic, their value must be established through education of the public. This will not happen quickly. In the meantime, their protection must be secured through legislative action. Professional archaeologists are too few in number to complete this task alone. Here the avocational groups can make their greatest contribution. Archaeology needs to have a solid block of dedicated persons to transmit the educational message to the public; when enough people become concerned about our cultural resources, legislative indifference to their protection and proper management will not be tolerated. In order to achieve this, mutual respect between the amateur and professional must exist. If professional archaeologists fail to recognize, encourage, and, above all, share the problems as well as the joys of archaeology with the amateurs, support and public concern over cultural resources will soon dwindle. Federal and state regulatory agencies need to operate closely with the amateur groups. Compliance with antiquities laws usually is better achieved through patience, education, and demonstrations of real concern over the resource rather than through threats and legal actions. The former course of action will also result in the greatest future benefits to archaeology. The conversion of a collector into a concerned avocational archaeologist is a rewarding experience that is apt to be emulated by others.

The Avocational Archaeologist as the Eyes and Ears of the Professional

The reality of archaeology is that professionals cannot keep abreast of all the developments that affect cultural resources. Professional archaeologists have little chance of being aware of more than a small fraction of the continual natural and manmade forces that destroy archaeological resources. The avocational archaeologists can and often do perform admirably in watching all forms of earth disturbances. They can watch locations such as stream banks, road cuts, basement excavations, trenching operations, areas eroded during flooding, and innumerable other situations for archaeological manifestations that should be investigated. Although such work cannot be described as "problem-oriented archaeology," it still concerns the salvage of a significant part of the data base. The most visible archaeological sites are often found in this manner and have been especially valuable in interpreting the archaeological record.

The perceptive eye of the knowledgeable amateur archaeologist can seldom be matched by anyone but the best survey archaeologists. They have learned to associate soils, land forms, vegetation types, and many other natural features of the environment with the lifeways of prehistoric inhabitants. Many have developed expertise in related subjects, such as geology, soils, paleontology, and plants, and are able to employ these talents toward the documentation of cultural resources. Unfortunately, the body of rules and regulations adopted by state and federal regulatory agencies has largely excluded use of avocational archaeologists because of lack of academic qualifications. This is unfortunate because it rules out the use of a reservoir of expertise that can be acquired only by experience.

Support of Foundations and Scholarships

Support for academic research is becoming increasingly difficult to obtain, as is support for students at both graduate and undergraduate levels. Many avocational archaeological groups perform a notable service to the profession by getting young students interested in archaeology and then providing scholarships as an incentive for continuing study. Many students have received their "baptism of fire" by presenting papers at the local or state archaeological society meeting, a valuable experience for future professional presentations. Professionals and amateurs need to work closely to encourage the proper students and to achieve the most from limited funds.

Some amateur societies also support foundations that provide research money for the professionals' use. Small amounts of monetary support at a critical point can often spell the difference between a good research effort and a mediocre one. Society members regularly donate significant amounts of their time and effort toward projects in order to raise money for foundations. They also manage these funds to realize the maximum return. Amateurs often remember these foundations in wills and influence others to do the same. More and more archaeological research support must come from such private sources.

The Future of Avocational Archaeology

We can only speculate about the future for the amateur archaeologist. The ever-increasing demands in the methodology of data recovery, the development of more specialized means of collection and analysis, the necessity for a more careful adjudication of a disappearing data base, and the continual development of improved theoretical models all remove the avocational archaeologist further from the mainstream of the profession. Archaeology must be practiced continually or the necessary skills will be lost. We must discourage exploitation of the remaining data base by those without the proper facilities and expertise.

On the other hand, the processes of data destruction, both natural and manmade, will continue. The interest of amateurs will continue also and their efforts must be channelled into positive activities. Land ownership status, state and federal laws, topographic and vegetative cover, population density, the nature of the data base in any given area, and numerous other factors affect the availability of archaeological resources and the nature of avocational participation. Avocational interests reflect all of these different influences; consequently, amateurs cannot be placed into a single mold any more than professionals can. All who are interested in archaeology must look ahead toward the best interests of the threatened resource. This means that there are serious responsibilities, as well as many personal rewards, in becoming an avocational archaeologist.

Conclusion

Archaeology arouses the curiosity of persons in all professions, life styles, and social strata. These people tend to form informal and formal groups in pursuit of their common interest. It is the rule rather than the exception to see people of very disparate backgrounds, with no other common interest or contacts, discussing archaeology at a monthly society meeting. It is possible also for these persons to become quite knowledgeable in the discipline.

The relationship between amateur and professional archaeologists must be one of mutual respect and support, or archaeological resources will suffer. The relationship cannot be taken for granted; the avocational archaeologists devote time and effort and expect proper recognition for their efforts. It is unfortunate that as the methodology of archaeology becomes ever more esoteric, amateurs are excluded more and more from the processes of data recovery and analysis. Consequently, they must either acquire the necessary expertise or find other ways to participate. The professionals must concern themselves with this problem and seek workable solutions or the amateurs will drift away from their archaeological interests and even develop antagonistic attitudes toward the professional.

The amateurs comprise a group of sufficient size and determination to strongly influence the future of archaeology. Besides participating in archaeology for personal satisfaction, they can help the professional and the profession in many ways. They can be politically active and aid in the passing of legislation favorable to the management and protection of archaeological resources. They can be the eyes and ears for the professionals by collecting information concerning archaeology. They can be a major source of monetary support for research. Professional archaeologists cannot afford to jeopardize this source of help.

22

Value Conflicts in Osteo-Archaeology

Annetta L. Cheek and Bennie C. Keel

The "Native American Movement" is one of the most emotional issues in archaeology today. The following essay focuses on its ethical ramifications for archaeologists. The subject is complicated by the differences of opinion and approach within each camp. The most extreme Native American position is that their cultural heritage is defiled by exposure and examination of any Indian cultural materials. Thus, any archaeological excavation would be ethically unacceptable. The more common position is that excavation of religious materials and disturbance of sacred locations diminish their sacredness, and that osteological remains are defiled by exposure and analysis.

The Native American ethical position has been increasingly politicized, particularly after passage of the American Indian Religious Freedom Act, which led to several instances of Indians' use of governmental agencies to try to accomplish their aims. A recent example occurred in California when several state agencies attempted to rebury 871 skeletal remains and 10,000 associated artifacts—materials that had been excavated by and stored at California universities over the past several decades.

These issues clash with the most basic archaeological ethics and values: that knowledge gained from scientific data retrieval is valuable to mankind in general, that destruction of the resource is unethical, that true inquiry requires complete data, and that the resource is part of the public trust. At issue is the freedom to pursue knowledge and scientific inquiry without political pressures and legal restraints.

In most parts of the country, archaeologists have adjusted their ethical code to integrate the Native American position that historic Indian burials of known tribal affiliation will not be excavated unless they are threatened by vandalism or some other impact. In some locations, however, the situation has become so rigidified and politicized that archaeologists have had to choose between support of the Native American position and that of professional ethics and values. Where this has occurred, it has polarized the discipline.

ARCHAEOLOGISTS AND PHYSICAL anthropologists have long considered archaeological human remains to be an important source of information about both biological and cultural aspects of prior human populations. Data derived from human remains of all ethnic and socioeconomic groups are critical to our understanding of many aspects of modern human biology, as well as to the field of forensics. In recent years, the use of human osteological collections derived from archaeological investigations as objects of scientific inquiry has been questioned by elements within large national populations. For example, Orthodox Jewish rabbis in Israel have objected to the excavation of human remains. In the United States, some Native Americans have objected to the uses of human remains from archaeological Indian sites for scientific purposes. In this presentation, we shall restrict our consideration of this problem to the United States.

The relationship between anthropologists and Native Americans has received increasing attention over the past couple of decades. Native American peoples are becoming increasingly concerned over their heritage and the role that anthropologists, including archaeologists, play in the interpretation of that heritage. A consideration of both the popular and professional literature reveals the development of these concerns (see especially Rosen 1980; Trigger 1980; Winter 1980).

Native American complaints about their relationships with anthropologists in general, and with archaeologists in particular, follow several identifiable themes: (1) the disrespectful treatment of burials, (2) the implied attitude that Indians are laboratory specimens, (3) the failure of anthropologists to consult Indians concerning the design and execution of research, and (4) the "looting" of Indian heritage properties by archaeologists (Johnson 1973).

Clearly, the problem of American Indian burial sites encompasses all of these concerns, and the excavation and subsequent treatment of remains from such sites pose significant ethical and legal problems. The following discussion will attempt to describe the issue and acquaint the reader with the different factors that contribute to the complexity of the problem. It is hoped that this will help the individual professional to analyze particular situations and develop appropriate responses. It is unlikely that any one solution to the overall problem is possible, and certainly no attempt is made to present one here.

Background

American Indians are becoming increasingly articulate about the treatment that their heritage receives at the hands of the "white man," professional and layman alike. Although one might expect that the charges made against anthropologists in this matter, including archaeologists, are to a great extent overdrawn, there is little in the history of our discipline that enables us to refute the charges in general. Specific cases have demonstrated that the possibilities for an improved relationship exist, however.

Trigger (1980) has analyzed the reasons for what he views as a lack of contact between archaeologists and the peoples whose material remains are the major subject of the discipline. Briefly, he contends that the 19th-century social science view of Indian peoples as static and backward—and therefore of little interest to social scientists—gave way in the early 20th century to studies of chronology and the formal definition of artifact types, neither of which encouraged or required contact with contemporary Indian peoples. Most recently, Trigger continues, the development of processual approaches has, if anything, increased the emphasis that archaeological sites are "laboratories" of paramount importance in our attempt to establish generalizations about human behavior and cultural change that will serve us in managing our contemporary world; but the living descendants of the people who created the sites are still held to be of little interest in their own right insofar as they relate to the archaeological record.

Thus, in spite of our professional training—which, in most educational institutions, continues to emphasize an approach involving archaeology, cultural anthropology, physical anthropology, and linguistics—most archaeologists either know very little about the cultural and religious values of living Native Americans or fail to carry over "classroom" knowledge into positive actions in dealing with Indian burial concerns.

Anthropological and archaeological workers from Lewis Morgan and John Wesley Powell to Florence Ellis, Lewis Binford, and others suggest that Trigger's statements may not be completely accurate. Nevertheless, it does seem to be true that archaeologists have paid minimal attention to extant Native Americans, either as possible sources of information or as groups of people whose values should be considered by professional archaeologists in the pursuit of their work. In the last decade, ethno-archaeology has become a common approach to understanding archaeological phenomena. Since about 1970 archaeologists have been forced to pay greater attention to the desires and claims of some Native American groups. This new awareness of Indian sentiments results both from an awakening on the part of archaeologists and from the political pressures brought to bear by native peoples.

Current relations between archaeology as a profession and Native Americans as a group are not good, although certainly numerous individual cases of cooperation and mutually satisfactory solutions could be cited. In many instances, native groups have successfully challenged the right of the profession to work at archaeological sites, especially those where burials occur. Even when legal actions are unsuccessful, the delays can be very time-consuming and costly, and considerable adverse publicity for archaeology can result.

More and more state and local statutes restricting what can be done with archaeological burials are being promulgated. We now read frequently of instances in which Indians have been successful in their requests to have previously excavated materials reburied, to negotiate a reburial agreement before permission to excavate a site is given, or even to prevent excavations altogether. We are coming into more and more conflict, in specific cases, over control of archaeological sites and related materials that are valued by Native Americans as components of their cultural heritage.

Value of Human Remains

Given the foregoing facts, it is apparent that archaeology must confront the dilemma presented by human burials and attempt to work out a solution that is satisfactory both to the profession and to concerned interest groups. An attempt to break this issue down into several factors can aid the professional who must deal with a particular situation involving human burials.

It may be useful to view the general issue as a case of value conflict, since each group unquestionably believes the sentiments it holds are of great merit and worth, and the solution as an attempt to reconcile the conflicting values to the maximum extent possible. We shall discuss two types of values associated with human burials which frequently come into conflict with each other: (1) scientific values, and (2) religious and cultural values. We shall also consider the legal context of the problem.

Scientific Values

The scientific values associated with human burials unfortunately are poorly known and unappreciated by the nonscientific community and even by many archaeologists who are unfamiliar with the volumes of scientific material derived from burial populations. This material has been developed by physical anthropologists and archaeologists over many decades of work with populations from all over the world, and deals with topics as diverse as residence patterns, diet, mortuary practices, social stratification, population movements, demography, mortality, and longevity.

The Canadian Association for Physical Anthropology (CAPA) (1979) has presented a good summary of types of information that can be obtained from human remains. The Association discusses three areas that derive information from such human remains: archaeology, medicine, and forensics. Archaeological information is further subdivided into six categories: (1) physical characteristics of the population being studied, such as stature and body build; (2) biological features or genetic elements, which enable the study of degree of relatedness among earlier populations; (3) demographic factors, which produce information on the structure of the population, such as sex ratio, death rates, and longevity; (4) pathological evidence, which provides information on diseases and accidents; (5) evolutionary processes, which have shaped the development of modern man; and (6) treatment of the dead, which reflects social organization, societal mores, and religious life.

As an example of the last type of information, recent studies in the Southeast have shown that only individuals of high social status, as evidenced by sumptuous mortuary treatments and grave goods, enjoyed diets that were relatively high in animal protein. This suggests that at least during the late prehistoric period, social position had become in part a matter of ascription rather than personal achievement. Such findings shed light on the development of the more complex native societies encountered by European explorers of the 16th century (Schoeninger and Peebles 1981).

Medical information from archaeological skeletal populations is important because such populations provide information on disease *processes* and sequential changes of certain diseases of the skeleton. These data are not readily obtainable from clinical study of living people or from autopsies. Such studies also provide information on the relationship between diet and lifestyle.

Medical information derived from archaeological skeletal collections clearly is useful not only to our interpretation of the past, but also to our management of the present and future. The study of skeletal pathology in archaeological materials can provide a time depth to our understanding of disease and contribute to our understanding of the role of disease in human adaptation (Ortner and Putschar 1981). For example, the low frequency of cancers of the bone in earlier populations has important implications for the study of the current health status of world populations and the relationship of this status to modern environmental factors (Buikstra 1981: 27). The study of the effect of diet on dental caries has been greatly advanced by the study of archaeological populations from different cultures utilizing varied means of adaptation.

Forensic practice requires the identification of unknown deceased individuals, often in cases where only parts of the skeleton are present. Initial analysis of such specimens, which is critical to the eventual identification of the individual, involve the determination of age, sex, and race, as well as the assessment of other characteristics. Such analysis depends very heavily on information obtained from the analysis of archaeological skeletal collections from many different cultures around the world.

Such information has been derived not only from recently excavated materials, but also from the study of osteological collections in the nation's museums. Buikstra and Gordon (1981) have summarized the use of museum collections of human osteological materials, as evidenced by the professional literature from 1950 to the present. Their article was in part a response to the increasing pressure from Native Americans to rebury collections following a period of analysis, and clearly shows that repeated reexaminations of collections produce important new information as new techniques and research problems are developed and used. For example, reexamination of burial collections from certain New York State sites utilizing new techniques of isotopic analysis have allowed the identification of prehistoric diet by the proportional concentration of C14 and related isotopes in the bones (Vogel and Van De Merwe 1977). In over half of the cases reported by Buikstra and Gordon, new conclusions were reached by restudying previously collected materials. Obviously, much important information would have been lost had these collections been reburied. By extension, much important information has already been lost by reburials.

One type of information not discussed in the CAPA article is that relating to Indian land claims. Along with general cultural and archaeological information, information from studies of burial populations has provided evidence favorable to Indians in the numerous land claim cases of the 1950's and 1960's in the United States. Such evidence continues to be used in judiciary proceedings to correct previous injustices.

Because of the scientific importance of human remains, and the increasing pressure to consider the cultural and religious values of Native Americans regarding those remains, various interest groups have promugated policies relating to this issue. In June 1973, the American Association of Museums (AAM) (1973: 9) adopted a resolution stating that there is merit in continuing the study of burials, but that such studies must be undertaken with dignity and sensitivity: "It is presumptuous to interpret people unless we respect their rights and intrinsic dignity. . . . The curiosity of the visitor is no justification for the violation of beliefs concerning the dead."

Statements of ethics by the American Archaeological Association (AAA) covering the responsibility of a professional anthropologist to those studied can be taken to cover situations involving human remains. In 1974, R. E. W. Adams, then Secretary of the Society for American Archaeology (SAA), recommended that the Society take an active role in developing a policy toward human remains that is mutually agreeable to Native Americans and archaeologists (1974: 668). Currently, a special committee of the SAA executive board is considering several aspects of the problem, including the need to adopt a resolution concerning human remains (SAA 1982).

In early 1982 the American Association of Physical Anthropologists (AAPA) passed a policy statement on human remains. This statement takes a stand against the reburial of skeletal materials, which are considered to be essential to the understanding of humankind's past. The

AAPA policy does state that when living descendants desire the remains to be reburied, this should be done, and it generally encourages communication with Native American communities. In February 1982, the Anthropology Section of the American Academy of Forensic Science adopted a resolution (Angel and Suchey 1982) stating that "burial of skeletons by people who are not descendants of the skeletal populations is disrespectful, contrary to scientific needs, contrary to the respect which all should show to the dead, and contrary to the best long-term interests of the people performing such destruction."

Buikstra (1981) has spoken eloquently against the trend to rebury osteological collections. McGimsey (1972: 5) has stated that "no individual may act in a manner such that the public right to knowledge of the past is unduly endangered or destroyed. This principle is crystal clear." Certainly, reburial of osteological materials represents destruction of our scientific knowledge of the past. Although it has been suggested that reburied materials could be reexcavated later, it seems likely that costs to retrieve buried materials would be prohibitive and the condition of such material would be inferior to that of skeletal collections curated properly in controlled museum conditions. Reburial of skeletal materials means that they are no longer available for scientific study, for training young scientists, or for forensic purposes.

On the other hand, there are instances where there is no apparent reason to oppose the reinterment of archaeological remains. For example, reburial in response to Indian wishes has been carried out when the remains were extremely decayed, there was no cultural context, and the remains had no analytical value. Under the limits set by current state-of-the-art techniques and due to the condition of the remains, they were judged to offer no important advance in knowledge. In such a case there appears to be no good reason for the scientist to maintain a position that the remains should not be reburied, since no scientific value remains. Additionally, there are certainly cases where the ties of living individuals or groups to the remains in question are clear and whose desires should be considered in deciding on the disposition of the remains.

Cultural and Religious Values

Some Native Americans claim that their religious beliefs are violated and important aspects of their heritage destroyed by the collection and curation of burial materials. Some, through a "Pan-Indian" redefinition of sacredness, now consider all human skeletal material to be sacred (Zimmerman and Alex 1981a). Others believe that in particular instances the religious values of their own specific group are being violated. Some of these claims are reasonable and are based both on religious or cultural values and on definable ties to the remains in question.

The views of Native American peoples toward the dead, toward skeletal material, and toward the soul are highly varied. Classic anthropological studies of Indian religious beliefs as they relate to the remains of individuals clearly illustrate that this area is especially complex. Beliefs range from disregard of the mortal remains to a belief that the spirit or soul is tied to those remains as long as there is any physical integrity whatsoever. Treatment of the dead ranges from burial rituals that serve to free the spirit from this world so that it can return to the spirit world to serve as a benevolent helper of the group, to purification ceremonies designed to prevent malevolent actions by the ghost of the deceased. The influence of acculturation, amalgamation, and Christian missionary efforts has created greater confusion in understanding current Indian religious beliefs as they relate to human remains.

An extensive explication of these views is beyond the reach of this essay, but clearly archaeologists and physical anthropologists should become familiar with the views and values of the particular group with which they are working. Archaeologists must acquire sensitivity and be prepared to deal with Native American concerns about human remains with understanding and fairness. If we do not have this basic understanding, we can hardly respect the rights and intrinsic dignity of the people we study. Futhermore, such an understanding increases the likelihood that any conflict between the scientific values and cultural/religious values can be resolved positively.

Legal Context

The legal context of Native American burials is also quite complex (Rosen 1980). In addition to dealing with general federal, state, and local legislation and regulations, the archaeologist must often deal with individual agencies with varying policies toward the appropriate treatment of human remains. In some cases, regional offices of agencies, particularly federal agencies, may implement their own policies and procedures. Because of this, an important first step in dealing with burials is to find out which agency has jurisdiction in the case, and what the policies of that agency are.

Legislative mandates are enacted to insure through law that the rights of individuals or of society are defined and protected. At the level of federal legislation, there are numerous acts and implementing regulations that relate to human burials. These laws and regulations address almost exclusively the scientific values of burial sites. Two pieces of legislation deal to some extent with cultural and religious values.

The Joint Resolution on American Indian Religious Freedom (1978, PL 95–341; 92 Stat. 469) expresses the philosophy that federal agencies, in the pursuit of their individual missions, should consider the impact of their actions on Native American religions and on the sites and objects necessary to those religions. Although the impact of this resolution on federal activities cannot be specified in the absence of implementing regulations, certainly it sets the stage for increased attention to Indian religious concerns, including the disposition of burials.

The Archaeological Resources Protection Act of 1979 (PL 96-95; 93 Stat. 721) is primarily directed at the preservation and exchange of scientific data represented by archaeological sites on "public and Indian lands." It achieves this by requiring that a permit be obtained for excavation or removal of antiquities on such land and by setting requirements that must be met before permits will be issued. The act also establishes special conditions on the issuance of permits for Indian lands. It specifies in Section 4(g)(1) that when an Indian tribe has established its own tribal law regulating the excavation or removal of archaeological resources on its lands, no federal permit is needed for the tribe or an individual of the tribe to undertake archaeological work. Additionally, Section 4(g)(2) specifies that federal permits for work on Indian lands cannot be granted without the permission of the Indian or tribe owning or having jurisdiction over the land in question, and that the Indian or tribe can attach any terms or conditions to the permit. Since all archaeological work on Indian lands requires a federal permit (including work undertaken on behalf of a federal agency or a tribe), this Act requires the archaeologist to consider the values and attendant desires attached to burial sites by native peoples. No matter how important the scientific values of a property on Indian lands, we must defer to the desires of the individual or tribal landowner, as defined by law.

Another significant piece of federal legislation that relates to burial sites is the National Historic Preservation Act of 1966, as amended (PL 89-665; 80 Stat. 915). The most important part of this act and its associated regulations are those portions establishing the National Register of Historic Places and National Register criteria. Federal regulations list four major eligibility criteria for inclusion in the Register. Criterion D is most commonly used with archaeological properties. This states that properties are eligible if they "have yielded, or are likely to yield, information important to prehistory or history." However, "ordinarily cemeteries, . . . or graves . . . shall not be considered eligible." A grave may be considered eligible if it is of an important historical figure and if there is no appropriate site or building directly associated with the person's productive life, and a cemetery may be considered eligible if it "derives its primary significance from graves of persons of transcendent importance, from age, from distinctive design features, or from association with historic events" (36 CFR 60.4). The fact that the potential information content of cemeteries is not recognized by the regulations can on occasion cause problems, as in a case in Arkansas where a federal agency maintained that a cemetery associated with a black settlement dating to approximately 1850 was not eligible since it contained no famous individuals, had no distinctive design features, was not associated with historic events, and was not particularly old. Ultimately, this property was listed, based on its information content (criterion D). Although this decision may not be entirely consistent with the letter of the regulations, it is probably consistent with the spirit of the law. Other cases, however, may not have the same outcome.

At the state and local levels, the picture is much more complex, and neither space nor time permits a full discussion of individual statutes. The most recent and comprehensive coverage of state legislation (McGimsey 1972) is now considerably out of date. A noteworthy piece of legislation aimed at protecting both scientific values and the cultural/religious values of Native Americans was a bill passed in 1981 in North Carolina (North Carolina General Statutes, Chapter 70). Briefly, the bill provides for notification procedures, archaeological investigations of human skeletal remains, and consultation with the Native American community. It provides a period of up to two years for study of human remains, after which they may be reburied. The authority to decide upon the final disposition of archaeological human remains, including the decision to rebury, ultimately rests with the Executive Director of the North Carolina Commission of Indian Affairs. This decision is made in consultation with concerned Native American groups and other interested individuals. Extant collections were excluded from the requirements of the statute.

Many individual localities, particularly in California, address the problem of archaeological remains, including burials. For example, an ordinance passed in Inyo County, California, in 1967 requires that permission to excavate archaeological burials be obtained from the Board of Trustees of the local Indian group and from the Board of Supervisors of the County (McGimsey 1972: 230–32).

Some tribes have established a section of tribal code dealing with archaeological remains, including burials. For example, the Navajo Tribal Code (1972, Section 233) requires permission of a majority of the district councilpersons and of the Chairman of the Tribal Council prior to the issuance of a Federal Antiquities Permit.

Rosen (1980: 6) points out that from the judicial point of view, four sets of issues arise: (1) the nature of the burial site and the basis for permissible disinterment, (2) the legal standing of any parties seeking judicial relief, (3) the right of privacy of those involved in the dispute, and (4) the status of an action to prevent the display of burial remains. Rosen covers these points at length; only two important points will be recapitulated here.

First, the legal designation of a burial site as a "cemetery" has a very important bearing on the legal status of burials. If burial sites are not considered cemeteries, much of the legal protection offered such recognized burial locations may be denied them. On the other hand, once burial sites have been granted designation as cemeteries, courts are very hesitant to permit the removal of any human remains for any reason (Rosen 1980: 6–8), unless the site is about to be destroyed, in which case the court may require removal and relocation. Since the definition of a cemetery—as well as the specific nature of the protection afforded a cemetery—may vary depending on which federal, state, or local statute is applicable, the concerned professional should determine the legal context of each individual situation.

Second, establishing a party's legal standing to sue is often a difficult matter. When human remains are of known individuals, the descendants of such individuals are generally considered to have legal standing. The situation is much less clear in cases in which the burial is of unknown or prehistoric origins. In such cases, the burden of demonstrating affinity—and thus legal standing—may rest upon any individual or group desiring to prevent excavations of the human remains. However, this is not necessarily the case, and the outcome of any legal proceeding may depend upon a wide variety of often unpredictable factors (Rosen 1980: 8–10).

The use of case law to provide guidance on human burials is often complex and even contradictory. The last few years have witnessed a burgeoning of federal, state, and local burial laws in response to the mounting public pressures from both Native American and professional groups.

The complexity of these judicial proceedings is exemplified in an ongoing California reinterment case. The basic issue that led to the conflict between archaeologists and some members of the Native American community was the desire of certain Native Americans to require that all native California burials being curated in state institutions be reinterred, along with all their burial goods. In response to this pressure, the Director of the California Department of Parks and Recreation committed the Department to the reburial of some 871 human remains. Those without associated grave goods were to be buried immediately without study; those with associated grave goods were to be buried after the associated grave goods had been replicated and studied through volunteer and citizen action. This reaction and response to Indian concerns did result in the reburial of some remains, the reclaiming of materials collected from federal lands by federal agencies, at least one lawsuit against the State of California by the American Committee for the Preservation of Archaeological Collections (ACPAC), and formal protests from some California Indian groups who disagreed with the manner in which the reburial ceremonies were conducted. In the suit instituted by ACPAC, the Superior Court of the State of California for the County of Los Angeles found that requisite California procedural requirements had been violated by the Department of Parks and Recreation and ordered the reinterment program halted until the state had fulfilled the requirements of the California Environmental Quality Act. The final outcome of this litigation is difficult to predict since, under this statute, the state will have to consider the concerns of a wide variety of interested parties. This case may well reach the Supreme Court of the United States.

The basic legal claim that is most likely to be made once a group demonstrates that it has legal standing to bring a suit concerning human remains is the First Amendment, which prohibits establishment by the government of any religion and provides for the free exercise of religion. Case law studies indicate that dealing with these two legal concepts requires extremely sophisticated judicial judgments. Other constitutional considerations, such as the Fifth Amendment (equal protection) and the Ninth Amendment (which specifies that certain constitutional rights shall not diminish or deny other rights retained by the people), may be injected into such suits.

A notable case in respect to constitutional rights is that of *Sequoyah v. The Tennessee Valley Authority*. The plaintiffs, Cherokee Indians, sued TVA to halt the impoundment of waters behind Tellico Dam on the Little Tennessee River. The Cherokees claimed that the lands to be flooded were sacred to them for a variety of reasons, including the presence of graves of their ancestors, a First Amendment issue, and that TVA's refusal to rebury Indian skeletal material was based solely on race. The Court of Appeals for the Sixth Circuit (1980) gave an opinion that stated:

> Examination of the plaintiffs' affidavits discloses no such claim of centrality or indispensability of the Little Tennessee Valley to Cherokee religious observances. Granting as we do that the individual plaintiffs sincerely adhere to a religion which honors ancestors and draws its spiritual strength from feelings of kinship with nature, they have fallen short of demonstrating that worship at the particular geographic location in question is inseparable from the way of life (*Yoder*), the cornerstone of their religious observance (*Frank*), or plays the central role in their religious ceremonies and practices (*Woody*). Rather, the affidavits disclose that medicines are obtainable there which may be found at higher elevations in other locations, that it is believed by some that the knowledge of previous generations will be lost if graves are disturbed or flooded and that the locations of Chota and other village sites are sacred places. These affidavits appear to demonstrate "personal preference" rather than convictions "shared by an organized group." *Yoder, supra,* 406 U.S. at 216, 92 S. Ct. When the affidavits are "indulgently treated," *Bohm Aluminum & Brass Corp. v. Storm King Corp., supra,* 303 F. 2d at 427, at most they establish a feeling by the individual affiants that the general location of the dam and impoundment has a religious significance which will be destroyed by the flooding. The claim of centrality of the Valley to the practice of the traditional Cherokee religion, as required by *Yoder, Woody and Frank,* is missing

> from this case. The overwhelming concern of the affiants appears to be related to the historical beginnings of the Cherokees and their cultural development. It is damage to tribal and family folklore and traditions, more than particular religious observances, which appears to be at stake. The compliant asserts an "irreversible loss to the culture and history of the plaintiffs." Though cultural history and tradition are vitally important to any group of people, these are not the interests protected by the Free Exercise Clause of the First Amendment.

In addition to legislative and judicial considerations, numerous official policy statements have been adopted by a variety of organizations. The Department of the Interior has developed a policy applicable to the discovery of human burials on archaeological sites. Briefly, the policy sets forth with whom, and under what conditions, departmental bureaus should consult about the ultimate disposition of human remains found on archaeological sites. The basic assumptions of the policy are that all burials should be treated with respect and that, the closer the relationship of the burials is to living individuals or populations, the more imperative is the need to consider the wishes of the descendants in determining the final disposition of the materials.

The legal issues surrounding human burial situations are both diverse and complex. Archaeologists who wish to deal with human burials must first assess the latter's legal context in all its complexities. Regardless of conflicting cultural, religious, or scientific values, if the situation necessitates a legal decision, the courts will consider only legal issues.

Discussion and Conclusion

This essay has presented the central issues in the conflict between scientific values related to the study of human osteological material, and the reverence with which such remains are held. The legal context of these issues has also been discussed.

It is imperative for the concerned scientist to be aware of all the aspects of this problem as they relate to each specific case in which he or she may be involved. Some cases may be straightforward and relatively simple to resolve. Others may be more complex and have no obvious, clear-cut, "right" solution.

It often may be difficult to distinguish between Native American objections stemming from sincere beliefs in particular religious and cultural values and those arising from a desire for economic or political gain. As Winter notes, "it is very difficult at times to separate the genuine Native American concerns from the insincere, self-aggrandizing concerns" (1980: 126). Certainly, in many instances, the motives of the Indian groups objecting to archaeological research derive, not from a sincere concern with tradition and belief, but from a desire to receive recognition of generalized grievances, to obtain some sort of remuneration for the withdrawal of objections or from participation in a field project as "paid observers," to obtain "restitution" for perceived wrongs, or to achieve other social or political aims. In some cases, the feelings generated by the excavation of skeletal materials have been used to galvanize local native groups and to encourage an increased concern about Indian values.

Increased awareness and concern on the part of Native Americans for Indian traditions, values, and culture, usually welcomed by the professional cultural anthropologist, may result in a peculiarly difficult conflict of professional interest and objectivity when they lead to the disruption of an archaeologist's excavations. It is hard to retain objectivity about such value conflicts because they involve our own scientific values. Nevertheless, it should be possible for us to achieve a greater understanding of the conflicts involved in these situations, and to work toward mutually satisfactory solutions, at least in individual cases.

Sometimes it appears that archaeologists treat all objections to their research as being based on ignorance and violating some inalienable right of scientists to pursue their work wherever and however they choose. As anthropologists we must recognize that the "individuals [whom we study] must come first" (American Archaeological Association 1973:1).

The archaeologist who becomes involved with the excavation of human remains in which some specific Native American group is interested should become familiar with the cultural and religious values of that particular group as well as with the specific legal context in which the work is being done. Awareness of the particular values involved is necessary to resolve any conflict between those values and the scientific values held by the archaeologist. If we give greater consideration to legitimate values we may not end up having to "respond positively to Native Americans, just because they are Indians" (Winter 1980: 126).

There is a need to develop a more cooperative relationship with Native American groups, since they can be a valuable ally in attempts to preserve archaeological resources, and since the information developed by archaeologists and physical anthropologists can be so useful to such groups, who want to revive their own cultural traditions or substantiate claims to traditionally held areas. From the point of view of the conservation ethic, there should be few cases in which the differences between the views of the archaeologists and the Native Americans are irreconcilable.

23

Archaeology: Science or Sacrilege?

Clement W. Meighan

Controversies surrounding archaeological excavation of prehistoric Indian sites exist throughout the United States but are probably more prevalent, pronounced, and varied in California than elsewhere. Therefore, selection of that state as a microcosm to analyze the ethical implications of these issues allows us to examine the range of positions, any one of which has or could be voiced in another state.

After reviewing the historical background of the controversies, Meighan presents the diversity of opinions which exists in both the Indian and the archaeological communities. He then focuses on specific ethical issues, such as archaeological obligations to Indians, attempts of governmental bodies to regulate these kinds of ethical questions, and respect for the dead.

It should be noted that the situation in California has been undergoing such rapid political and judicial change that it may be somewhat different currently than it was a year ago, when this essay was written.

THE CONTROVERSIAL AREA of Indian concerns has its share of moral dilemmas for archaeologists. There have been increasing conflicts in recent years between the obligations of archaeology to the people studied and to professional scholarship. The present discussion cannot resolve the difficulties; rather, it is an effort to review the status of the problem and explain some of the alternate perspectives.

The focus is on issues of ethics rather than a review of the legal literature. Most of the laws are general statements that do not directly address the ethical issues. Further, with the increase of regulatory efforts, many of these "legal" standards are in fact policy statements and "guidelines" generated by nonarchaeologists; they often do not have the force of law and some have been demonstrated to be contrary to ex-

This essay was read in draft by several colleagues who generously contributed suggestions and comments; particular thanks are expressed to Keith Dixon and Travis Hudson for their help.

isting laws. Finally, the legal positions are often incomplete and sometimes contradict one another. For example, the U.S. has strict and thorough laws in all states concerning the disturbance of cemeteries and graves. On the other hand, case law has often judged grave-robbing laws to be inapplicable to archaeological graves. In California, as recently as 1980 the Superior Court of San Joaquin County ruled that an Indian burial site in Stockton "is not and never was a cemetery under California law."

Historical Background

Much of the archaeology done in the United States has paid little explicit attention to Indian concerns; this is one of the principal complaints of Indian spokesmen about archaeological study. However, in many cases archaeology has been done at sites where the native population was extinct (starting with Thomas Jefferson's opening of an Indian mound on his plantation in Virginia). With the recent development of organized political entities among Indian groups and the Pan-Indian movement that proclaims all Indians to be brothers, there are some living people who claim to speak for the now extinct tribal groups. Indeed, many groups considered to be culturally extinct for many years now have "tribal members" based on ancestry, even though the culture itself is long gone and the "tribal members" are not recognized legally as "Indians."

Archaeologists also have failed to consider viewpoints of living Indians because of the time frame within which the studies were conducted, and the belief that living people could not demonstrate any direct connection with ancient archaeological remains. This historical and scientific conclusion about archaeology is vigorously contested by some Indian spokesmen who claim a spiritual connection with all archaeological remains in the United States, regardless of area or age of the remains.

The shift from tribal organization to political organization has placed the role of the Indian in a new light and has led to political action to assert Indian rights over territory, resources, and traditional beliefs. With respect to archaeology, the Indian claims are essentially for control over their heritage, based on the observation that it is their history that is being studied, their bones and artifacts that are being dug up and displayed in museums, and their traditional beliefs that are being ignored.

In the 1960's, Indians began to register objections to the display of bones and artifacts considered to have ritual meaning, to the excavation of archaeological sites—particularly those of the historic period (since Columbus)—and even to the study of archaeology as a discipline. One

Indian spokesman in Southern California stated his objections to field classes and viewed the training of new archaeologists as an essentially immoral act because those trainees were going to go out and dig archaeological sites. This is an extreme view not shared by most Indians, but it represents a condemnation of archaeology as an immoral occupation, and a view that the world would be a better place if there were no archaeologists.

This viewpoint was given some support by inflammatory statements appearing in the national Indian press. The newspaper *Wassaja* made frequent reference to the "vulture culture," referring to the American interest in archaeology as an insensitive treasure hunt and looting of Indian sites (see *Wassaja* for July 1975: 3 and August 1975: 1, 8, where "vulture culture" is linked to a story headlined, "How to Make a Dollar on Indian Graves"). The newspaper also published a couple of letters to the editor which objected strongly to this terminology, but these letters were clearly not the editorial position of the paper at that time.

This period also saw numerous sit-ins by Indian groups in various museums around the country, along with the issuance of a set of "demands" for actions and reparations. The most common demand was for the removal of Indian bones from display and the return of various classes of objects and artifacts deemed to have ritual importance. The latter claim frequently applied to ethnographic and ethnohistoric specimens as well as archaeological ones. In a few cases, the demands included various other kinds of museum concessions—the political action group that occupied the Southwest Museum (Los Angeles) in 1971 issued a printed list of 20 demands, including: "Permanent removal of our ancestral bones from public view"; "That archaeological expeditions be screened by our traditional Indians to prevent further desecration of our Ancestral burial grounds"; and "That traditional orientated Native Americans replace non-Indian employees."

Diversity of Opinions

Indians

The spectrum of Indian opinion is quite wide and includes many divergent ideas. The most extreme position is that all archaeology is a desecration of, and a transgression on, Indian beliefs. A more moderate position is that some archaeology may be desirable, but that it should be strictly controlled by Indians, should not allow recovery or study of any burials or burial data, and should transfer possession of everything dug up to some Indian group. Then there is the neutral view, probably held by the majority of Indians, which is little concerned about archaeology, seeing it as not very critical to the more pressing problems of everyday life (this is certainly the majority view of the non-Indian population).

Finally, there is the view of some people of Indian descent that archaeology is valuable and useful in recovering Indian history, that preservation of archaeological collections in museums (Indian or non-Indian) is not a sacrilege but a recognition of cultural values of the nation and an important teaching resource for Indians and non-Indians alike. This view has led to the construction and operation of Indian-owned museums, many of which have high standards of curation, display, and education.

Religious arguments have been advanced repeatedly by Indians as the primary basis for asserting control over archaeology. Such arguments are deeply held emotional convictions and are not subject to intellectual reasoning. They are rarely subject to compromise either, and efforts to find a middle ground between science and religion have been no more successful with this issue than they have been with Creationism or other beliefs that are in polar opposition to investigations.

Following is an example of the statements documenting the religious objections to archaeology:

> One of Wiyot's teachings is that buried Indian artifacts and human remains should be left alone and untouched both by Indians and non-Indians . . . the uncovering of these materials, either deliberately or accidentally, is a violation of this principle which strictly forbids this type of activity. The Luisenos believe that even the sanctioning of the unearthing of any Indian material is taboo and will result in harm or death to the Luisenos and to those persons responsible. Therefore, the Luiseno Tribe cannot sanction the excavating, examining, or preserving of any of the materials or remains that may be buried in the four sites along Interstate 15 [California Indian Legal Services n.d.].

The religious basis for claims on archaeology has often been supported by non-Indians. For example, an archaeological site in Santa Barbara on public land was "leased" at no cost to the Santa Barbara Indian Center; the city's mayor commented that this action was "one of the more significant things we can do for them. . . . The very purpose of this agreement is to prevent [any further archaeological excavation]" (*Santa Barbara News Press,* Nov. 6, 1981: B–1).

In deciding to order the reinterment of all the collections in California's Departments of Parks and Recreation (over 870 burials and many thousands of artifacts), Director Peter Dangermond "acknowledged that the archaeological community was concerned about reinterment. He said, however, 'I feel that when the choice is between added information and a human or religious standpoint, we should do what is right; we should opt for the religious and human standpoint.' " (*News and Views* 1981: 3). The contrast drawn here is between the right-thinking religious Indians and the wrong-thinking searchers for additional knowledge, who by implication are irreligious and inhuman. Archaeologists are stereotyped in this view as "evil scientists" whose concerns should not carry any weight in the decisions of state agencies.

Archaeologists

The spectrum of archaeological opinion is also quite wide. Strongly held viewpoints maintained by archaeologists include the following:

1. All collections must be preserved; archaeological decisions are scholarly matters that should be made by archaeologists.
2. Archaeology should be conducted only with the consultation and consent of some representative of the Indians.
3. Some parts of archaeological collections can be given away for destruction, particularly human bones and anything labelled sacred by Indian spokesmen.
4. All of the archaeological collections rightfully belong to Indians and should be given to them to use as they wish (most archaeologists do not object to Indian ownership of collections that are preserved and properly curated in a museum; the controversy is over whether collections should be reburied or otherwise destroyed and dissipated).
5. Archaeological excavation should be avoided whenever possible, partly on conservationist grounds and partly to avoid the conflicts inherent in the viewpoints above. This also leads to the "no collections strategy" in which archaeology is to be done without collecting anything.

Individual archaeologists have handled individual situations in accord with all of the above positions. The positions of archaeological organizations, however, have in general stressed preserving collections and keeping them accessible for study by qualified scholars. In California, the only archaeological organization to take a position in favor of reinterment of collections was the Society for California Archaeology (resolution of the Executive Board of Nov. 14, 1981), which concludes that "while scientific inquiry is legitimate, human dignity is of paramount importance." This resolution also states that "such remains [burials] contain spiritual as well as scientific significance," that any storage and study of skeletal remains shall be done in a "dignified and professional manner," that no human remains shall be displayed, and that reinterment shall be in "accordance with the wishes of the descendants." This resolution was overturned by a subsequent meeting and is no longer an official position of the organization. It does indicate the deep divisions of opinion, though, particularly in local organizations of limited membership.

The opinion that no excavation should be done and no collections should be made has been put forward, but since this is essentially a position to terminate archaeology as a field of study, it is a view more popular with nonarchaeologists (bureaucrats, regulators, and Indians) than within the scholarly profession itself.

Some areas of confusion in the developing controversy merit discussion. Archaeologists have been blamed for all site disturbances, including those by looters and pothunters, and for other problems that are not primarily archaeological responsibilities (such as the way bones were stored in museums after they were collected). In addition, some have been under the impression that archaeologists are digging up "someone's grandfather," even though the majority of American archaeologists have little or no experience in digging sites of the historic period. A major difficulty is the inability of archaeologists to communicate to anyone the distinction between burials that are 200 years old and those that are 2000, 5000, or 10,000 years old. Initially, this message got across, as in the California legislature's adoption of a resolution calling for a moratorium on archaeological investigations at sites less than 200 years old. However, since the issue is emotional rather than intellectual, the claims in California soon grew to include all Indian remains, regardless of age, and newspaper accounts quote Indian political appointees as seriously considering making a claim for the bones of Del Mar Man in the San Diego Museum, a find claimed by some to be 49,000 years old and the oldest known human remains in the New World.

Another souce of confusion is in the dual role of most American archaeologists. Trained as anthropologists in anthropology departments (where the archaeology faculty is generally a small minority of the staff) and holding advanced degrees labelled "anthropology," American archaeologists must confront the conflict between their role as anthropologists and their role as archaeologists. In general, cultural anthropologists outside of archaeology have not taken any position with respect to archaeological study. In the various newsletters, pamphlets, and statements made by California anthropologists, however, it is often stated that the local *anthropological* community supports Indian perspectives. Archaeologists may therefore be forced to defend their position about their scholarly obligations against their own colleagues—not an easy task.

The Reasons behind Regulatory Efforts

The confusion and growing conflicts over archaeological research have led to a proliferation of regulatory efforts, which will be discussed later.

Let us now examine the three factors that have contributed to this phenomenon.

First, professional archaeologists began reexamining their premises and considering how the Indian concerns should be handled by scholars in archaeology. Numerous statements appeared in local and national archaeological journals; Sprague's article (1974) is typical of archaeological efforts to find a middle ground and recognize and respond to Indian concerns.

An early statement of professional ethics in archaeology was the "Four Statements for Archaeology" (Committee on Ethics and Standards, 1961), whose guidelines do not mention Indians at all; clearly this was not an issue in 1961, since no member of the organization raised the question of consultation with Indians. It made clear, however, that ethical archaeology requires adherence to laws and statutes, as well as the explicit permission of property owners. Hence, even under these guidelines, Indians had the authority to deny permission for archaeological studies on lands under their control.

The Society of Professional Archaeologists has a three-page "Code of Ethics" and "Standards of Performance" which all applicants for membership are required to sign (reprinted elsewhere in this volume—ed.) Indians are not mentioned specifically, but there is a statement calling upon archaeologists to "Be sensitive to, and respect the legitimate concerns of, groups whose culture histories are the subjects of archaeological investigation." This is too vague to be useful since there is no clarification of what "sensitive" means, what the "legitimate concerns" may be, or who has a claim on any specific "culture history."

Second, the proliferating business of "cultural resource management" in government agencies led to the development of "guidelines" to control archaeological research. Since the "managers" are rarely scholars and are often responsive primarily to political concerns, it was easy for this group to dictate restrictions on archaeological research and to require the appointment of Indian consultants and "monitors," who were sometimes given total control over archaeological excavations conducted on public lands (cf. Malibu Creek State Park n.d.). Several counties in California have written ordinances and regulations governing archaeological excavation, as have planning commissions and other bureaucratic agencies. The majority of these regulations *require* "consultation" with "Indians" (generally, tribal affiliation, degree of Indian ancestry, and knowledge of Indian culture are unspecified). While these regulations are often called "guidelines" and do not have the force of law, they can be used to deny permission for archaeological research. In some exceptional cases (such as Monterey County), archaeologists may have to obtain a use permit before conducting excavations.

Third, the Indian approach, primarily in California through the Native American Heritage Commission (The Governor's Office, Sacramento), has been to exert pressure on the groups above and, more importantly, to move in the direction of introducing legislation designed to prevent as much archaeology as possible.

Obligations to Indians

In practical terms, archaeologists who have been willing to concede that they ought to work more closely with the Indian community have sometimes been frustrated in their attempts to do so. There is first the difficult problem of *which* Indian spokesmen one should listen to; even tribal communities on Indian reservations may have several factions. Generally, one faction of the community sees archaeology as possibly contributing to the Indian heritage and therefore supports (or at least does not oppose) archaeological studies. Another faction generally does not want any tampering with the remains of the past and feels that it is better for sites to remain unstudied. The archaeologist has little to say about such disputes. (Additional comments on this issue are in the essays by Ferguson and Adams in this volume—ed.)

Where there is no reservation and no tribal government, the problem is much more difficult. For example, California is said to have 160,000 Indians at the present time. This is not far from the number of Indians who inhabited California in pre-Spanish times. The difficulty is that most of the contemporary Indians are urban; less than 10% live on the widely scattered reservations in the state. Furthermore, few of these Indians are of California descent. Of the few claiming California Indian ancestry, a considerable number are from tribes that have been culturally extinct—i.e., there is no tribal community, no one speaks the native language, and the native beliefs and behavior survive only as fragmentary remnants—for eight generations. In addition, many of the spokesmen in California are not on tribal rolls and have very limited Indian ancestry; they are comparable to Californians of European descent who claim to be German or Irish but whose ancestry of the past few generations actually includes people from many European and non-European backgrounds. Hence, while one may be willing in principle to consult with Indians, one may be less willing to consult with self-proclaimed Indians, Indians from other parts of the United States, or Indians who have no particular knowledge of their traditional culture except what they get out of reading anthropological reports.

An example of the problems that can arise is seen in the case of the Candelaria Indian Council of Ventura County, in Southern California. This group came into existence less than 10 years ago and is not a tribal organization of California Indians but a social and political organization made up primarily of people who have no historical connection with the county or its archaeology. According to *Wassaja,* which reported in detail on the organization of the group (Feb. 1976): ''With a majority of the nation's tribes represented, and a few from Mexico, the task assumes the complexity of a Pan-Indian movement. These local Indians are as diverse as the Yaquis of Sonora and a lone Mohegan from Connecticut.'' Additional discussion in this same article lists 17 persons who are officers or candidates for the board of directors of the new organization; of these, only two claim any Chumash ancestry (the tribe that occupied Ventura County in ethnohistoric times). The other 15 include persons identified as Potawatomi, Sioux, Creek, Chippewa, Ute, Navajo, and other Indian ancestries. One person is even identified as ''non-Indian.'' Is it ''consultation'' with Indians to defer to the judgment of such a group relative to the archaeology of Southern California? State agencies believe so and have given this group near-total authority over excavation programs (Malibu Creek State Park n.d.).

To complicate this matter still further, there is the claim of the Chumash reservation Indians (Santa Ynez Indian Reservation, the only existing Chumash tribal group), who asserted their authority in an open letter (Olivas 1977) that was widely distributed and published in the Indian newspaper *Wassaja.* The letter concludes: ''the Santa Ynez Reservation is not represented or *does not recognize* any Chumash medicine man, spiritual leaders, or traditionalists. These sacred and anciently honored positions have unfortunately passed on with time.'' So what is the archaeologist to do when he is confronted by someone claiming to be a Chumash medicine man who wants to be hired as a monitor of an archaeological excavation and/or wants to claim all the remains from an archaeological excavation? It is easy to assert that there is an obligation to ''Indians'' in an abstract way, but what is the obligation to individuals and groups of the kind listed above?

The Indian pattern of social and political, rather than tribal, entities is the rule rather than the exception in California, particularly in urban areas. Following are two other examples of control of archaeology by political groups:

> Ohlone Native Americans, members of the Northwest Indian Cemetery Protective Association, the Bay Area AIM, the San Jose Indian Center, and the local anthropological community all cooperated together in the excavations, which eventually resulted in the reburial of the remains of 40 skeletons and the return of all native American artifacts to the Ohlones [Winter n.d.].

> The bones of 66 Indians which were dug up at the site of the Diablo Canyon nuclear power plant will be reburied in a Chumash cemetery in a sacred, secret ceremony. . . . The Chumash groups decided to accept the bodies without the artifacts . . . ''But we're going to get those artifacts back

if we can. These artifacts are religious and do not belong in a museum" [*San Luis Obispo Telegram Tribune* Dec. 17, 1977: B–1].

Respect for the Dead

We have many forms of showing respect for those who have gone before, ranging from the construction of elaborate mortuary monuments to commemorative ceremonies such as celebrations of the birthdays of important people. Indians have complained that archaeologists respect their own ancestors but that they (and the rest of the "vulture culture") are discriminatory since they dig up only Indian graves and never the graves of their own ancestry. The latter statement is patently false but sounds convincing to many people because in the United States there are no *archaeological* sites of non-Indians in areas where white settlement is very recent. Recent Indian cemeteries are protected by the same laws that protect recent cemeteries of the rest of the populace, but this is irrelevant because archaeologists are dealing, for the most part, with bones that are in a class with paleontological specimens rather than anyone's identifiable ancestors. It is very difficult for most archaeologists to accept the notion that the study, preservation, and display of the 9200-year-old skeleton found at the Pleistocene fossil site of the La Brea tar pits constitute violation of a grave or racist exploitation of minority beliefs.

Aside from disturbing the dead, collecting and displaying objects placed in prehistoric graves is considered by some tribal groups to be immoral and, indeed, dangerous, because uncontrollable powers may be tampered with by persons ignorant of the correct religious and ceremonial procedures. This is a religious or spiritual belief that anyone is free to entertain, but it is not part of the beliefs of scholarly archaeology. The notion that it is somehow spiritually dangerous to investigate ancient sites is a view common among uneducated people and is perhaps best known in our popular literature from the "mummy's curse" stories about ancient Egypt. Are such beliefs justification for archaeologists to refrain from pursuing their studies of the past? If archaeologists do not believe in such notions, should they be compelled to accept them as a basis for their actions? (This question is also discussed in the essay by Ferguson in this volume—ed.)

It must also be noted that there is great variability in the beliefs held by different Indian cultures about what is proper respect for the dead, what happens to the soul after death, and other beliefs pertaining to death. There is no one "Indian religion" any more than there is one "Indian language," and beliefs about death are exceedingly diverse among Native American peoples. Corpses have been interred, cremated, exposed on platforms, dug up and treated to secondary funerals, and dealt with in many ways. Among Southern California Shoshoneans, proper funerals included a reenactment of the death of the culture hero, and *that* included the performance of a special mortuary functionary who ate a piece of the corpse from the funeral pyre. Bones and cremations were often dug up, treated to secondary rituals, and reburied. Sometimes they were ground to a powder or otherwise used in ritual. Archaeologists are well aware from the evidence of their own investigations that ancient burials were often disturbed by later graves, the bones of the previous person being thrown out and scattered about. Human bones were also used as artifacts in many cultures, including that of Early Central California (ca. 4000 years ago), where bowls were made of human skulls, daggers and other artifacts were made of human bones, etc. It is doubtful if this activity was considered disrespectful of the dead at the time.

Research into California ethnography shows that most California Indians had a belief about souls which was comparable to the Christian notion that the soul exists separate from the body and that the body is merely a temporary habitation for the soul. The details varied considerably, but the general belief was that the soul left the body after death (sometimes it waited a period of time before departing) and went to live in an afterworld with other souls. The point is that after death the body no longer had any special meaning in the native cultures.

The archaeologist cannot forget the factor of time and the reality that religious beliefs change through time, along with other aspects of human life. Many of these changes can be seen in the archaeological record (the shift from burial to cremation, for example); a large number of dramatic changes are fully attested to in the ethnohistoric record, which is full of new prophets, new religions, and shifts in religious beliefs. The tremendous changes in religious belief brought about by the lives of Christ, Buddha, and Mohammed are all within the past 2000 years. For living people to assert that contemporary beliefs are the same as those of peoples several thousand years in the past, and that "traditionalists" are pursuing the life of peoples who lived as recently as even a couple of hundred years ago, is fallacious. This is well documented by Ward (1982), who studied Navajo burials from the late 18th to 20th centuries and found that the archaeological record was often found to be in direct contrast with informant data and/or various ethnographic accounts of what one is supposed to do in given circumstances pertaining to death and burial. The only way we can discover the behavior of the peoples of the prehistoric past is through the evidence of archaeological investigation. If we consider that the ancient beliefs and practices are worth knowing about, then we cannot give up archaeological study in favor of hearsay from contemporary people.

Legal Action, Government Regulations, and Policies

As stated earlier, this discussion does not attempt to review all of the legislative and governmental decisions affecting archaeology. Since such decisions reflect views of proper and legal activity, however, a very brief discussion is in order.

Federal legislation dates back to the Antiquities Act of 1906, which provided permit regulations for the conduct of archaeological studies on federal land. It and numerous subsequent federal statements (cf. the Archaeological Resources Protection Act of 1979, 36 CFR Part 1215, and PL 96–515, 1980) adopt the position that archaeological resources are part of the historical and cultural heritage of the nation. Archaeological collections are therefore considered to be the property of the citizens, and private ownership and disposition are disallowed. Recent acts have stated explicitly that applicants for a permit to perform archaeology on federal land must submit evidence that "the university, museum, or other scientific or educational institution proposed as the repository [of archaeological collections] possesses adequate curatorial capability of safeguarding and preserving the archaeological resources and all associated records." Discussion of the Archaeological Resources Protection Act of 1979 (Federal Register, Vol. 46, No. 12, pp. 5566–5576) includes the statement, "Neither the Act nor this proposal require that religious or cultural concerns prevail over other interests."

The implied ethical obligations of the archaeologist are therefore to data first, and to other interests second. Contrast this notion of public ownership with the provisions of California AB 3007 (introduced by Assemblyman Keene in 1978), which specifies that a "California Indian cultural artifact found on state land or on the property of a local agency is the property of the descendants of the California Indian group which created it." This legislation did not pass, but it is an example of several similar attempts in California to deny the "national heritage" aspect of archaeological study and to define such study instead as an intrusion on the property rights of Indians. This "artifacts bill" was followed by several others dealing with mortuary remains, two of which are before the California legislature at this writing.

The burials bills would amend the California laws on grave-robbing by inserting the prohibition on "prehistoric" graves as well as historic ones, thereby making it illegal for any archaeologist to examine any human remains, regardless of age. The moral stance taken here is one of repugnance to the study of human remains. Earlier versions of today's bills were introduced in 1977 and defeated; the 1982 versions were introduced by the same coalition of interests.

To shift from the concept of public ownership to the concept of private ownership, even when the archaeological remains are on publicly owned property, forces some serious shifts in archaeological thinking. It also creates major confusions in performing research, since the federal policy may conflict with state policies. Indeed, the study of archaeology is up for grabs since all levels of government have decided to regulate it; in California, there are not only state and federal codes but also county and city ordinances, regulations of several state agencies, planning commissions, zoning commissions, etc. These independent regulations often bear little resemblance to one another. Furthermore, the question of private property remains unclear; some regulatory agencies in California refuse to allow archaeological investigations even on private property when the property owner is willing to consent and underwrite the excavation! Agencies that manage public property can decree that no archaeological study be conducted on lands under their jurisdiction. The policy statement of the California Department of Parks and Recreation (of May 10, 1978) says that the department "shall endeavor to preserve intact any Native California Indian cultural resource in the State Park System." This appears to be a harmless conservationist statement, but it can be used to deny any archaeological study in extensive areas of the state, and is in fact used that way. (It must be noted that prevention of archaeology does not preserve the sites; numerous well-known California sites under the supervision of agencies "preserving" them have been destroyed by weather, pothunters, and even misadventures with bulldozers run by the preservation agency.)

Meanwhile, the environmental impact legislation takes the position that a site scheduled for destruction must have an ameliorative study performed. Again, the rationale is that it is in the public interest for archaeological data to be preserved—if that were not the intent, there would be no point in worrying about whether sites were destroyed or not. Property owners are therefore caught in the middle—on the one hand, they are told they must pay for archaeological study of a threatened site; on the other hand, they may not be able to get a permit to conduct the study. And if they do conduct it, they may be required to turn over all of the collections for destruction by Indians, at which point they have *not* ameliorated the damage but are back to the beginning, wondering what it was they paid for.

The individual archaeologist is confronted with differing rules of ethical behavior depending on the land involved. If the site is on federal land, the principle of public ownership still holds; if it is on state land in

California, the principle of public ownership *may* hold, depending on the agency guidelines, or the contract may dictate destruction of the collection and avoidance of any research decisions that might offend a local group. If the site is on private land, it may be under some state jurisdiction (like the Coastal Commission), or it may be governed by county and local ordinances. In dealing with these diverse guidelines, the only way archaeologists can develop a consistent set of ethical guidelines is to forego research in some areas and decline contract work that violates their sense of scholarly ethics and responsibilities.

Some archaeologists have avoided these personal conflicts by doing "sampling"—selecting archaeological samples and research designs that will not get them into any conflicts (i.e., minimal excavation of one or two test pits, avoidance of all mortuary data, and the collecting of little or nothing from the site so that the problem of disposition of collections will not exist). Some people, including this author, believe that this has had a serious detrimental effect on the quality of research results over the past few years; many sites have been destroyed after only the most minimal and trivial study.

An interesting effort to clarify some aspects of the conflict between science and religion is continuing in California at present. A private group of archaeologists and supporters (American Committee for the Preservation of Archaeological Collections), brought an action against the State Department of Parks and Recreation in order to stop the proposed destruction of state-owned archaeological collections (the case referred to earlier in this essay, in which Director Dangermond decided that it was a moral imperative to return to Indians the 871 burials and thousands of associated artifacts so that they could be destroyed by reburial). As one of the numerous plaintiffs in this court action, I can say that the burial action was stopped by injunction and a writ of mandamus, but whether it is permanently halted is still not resolved. The court ruled that the decisions of the state bureaucrats were an abuse of authority. However, as of this writing, the state is continuing with its efforts to prepare environmental impact reports and meet other requirements so that it can go ahead with the reburial plan; there has been no reversal of state policy. It will probably require additional legal decisions to resolve the issues of public ownership, freedom of archaeologists to conduct their investigations, and related matters. In the interim, the California decision of 1981 does recognize that archaeologists have rights also, and furthermore that it is not the responsibility of the archaeologists to resolve all Indian complaints before undertaking their studies.

Before legal action could be taken in the above case, the state did hastily reinter two archaeological collections, one in Patricks Point State Park in Northern California and another in Cuyumaca State Park in

San Diego County. One of the interesting complexities of the religious and ethical arguments in this case is that one group of Indians from the latter area was deeply offended by the way the reinterment was conducted, and these people came to testify *for* the archaeologists in the court case. They are further conducting their own lawsuit against the state to get the reburied remains dug up again and treated with appropriate funerary ceremonies.

Conclusion

It is clear that archaeologists have not been very effective at getting across their viewpoints about preservation of collections, since powerful political forces are successfully preventing and restricting archaeological studies. The cases discussed for California are not unique; the same things are going on in other states, and precedents established in one area can well be used to justify similar actions in other areas.

In spite of this, it is this author's opinion that when the public is adequately informed and has an opportunity to state its position, archaeology will be supported as desirable and valuable. The position of those opposed to archaeology is understandable in emotional terms, but in intellectual terms it is not acceptable. It is nonintellectual in that it places no value on public ownership and preservation of the evidences of the past. It is anti-intellectual in that it proclaims that everything we need to know is already known. Introduction of the notion of private ownership is contrary to the position taken by federal legislators over the past 75 years; it also raises very serious conflicts over conflicting claims from *other* private interests (property owners, dealers, relic collectors, local museums and community interests).

Federal insistence on public ownership is well summed up in one California conflict about which the Department of the Interior said:

> The resources should be kept in the public trust. A reversal of this policy has serious implications not only for this and future collections of scientific data, but for the thousands of collections made since the beginning of the highway salvage program throughout the Nation. . . . We therefore recommend that such scientific collections be kept intact by CALTRANS in such a manner that their integrity can be maintained and at the same time be accessible to Native Americans, scholars, and the general public [Gordon n.d.].

In another case, occurring in 1982, in which California officials decided to dispose of public archaeological collections, a request was made from the federal government for the return to federal custody of all of the affected collections that had been acquired under federal permits. This action seems to indicate that the principle of public ownership will be upheld and that the common good will be held to outweigh the concerns of private interests.

Serious conflicts will continue, however, until a clear-cut judicial decision defines the rights and obligations of archaeological study. For the present, archaeologists can work with the existing statements of ethics and professional standards as published by the national archaeological organizations. When professional standards conflict with local requirements or political guidelines, scholars must make individual decisions about how, or whether, to participate in proposed programs.

24

Archaeological Ethics and Values in a Tribal Cultural Resource Management Program at the Pueblo of Zuni

T. J. Ferguson

Archaeologists are highly trained in the techniques of locating, analyzing, and interpreting cultural phenomena. Rarely, however, are we trained in the skills of dealing with people. Yet many of the changes in the profession in the last few years have involved increased contact and coordination with nonarchaeological segments of the public. Often these groups don't understand the goals and methods of archaeology and, in fact, may hold incorrect notions about the discipline.

Because of our lack of training in "people skills," at times these encounters have developed into conflicts between different value systems. Archaeologists sometimes lack the flexibility to adjust to different requirements and values, or fear that such an adjustment will compromise their professional ethics. When they do take the risk, however, they often discover that their professional ethics are not threatened and that they are allowed to work on cultural materials that would not be available for study otherwise.

The following essay examines ethical issues in the archaeological research and cultural resource management of the Zuni Archaeology Program operated by the Pueblo of Zuni.

UNTIL RECENTLY, the ethics and values of the American archaeological profession have stemmed almost solely from interaction between the academic discipline of anthropology and the Euro-American cultural background of most archaeologists trained in universities and museums. As a result, the professional ethics and values of American archaeology have almost exclusively reflected the values and beliefs of the Euro-American culture. Today this situation is changing. In the last decade, several Indian tribes have instituted professional archaeological research programs in response to the federal mandate for cultural resource management. These tribal archaeological programs have employed both non-Indian professional archaeologists and tribal members to conduct archaeological research, and to formulate and implement tribal policy concerning the management of cultural resources. Inasmuch as the beliefs and values of many Indian people regarding archaeological phenomena differ from those of Euro-Americans, it can be expected that the professional ethics and values pertinent to the practice of archaeology conducted by Indian tribes will differ in some respects from the ethics and values of the profession at large. This is because the professional ethics and values guiding tribal archaeological programs derive as much from an interaction between anthropology and tribal culture as they do from interaction between anthropology and the Euro-American culture.

The new archaeological ethics and values that are being defined and implemented by tribal archaeological programs demonstrate that the professional needs of archaeologists can be positively integrated with the concerns of Indian people. This is important, for today all archaeologists have the ethical responsibility to "be sensitive to, and respect the legitimate concerns of, groups whose culture histories are the subject of archaeological investigations" (SOPA 1981). The professional archaeologists and their Indian coworkers in tribal archaeological programs are working out on a daily basis the research and behavioral standards this ethical responsibility implies, and the processes and results of this interaction merit attention.

This essay examines how ethical issues have influenced archaeological research and cultural resource management at the Zuni Archaeology Program operated by the Pueblo of Zuni. A brief history of the Zuni Archaeology Program is presented to outline its goals and activities, and the multicultural aspects of the program are discussed. Following this, consideration is given to three ethical issues that have been influenced by the beliefs and values inherent in Zuni culture: (1) the excavation and study of human remains; (2) the design of appropriate research and tribal review; and (3) the management of religious artifacts and sites. The ideas and perspectives presented here are based on five years of employment with the Zuni Archaeology Program between 1976 and 1981.

History and Goals of the Zuni Archaeology Program

Interest in establishing a tribal cultural resource management program at Zuni developed in the early 1970's in response to federal environmental legislation requiring archaeological clearance investigations and cultural resource studies on land-modifying projects with federal involvement. Due to the very high site density on the reservation, virtually every federally funded project requires archaeological services. Rather than rely on outside universities and museums to provide these needed services, the Pueblo of Zuni decided it would establish a tribal archaeological program to train and employ tribal members in this work. With the assistance of the National Park Service, some initial on-the-job training of tribal members was provided through the Arizona State Museum, which fielded one archaeologist for the summer to conduct archaeological clearance surveys on the reservation with a group of young Zuni. Following this, the tribe began its own program in 1975.

Four goals were set for the tribal archaeological program: they were to (1) provide tribal members with increased employment and career opportunities; (2) enhance archaeological and historical research about Zuni by involving tribal members in the design, implementation, and dissemination of that research; (3) facilitate development of the 638-square-mile Zuni reservation by having a locally based professional organization available to provide needed services efficiently and quickly; and (4) develop and implement cultural resource management policies that respect Zuni values and beliefs.

The first few years of the program's operation were directed toward training tribal members in archaeology and other subfields of anthropology. This included a valuable year of formal classroom instruction, which provided a group of Zuni with the vocabulary and basic concepts necessary to communicate professionally with non-Indian archaeologists (Dodge and Ferguson 1977). Following formal instruction, Zuni tribal members employed in the archaeological program received on-the-job training in archaeological field techniques, laboratory analyses, and report preparation. This training program has enabled Zuni tribal members with only a high school education to become skilled archaeological fieldworkers. A core staff of four Zuni tribal members has become proficient in conducting and reporting small projects.

Over the past several years, the Zuni Archaeology Program has conducted over 170 projects on the Zuni reservation and in adjacent areas in West-Central New Mexico. At the same time, the program has played an active role in the management of cultural resources by assisting the Zuni Tribal Council in the development of policy, and by reviewing and commenting on matters related to cultural resources.

From the outset, the Pueblo of Zuni has been interested in sponsoring a tribal archaeological program that meets high professional standards. The permanent staff of the Zuni Archaeology Program has included, on the average, three non-Indian archaeologists, five trained Zuni assistant archaeologists, and two secretarial personnel. While the non-Indian professional archaeologists have played a key role in the development of the program, the importance of the Zuni staff members should not be underestimated. The contributions of the Zuni staff members can be seen in the fact that 42% of the 170 professional reports prepared by the Zuni Archaeology Program between 1976 and 1981 were authored or co-authored by Zuni tribal members.

Multicultural Aspects of the Zuni Archaeology Program

In its six years of operation, the Zuni Archaeology Program has employed 24 non-Indian archaeologists for periods ranging from 3 weeks to 5 years. All of these archaeologists have lived in Zuni Pueblo during their employment and, while they have not been engaged in ethnographic fieldwork, they have had an ethnographic experience. The Zuni people are bilingual, with English as the second language, and they maintain a strong pueblo cultural tradition. Living at Zuni Pueblo, even for a short time, immerses a non-Indian in a different value and belief system.

As a result of living at Zuni Pueblo, the archaeologists employed by the Zuni Archaeology Program form friendships as well as professional relationships with their coworkers and other community members. This social interaction acts as an important means of socialization, which to a very limited but nonetheless important degree incorporates the archaeologist into the community. Through both formal and informal means the non-Indian archaeologists become sensitive to and understanding of Zuni ethics and values regarding archaeological remains. As Wax and Cassell (1979: 88) describe,

> Fieldworkers enter the field as people mentally rooted within the professional world of a scholarly discipline and morally anchored as well in the cultural worlds where they were nurtured. In the course of fieldwork, if it be of the more participatory and egalitarian variety, they are gradually incorporated within the moral systems of those who are studied and so become increasingly sensible of, and governed by, the same moral codes as the hosts.

Information about Zuni values and beliefs relating to archaeological research and cultural resource management is elicited formally at Zuni in a number of ways, including interviews with the Zuni Tribal Council and tribal elders (e.g., Holmes 1980; Ladd 1980) and regular staff meetings at the Zuni Archaeology Program. One of the most powerful informal means of communicating what the proper behavior and ethical approach of archaeologists working at Zuni should be has been the verbal and nonverbal attitudes and behavior of the Zuni staff during the daily operation of the program. Almost everyone is affected by the way their coworkers act and feel, and the nuances of interpersonal relationships help define the boundaries of ethical behavior.

The Zuni tribal members employed the the Zuni Archaeology Program undergo a socialization process that is the obverse of that experienced by the non-Indian employees. In addition to studying the Zuni past, the Zuni tribal members have to study archaeologists and their professional culture in order to learn how to interact and communicate with their non-Indian coworkers. Zuni tribal members employed by the Zuni Archaeology Program are inculcated with new values concerning the study of the past, and the importance of material culture and archaeological sites.

At the inception of the archaeological program, it was necessary for the Zuni employees to redefine archaeology as it was generally seen in the eyes of the community. Prior to the Zuni Archaeology Program, archaeologists at Zuni were known as "Bone Diggers," a label stemming in part from the archaeological excavation of hundreds of burials at Zuni sites by Cushing and Hodge in the late 19th and early 20th centuries (Smith et al. 1966). The Zuni term "Bone Diggers" has a very negative connotation, implying serious antisocial behavior. The conservation orientation of the cultural resource management objectives of the Zuni Archaeology Program allowed Zuni tribal members to redefine the role of archaeologists at Zuni. The bulk of work conducted by the program in its first years involved archaeological survey oriented toward locating archaeological sites so they could be protected from the adverse impact of land-modifying projects, and this type of work reinforced a positive image of archaeologists as protectors and preservers of important material remains of the Zuni heritage. While the term "Bone Digger" is still widely used in a joking context at Zuni Pueblo to refer to archaeologists, many tribal members recognize and affirm the positive conservation and preservation goals of the program, and there is no stigma attached to the Zuni employed by the program.

Given the multicultural aspects of the program, it is surprising that there have been relatively few ethical conflicts between the goals and methods of archaeological research and Zuni values and beliefs. In general, there is a concurrence between the two, due in large part to the genuine interest the Zuni people have in their tribal history and culture. In addition to the tribal archaeological program, the Pueblo of Zuni sponsors a Tribal Historian and conducts other tribal programs in cultural research. The Pueblo of Zuni desires to maintain a "parallel culture" in which the Zuni people can benefit from the best things Euro-American culture has to offer while maintaining their own values, beliefs, and tribal culture. The Zuni Archaeology Program, with its goal to preserve, protect, and study Zuni cultural resources, is viewed as a means to maintain the "parallel culture" and learn more about the Zuni past (Pueblo of Zuni 1982).

Where there has been conflict between the traditional ethics and values of the archaeological profession and Zuni values and beliefs, the Zuni Archaeology Program has been guided by three principles:

(1) where Zuni and Euro-American values and beliefs differ, precedence is given to Zuni values and beliefs; (2) where issues concern specific Zuni individuals or groups, consultation with these individuals or groups is required; and (3) tribal policy is set by the Zuni Tribal Council. The remainder of this essay examines the interplay of these principles with three major ethical issues or problems the Zuni Archaeology Program has faced.

Ethical Issues in the Excavation and Study of Human Remains

The excavation and study of human remains was the first ethical problem to be defined and resolved collectively by the staff of the Zuni Archaeology Program. Most non-Indian archaeologists arrive at Zuni secure in the belief that the archaeological investigation of burials and human physical remains is a scientifically and legally sanctioned exception to the general cultural proscription against the disinterment of graves. Their scientific training has taught them to depersonalize and objectify human remains, transforming them into valuable data to be collected as often as possible. These values and beliefs run counter to those held by most Zuni people, however.

The ancestors of the Zuni play an important role in the Zuni religion, and the power of the dead is considered to extend to the physical remains in the grave. At Zuni, the disturbance of graves is to be avoided if at all possible, as is actual contact with human bones, which is believed to cause arthritis. Opening of graves is believed by some people to release sickness or disease, with potentially harmful effects on the living. Within Zuni culture, willful excavation of graves and handling of human skeletal material are associated with social deviants such as witches (Holmes and Fowler 1980: 292). The exposure of human remains, even by archaeologists who are clearly not regarded as social deviants, is abhorrent to most Zuni, who experience negative physical and emotional responses to such activity. Some Zuni people believe that when the dead "come back," as with archaeological excavation, they take one of the living with them when they return to the grave or are removed from Zuni land. More than once, some people have attributed deaths in the community to archaeological activity involving human remains.

Zuni values and beliefs regarding human remains and the excavation of graves are communicated through verbal and behavioral interaction that is difficult, if not impossible, for archaeologists to ignore if they are concerned with not harming people psychologically and physically. The archaeologists who work for the Zuni Archaeology Program generally come to believe that human graves at Zuni should not be disturbed simply to collect archaeological data.

An ethical dilemma arises, however, with graves that are to be disturbed through the impact of land-modifying projects such as road construction. In this situation, the graves will be disturbed whether or not an archaeologist is involved, and most archaeologists think it is professionally irresponsible not to collect the associated data that will be destroyed. Many Indians believe that human remains are treated with more respect if they are excavated by archaeologists rather than disturbed by bulldozers or other heavy equipment. Nonetheless, such archaeological investigation of human burials still creates a culturally valid apprehension on the part of many Zuni people. The basic ethical problem is twofold: it must be determined (1) what disturbance of graves warrants archaeological excavation; and (2) what comprises appropriate study and disposition of excavated human remains.

This ethical problem has been defined and discussed through many means at Zuni Pueblo. There have been numerous, sometimes cathartic, staff meetings within the Zuni Archaeology Program. Policy decisions and procedural directives relating to the ethical issues involved have been elicited from the Zuni Tribal Council. The Pueblo of Zuni also took legal action in 1978 to block the sale of a prehistoric mummified body offered in an auction of Indian art and artifacts, and this helped to clarify the issues involved. In this case, the Pueblo of Zuni successfully invoked New Mexico burial statutes to prevent the sale and cause the body to be buried (Ferguson 1979). This action set the ethical, if not legal, precedent for archaeologists at the Zuni Archaeology Program to regard human remains primarily as deceased people rather than objectified sources of data.

Over the years, the following ethics have been established as the professionally and culturally responsible guidelines for the excavation and study of human remains. In all work conducted by the Zuni Archaeology Program, human graves are not investigated archaeologically unless they will be, or have been disturbed by a direct impact of land-modification activities unassociated with archaeological research. A direct impact is one that physically damages a grave through the rearrangement or disturbance of the contents (e.g., bulldozer damage). Impacts such as innundation are not thought to disturb graves or warrant archaeological investigation.

For the Zuni, reinterment of archaeologically excavated human remains is the only ethical disposition of them, and the Zuni Archaeology Program has respected this. The ethics of reinterment extend to the grave goods associated with human burials. The Zuni believe these artifacts belong to the dead and therefore are of no legitimate use to the living. Consequently, they are reburied along with the human remains. There are no religious observances that need to accompany reburial, although the Zuni religious leaders have informally advised that it is best to rebury the human remains as close as possible to their original location. The reburial of human remains and associated grave goods mitigates the adverse impact of archaeological excavation and makes such excavation preferable to other types of disturbance during land-modifying activities.

When graves have to be disturbed, there is general agreement that archaeological study of them will yield important cultural information about Zuni mortuary customs which should be recorded prior to reburial if this does not lead to inordinate delays. Photographs and documentation of graves and associated artifacts are relatively innocuous, but osteological analysis involving extensive handling of skeletal material creates concern, and tribal policy dictates that the Zuni Tribal Council will decide what types of osteological analyses are appropriate on a project-by-project basis. The reburial of human remains and associated artifacts increases the responsibility of the archaeologists involved to record the materials as fully as possible to minimize the loss of data.

The ethics for archaeological investigation of human remains established by the Zuni Archaeology Program are the best solution to a difficult problem. When the program finds it necessary to excavate human remains, the actual labor is performed by the non-Indian staff. Zuni tribal members are not asked to participate directly in the archaeological investigation, but they nevertheless find it emotionally unsettling if they are present. Experience has shown that minimizing the amount of time a grave is exposed and reinterring the remains as quickly as possible thereafter help to reduce negative aspects of the situation. This creates logistical and scheduling problems for the non-Indian archaeologists, but these are minor concerns when the other factors involved are taken into consideration. Many of the non-Indian archaeologists employed by the Zuni Archaeology Program have expressed the fact that working for and with the Zuni people has qualitatively changed their values and beliefs regarding the archaeological investigation of burials. Although their professional responsibility still dictates archaeological investigation of burials that have been or will be disturbed, such investigation has become an emotionally ambivalent experience for them in many of the same ways it is for Zuni people.

Design of Appropriate Research and Tribal Review

Archaeologists who reside in Zuni Pueblo soon learn that their research has more than academic value for the Zuni people. In part, interest in archaeology at Zuni lies in the validation of Zuni culture, in the sense that many Zuni people have an interest in comparing Zuni traditional history with archaeological culture history. The Zuni's own history is important to them in ways (Trigger 1980) that archaeologists have sometimes not understood or valued. For the Zuni, the results of archaeological research are more than grist for the mill of hypothesis testing and model making; archaeological research provides an independent source of information about their own past. As archaeologists become sensitized to this value, they begin to carefully differentiate between data and interpretation, between facts and theories. The Zuni people seek both archaeological data and the archaeologist's interpretation of that data, and then develop their own interpretations. The archaeologists at the Zuni Archaeology Program have respected and encouraged this, as it will eventually lead to new and exciting research directions.

Many Zuni people think that much anthropological research concerning their religion has violated their right of privacy and that certain aspects of the sacred realm have been profaned through scholarly publication of esoteric information. Archaeologists who work for the pueblo are constantly reminded of this and become sensitive to which religious areas should not be studied. At the same time, there is much information about the Zuni religion and culture which the Zuni people want to share with others, and archaeologists are encouraged to use this in their work (e.g., Ferguson 1981a). Unfortunately, the boundaries of what is appropriate and inappropriate to research concerning the Zuni religion are neither well defined nor universally accepted, which creates a stressful and ambiguous situation for scholars. The research grant proposals of the Zuni Archaeology Program are reviewed by the Zuni Tribal Council prior to submission; this consultation is integral to the design of research that abides by community standards.

Given the Zuni values for their own history and religion, most archaeologists who work for the tribe develop a very cautious intellectual approach to facets of Zuni prehistory and history relating to the Zuni religion. This intellectual caution has at times been misunderstood, as in the following comments by J. Charles Kelley concerning a paper dealing with the emergence of modern Zuni culture and society in the protohistoric period (Ferguson 1981b). Kelley (1981: 436) comments:

> As good as the . . . paper is in the areas which it explicitly covers, I find myself uneasy about all of the things that are left unsaid or which are not touched upon. Are we as professionals to accept without question that there are archaeological problems that must remain mysteries because the sponsoring agency feels that there are sensitive items that cannot be discussed? I cannot easily accept an account of Zuni culture history which completely omits any reference to the Kachina cult (or to Zuni astro-religious practices). We may have here a critical conflict of ethical considerations—archaeological ethics on the one hand and anthropological ethics concerned with the privacy rights of the Zuni tribe on the other.

Kelley confuses an ethical conflict with ethical imperative—namely, the need to involve the Zuni people as consultants and principal investigators in research investigating sensitive aspects of their religion, something the Zuni Archaeology Program has done on several projects (Eriacho and Ferguson 1979; Ladd 1980). To date, the research priorities and funding of the Zuni Archaeology Program have not resulted in research on Kelley's particular interests. As archaeologists really know very little about the prehistoric development of pueblo religion, this topic was not treated in the brief paper he mentions; the purpose of this paper was to review the known data concerning protohistoric Zuni culture history. It is important to note that the intellectual caution applied in this case was self-imposed rather than dictated by tribal policy.

The Pueblo of Zuni has never formally decreed any restrictions on the investigation of archaeological problems by the Zuni Archaeology Program, and no Zuni tribal officials have ever censored archaeological reports or professional papers prepared by tribal employees. These activities would conflict with the scholarly objectivity and professional standards the tribe expects their archaeological program to meet. The archaeologists employed by the Zuni Archaeology Program have internalized community standards of appropriate research topics to some degree, however, and these personally internalized standards have guided the design of research problems. Any research limitations that the archaeologists employed by Zuni have experienced in their work have been individually determined rather than institutionally dictated.

Conducting archaeological research under the sponsorship of the Zuni tribe creates both the opportunity and ethical necessity to involve tribal members in the research of their own past. The more sensitive the topic, the greater the need for input from tribal members. At the Pueblo of Zuni, responsible ethics dictate that informed tribal members help design, implement, and interpret the research. Such involvement of tribal members positively enhances archaeological research, and promises to eventually expand our understanding of the past in new ways.

Cultural Resource Management of Religious Artifacts and Sites

The most important cultural resources the Zuni people have are the religious artifacts and sacred sites integral to the Zuni religion and way of life. Although the Zuni Archaeology Program is primarily involved in archaeological research and the management of archaeological sites, religious sites in project areas subject to impact from development are also of management concern. At the request of the Zuni Tribal Council and religious leaders, the Zuni Archaeology Program has also been involved with the management of religious artifacts that have been removed from Zuni land. The cultural resource management of religious artifacts and sacred sites by the Zuni Archaeology Program has increased since the passage of Public Law 95-341, The American Indian Religious Freedom Act (Ferguson 1981c).

One of the key ethical issues involved with the management of sacred cultural resources is making sure that the people responsible for the religious artifacts or sites participate in the decisions made about them. At Zuni this issue has been resolved through Tribal Council Resolution #M70-78-1020, which clearly identifies the Zuni religious leaders as the people responsible for making decisions about religious matters; it also affirms that the political leaders of the pueblo support the religious leaders in their decisions. The Zuni Tribal Council acts as a contact point for outsiders, involving the appropriate religious leaders when necessary.

In 1978, the Pueblo of Zuni invoked federal law (18 U.S.C. 1163) requiring the return of stolen tribal property to recover a religious artifact at auction in New York City. This religious artifact was communally owned and had been removed from Zuni land in violation of tribal tradition. Subsequent to this, religious leaders began to intensify concern for similar religious artifacts in museum collections. Zuni religious leaders reached a consensus on the handling of religious artifacts in museums during a project conducted in 1979 and 1980 with funding from the North American Indian Museum Association. In this project, one of the Zuni religious leaders contacted all of the other religious leaders and groups in the pueblo to gain their input and approval concerning recommendations for the curation of Zuni religious materials in museums.

Zuni concern for religious artifacts that have been removed from Zuni land indicates that at times there is a conflict between the use of these artifacts as art or scientific specimens, and their intended use in the Zuni religion (Eriacho and Ferguson 1979). The Pueblo of Zuni has taken the position that when this conflict in values precludes or violates religious use of the artifact, the conflict should be resolved in favor of religious use. The basic reasonableness of the Zuni concerns is attested to by the fact that the pueblo has been able to reach mutually satisfactory agreements concerning care and use of Zuni sacred artifacts with every museum it has approached to date. The Zuni religious leaders have explained their concerns and have considered the legitimate concerns of the museums as well.

The Zuni Tribal Council and the Zuni religious leaders determine the research tasks, goals, and methods in the cultural resource management of religious artifacts and sites by the Zuni Archaeology Program. In research concerning artifacts, the goal is generally to explain Zuni concerns in terms understandable to professionals. With regard to sacred sites, research has been directed toward locating sacred sites in project areas and identifying which religious leaders and groups should be consulted, if needed. Whenever possible, Zuni consultants have been used to define project impacts on specific sacred areas in enough detail to be useful to project planners, but without disturbing the sacred values of the sites (Ladd 1980). At other times, the Zuni Tribal Council has provided this information (Holmes 1980; Robertson 1980).

The cultural resource management of religious artifacts and sites is a valuable function of the Zuni Archaeology Program. It facilitates and is a model for the consultation called for in numerous federal regulations. By helping to present Zuni values in planning documents, it increases the Zuni's control over the cultural resources of greatest importance to them.

Conclusion

Zuni values and beliefs play an important role in the ethical guidelines structuring archaeological research and cultural resource management at the Zuni Archaeology Program. Non-Indian archaeologists who live and work in Zuni Pueblo come to understand and be influenced by Zuni values and beliefs through daily interaction with Zuni coworkers in a small group setting. Access to the Zuni Tribal Council and other tribal leaders facilitates clarification of Zuni values and beliefs when needed. The goal of the Zuni Archaeology Program is to respect Zuni culture while studying it.

Zuni values and beliefs impinge on archaeological research in two major ways: (1) the excavation and study of human remains is limited to graves impacted by development; and (2) an intellectual caution is developed with respect to research concerning the Zuni religion. Although such caution is not formally dictated by tribal policy. Zuni values and standards of research have been internalized by the non-Indian staff. Some might see this as a conflict between the archaeological ethic of freedom of scientific inquiry and the Zuni ethic that burials and certain religious materials should not be studied. In this case, the resolution is in favor of the Zuni standards. Archaeologists at the Zuni Archaeology Program have accepted the fact that, in order to remain sacred, some aspects of the Zuni religion need to be kept secret. To disregard this value would harm the people these archaeologists work for as well as study.

This situation does not preclude research concerning the Zuni religion, but it does necessitiate involving Zuni people in the design, implementation, and interpretation of such research so that all values can be respected. The value the Zuni people place on their own history, and the availability of knowledgeable Zuni consultants and researchers to implement research concerning sensitive topics, create new opportunities for archaeological research. In this author's opinion, the resolution of ethical issues in the Zuni Archaeology Program has been to everyone's benefit, which augurs well for the future.

25

Archaeology and the Native American: A Case at Hopi

E. Charles Adams

One classic conflict that must be overcome in working on tribal land is that between the archaeological ethic of freedom of inquiry into all categories of data without hindrance and the Native American ethics that remains of Indian culture belong to Indians, that it is tribal prerogative to decide what investigations are undertaken on tribal land, and that certain classes of objects are so sacred that their study would diminish their religious power.

Based on his experience in working on tribal land and for tribal governments, the author recommends principles to follow to avoid such conflicts and to integrate archaeological ethics with those of the host group. These guidelines would apply to any situation in which archaeologists work on lands of an ethnic group different from their own.

In 1875, John Wesley Powell became the first person to publish an anthropological study of the Hopi. Beginning in the 1890's, Alexander Stephen and Jesse Walter Fewkes published many other studies. Fewkes also initiated archaeological work in the area in 1895 with the excavation of Sikyatki, an ancestral Hopi village, followed by testing at several other ancestral villages.

Photographers began flocking to the mesas in the 1870's, capturing on film every aspect of Hopi life. The Hopi were offended when many of these photographs were published and, in 1911, photography was banned from most villages. Many photos were and are still taken, however.

In the early years, several publications detailed secret aspects of Hopi religion, much to the chagrin of the practitioners. As a result, information was withheld, inaccurate information was given, and some Hopi refused to talk to anthropologists. These lessons prompted most later researchers to take greater care in publishing their material and to show more sensitivity to the wishes of their informants.

A spurt of both anthropological and archaeological research occurred in the 1930's. These efforts were successful because the individual anthropologists and archaeologists earned the respect of their informants, employed Hopi, and did not threaten to expose existing institutions. Nevertheless, violations of trust and privacy of individual Hopi continue even now. By the 1960's, the Hopi had become much more politicized and were not afraid to speak out publicly against past and present anthropological research, as well as on other issues.

Political struggles and changing attitudes have caught many anthropologists and archaeologists in the middle. Many of the traditional religious leaders oppose anthropologists even working on the reservation, let alone publishing the results of their studies. Others freely admit that some of their own knowledge of their culture stems from reading anthropological studies and that research should continue, as long as it is properly policed. In general, the tribal government supports scholarly research; but if an individual is studying a specific village or consulting with individuals, the agreements are left to the scholar and the village or individuals. If asked by the village or individual, the tribe will act as a third party in most agreements.

By comparison with the problems of anthropologists, those facing archaeologists on the Hopi reservation have been minor. Generally, the people are indifferent to mildly supportive of work on prehistoric sites; objections may arise if the site is an ancestral Hopi village (i.e., has a place in the oral traditions of the people) or a modern village.

The Walpi Project, which functioned within this sociopolitical milieu, suggests mechanisms for cooperation between archaeologists of Euro-American descent and Native Americans. Certain aspects of the project will be described and principles that they illustrate will be discussed.

Groundwork for the Walpi Project

The Walpi Project involved the restoration of the ceremonial center for the First Mesa Hopi. Funding for the restoration came from the Economic Development Administration and permitted the crew to restore about half of the village. Because Walpi was eligible for the National Register of Historic Places, the Advisory Council on Historic Preservation determined that an historic architect and an archaeologist had to be on hand to record the village architecture before it was transformed and to recover any artifacts that the villagers would allow to be removed. The Walpi religious leaders agreed to this, and the Museum of Northern Arizona was subcontracted by the Hopi Tribe to do the work.

Before the project began, the archaeologist decided that he needed to research the Hopi, go to the village, and meet the people and the restoration crew. It was absolutely necessary to talk to the Hopi as equals. The archaeologist told them that they were his employers and that he wanted to learn from them.

The project lasted 18 months in the field and it took approximately 3 months to gain the trust of the Walpi people and their religious leaders. This trust enabled the archaeologist to ask questions about the use and meaning of artifacts and rooms, thus adding greatly to understanding of the material culture. During actual fieldwork, trust was secured by a completely open policy. Individuals were encouraged to visit both the site and the laboratory, to examine the materials, and to ask questions. If a religious leader indicated that an artifact should be returned to him or his clan, it was. Usually the religious leader offered information about the importance and use of the artifact and indicated why it should be returned. It is quite probable that more information was secured this way than would have been obtained from analysis alone. A sketch or photograph of the artifact was made before it was released.

This policy of openness minimized suspicion and distrust. At first, people feared that all the material was being taken off the reservation to be sold. When such gossip surfaced, the archaeologist immediately confronted it with the truth; for instance, inviting people to view the artifacts and setting up a community display. Because of this open policy and agreement that the artifacts were the property of the Walpi people, there was much less concern about their location and final disposition. Only 50 or so artifacts were removed from the collections, mostly for religious reasons.

The formal mechanism to recognize Hopi ownership of the artifacts was a Memorandum of Agreement signed by the museum, the tribal government, and Walpi religious leaders. This agreement stipulated that the artifacts would not leave the reservation, that the religious leaders would choose the areas to be worked, and that all artifacts could be examined by the religious leaders. An agreement of this sort is recommended for any project; it clearly outlines the responsibilities of all parties and can be referred to in case of disputes.

About every three months, a sample of artifacts from the excavations was displayed in the community building. One purpose of this exhibit was to acquaint the young people with material remains of their cultural heritage. It also helped in the identification of some artifacts, served to widen the archaeologist's and architect's personal identity, increased the appeal and understanding of archaeology, and acted to mitigate suspicions of what was being done with all the "junk," as most Hopi called the findings.

Through these processes, the archaeologist and architect became accepted members of the community. They took great care not to take sides in disputes, however; outsiders' involvement in personal problems tends to polarize the situation and make it even worse. This community acceptance broadened their acquaintances and, therefore, the pool of potential informants. It also allowed them to experience the workings of Hopi culture and to observe the use of some traditional material items.

The archaeologist served as a guide and spokesman to the innumerable tourists that came through Walpi daily. This served as an ideal forum for presenting the cooperative nature of the restoration enterprise and the mutual benefits to both Hopi and white, which showed archaeology to be a useful tool to the Native American.

At the conclusion of the restoration work, a new Memorandum of Agreement was signed which allowed the artifacts to be removed to the museum for further analysis and the preparation of reports. Another agreement signed in 1980 extended this loan until the Hopi build a museum to house the Walpi collection. This agreement allows the museum to use the Walpi collections for education and exhibits. It also grants the tribe and religious leaders the right to edit any reports before publication and to forbid publication on the Walpi artifactual material altogether. Unpublished reports are available to researchers on the museum grounds.

Ethics: Criteria and Problem Solving

The above discussion outlined the scenario of the Walpi Project and the resolution of day-to-day and long-term problems. Now let us focus on the ethical criteria that were used to arrive at decisions. Obviously, conflicts in values will arise in a situation in which an archaeologist confronts a different culture and excavates a site known to have been lived in by the local people. These conflicts cannot be solved by strict adherence to a "science is right" or "we have a legal right" stance. The only way conflict resolution can be achieved is through communication and compromise. Every attempt should be made to understand the cultural values underlying the position of the other side.

Whenever a conflict in values arose, the archaeologist first examined his own values. Then he tried to explain these to the other side and asked them to explain theirs to him. After that, they worked out a compromise. A good example is the return of artifacts mentioned above. There really was no choice; if the museum had not accepted this limitation, no agreement would have been signed and no archaeological work would have been done. The non-Indian professionals decided that the value to them was not the artifact itself, but the information that the artifact contained. By obtaining informant data on each returned artifact, plus a photograph, more inferential information was obtained than professional analysis alone would have provided. Viewed in this light, no archaeological values were violated. This is in keeping with the Code of Ethics of the Society of Professional Archaeologists: "An archaeologist shall be sensitive to, and respect the legitimate concerns of, groups whose culture histories are the subject of archaeological investigations" (Section I, Part 1.1e).

Work on Indian land and within a village is no different from excavation on private land. Work is done by the permission of the individual (or group) who owns the property, and all that is excavated belongs to the owner. The Hopi agreement allowed the archaeological crew to excavate, study, and prepare reports on the material, and to deposit the findings temporarily at the museum and permanently at Hopi, when a museum is built there. This was a compromise between the desire of many Hopi to have all of the material returned to them or their clan, and the desire of the archaeologists to have it at a museum with easy access for study and publication.

The bottom line is that Native American beliefs and values have as much credence in determining the scope of archaeological work in a Native American site as do the values of the archaeologist and the Euro-American scientific community. If these beliefs and values are understood and accepted, compromises satisfactory to both sides can be worked out. The passage of the American Indian Religious Freedom Act makes this even more imperative. The intent of this act is to insure Native Americans the same religious freedom guaranteed to all Americans under the First Amendment to the U.S. Constitution. On Indian tribal land, the American Indian has the right to deny or attempt to block archaeological work in an area deemed sacred or religious. Walpi is a sacred area; yet every aspect and artifact at Walpi is not sacred. With this understanding and the agreement to respect the wishes of the religious leaders of the village, it was possible to do extensive and scientifically valuable archaeological research there.

Therefore, the ethical criteria reside in communication and compromise. The archaeologist must be able to understand a situation in terms other than black and white. One must be able to look beyond the scientific value system to the end result. Will more valuable information result from compromise than from strict adherence to standards? Do the values of the other side have any validity? Why shouldn't they be as important as one's own values? On the Walpi Project, the professionals were never asked to compromise their standards, except for publication. In 1982 the Walpi religious leaders decided that under the Memorandum of Agreement with the museum no publication would be allowed. This involved only reports or papers describing the artifacts excavated from Walpi. As a result, many significant scientific studies of the Walpi artifacts cannot be published. However, the material has been analyzed and summarized in written form and the reports are available for reading at the museum. If the artifacts are returned to the Hopi, are lost, or are forgotten, the reports and analyses remain.

Of great value is the trust relationship that exists between the museum and the archaeological community, and the Hopi. Because of the Walpi Project, the Hopi's interest in and understanding of archaeology have increased severalfold. Before, there was little interest and no understanding of archaeology. Today the tribe is seeking funds for a museum, there is a travelling exhibit about Walpi (sponsored by the National Endowment for the Humanities) at the Hopi Cultural Center, attempts to begin a cultural resource program at Hopi have been made, several small archaeological projects have been successfully completed on the reservation, and excavations of one or more ancestral Hopi villages have been proposed by members of the tribe.

In 1980, a symposium of Hopi scholars was held to commemorate the three-hundredth anniversary of the Pueblo Revolt against the Spanish. One of the key issues at the symposium was conflicting views of cultural history. The Hopi complained that their views of their culture, and especially their history, were never presented. The white speakers argued that such claims were difficult to prove scientifically and that many of the details of Hopi history are kept private by the Hopi. A solution, of course, is to present both views in as much detail as possible. Obviously, this is easier said than done, but presenting the Hopi perspective would allow them to correct it or even write it themselves.

It is a responsibility of the Hopi to keep their oral histories alive. It should not be important to the internal workings of the culture that Euro-Americans have other opinions about the same events. The oral histories should be recorded in the native tongue and transcribed in the written form of the language. If this does not happen, the version in Euro-American books will have no alternative. While it is the Native Americans' responsibility to maintain their traditions, it is the responsibility of linguists and other anthropologists to record and check these oral traditions accurately. With these data available, it is the responsibility of the archaeologist and anthropologist to note the existence of alternative culture histories. Thereby, oral histories will provide an additional tool for the study of a culture and its prehistory.

Summary and Conclusion

When archaeologists work with Native Americans, they should be willing to communicate and compromise. Strict adherence to professional standards that make no sense to the Native American or, in fact, violate the beliefs of his culture may jeopardize the specific project, as well as future projects in the area, and damage the image of the archaeologist.

With early communication, it should be possible to explain the project to the people and work out a means of implementing it. The proper individuals at all levels of authority must be informed about the project. At Hopi, contacting the tribal government is not enough; the leaders of the individual villages affected by the project also have to be contacted.

If the project is of long duration, it is mandatory to gain the understanding and trust of the local people. Again, the long-term consequences of the program should be considered. A project cannot be considered a success if it alienates the people toward future archaeological programs. To gain this trust, one should be open and honest from the beginning. Explain who is doing the work, the reason for it, and the scope of the project. There is seldom a need to compromise archaeological values. If a conflict does arise, honesty will reap rewards in striking a satisfactory compromise.

26

Ethical Decision Making and Participation in the Politics of Archaeology

Ruthann Knudson

Although archaeology has been involved in one way or another with politics throughout this century, the amount of participation that we see today is relatively new. There has been an increase in the number of archaeologists with political skills, the amount of time spent in attempting to influence governmental policy, and the profession's awareness of these efforts. Professional societies such as the Society of Professional Archaeologists and the Society for American Archaeology have become involved in the political arena.

Even today most archaeologists think of politics as lawmaking only. Legislation is important, but a law rarely specifies how its mandates are to be implemented. Agency regulations tell the public how the law will be applied to that agency's operations. Therefore, work with federal, state, and local agencies forms an important arena of political activity.

In addition, once a law is passed, funds are necessary for its implementation and enforcement. Work with Senate and House appropriations committees and with the internal process of agency budgeting is also an important part of the political process.

To affect the political arena archaeologists need knowledge of both the formal systems, such as Congressional lawmaking, and the informal systems, such as the influence of Congressional staffs or which lawmakers are sympathetic to environmental concerns.

As the first Legislative Coordinator for the Society for American Archaeology, Ruthann Knudson has had firsthand experience in presenting archaeology to the political milieu. She outlines several areas of political activity and suggests ways archaeologists can fulfill their ethical responsibility to affect these areas for the benefit of the discipline.

ARCHAEOLOGISTS HAVE an ethical responsibility to participate in the development and implementation of public policies about the management of our prehistoric and historic archaeological resources, and can do so appropriately within a framework of situation ethics. A situationist first posits that the conservation of a significant portion of our cultural heritage is good for the human community, and then deals with specific instances or situations of decision making pragmatically and relatively. Archaeologists have a particular responsibility to aid in public policy making because they are members of the general community that benefits from cultural resource conservation, have personal and financial commitments to the derivation of knowledge from archaeological materials, and have the technical expertise to assist in the development of alternative conservation strategy and tactics.

Public policies are legislated by Congress and implemented by the Administration through its programs, budgets, personnel policies, and scheduling. Archaeologists can and should participate in this public decision making by developing coherent professional positions on issues and presenting them in a credible way to Congress, the Administration, and other special interest groups. In addition, archaeologists should provide individual review and comment on issues to the extent allowed by their specific professional roles. Historically, archaeologists have been successful in developing broad public policies of archaeological resource management without explicitly working with the whole governmental system as a nationally representative special interest group. The present and future competition for limited economic resources, and the growing complexity of governmental entities and systems, require us to accept greater responsibility for broad participation in the development and implementation of public management policies.

Most archaeologists have developed their own personal ethical rationale for the professional decisions they make. These rationales are supported by statements of ethics from professional and social societies, and have traditionally focused on the intellectual or technical questions that arise in the conduct of archaeological study. Those who participate in the development of broad national policies about the public treatment of archaeological resources often have to implement an ethical rationale about public goals without having an explicit consensual statement of those ethics. The number of public policy developers has grown exponentially in the past decade, as "public archaeology" has similarly expanded in federal agencies and environmental protection programs.

Any essay such as this is a function of the personal and professional growth its author has achieved over a number of years, and hence of the people who have encouraged that growth. Special thanks are due to colleagues Fred Wendorf and Jimmie Griffin, and to nonarchaeologists Loretta Neuman, Dennis LeMaster, Nellie Longsworth, Bob Terrell, Larry LaRocco, Don Miller, and Roger Ryman for their thought-provoking questions and insight into the pragmatic possibilities of public archaeological conservation.

This essay is intended to serve primarily as a guide to actual participation in the development and implementation of public archaeological policy within an explicit ethical rationale. It focuses on national policy forums and questions, but the basic ethical propositions and operational guidelines should be broadly applicable to international, regional, state, or local situations.

Basic Approach

The ethical system subscribed to in this essay is *situation ethics,* described by Joseph Fletcher (1966: 26–39) as follows:

> The situationist enters into every decision-making situation fully armed with the ethical maxims of this community and its heritage, and he treats them with respect as illuminators of his problems. [He or she] accept[s] reason as the instrument of moral judgment . . . decisions are hypothetical, not categorical . . . from the situationist's perspective, . . . it is possible to derive general "principles" from whatever is the one and only universal law . . . , but not laws or rules.
>
> . . . [Situation ethics] is empirical, fact-minded, data conscious, inquiring. It is antimoralistic as well as antilegalistic, for it is sensitive to variety and complexity. It is neither simplistic nor perfectionist. It is "casuistry" (case-based) in the constructive and nonpejorative sense of the word.

Let us look at the way the paradigm of situation ethics can appropriately be applied to ethical decisions about our participation in public policy. Our first proposition is as follows:

> There is a worldwide moral consensus that the long-term conservation of a significant portion of our cultural past is good for the human community. As a corollary, loss of our nonrenewable heritage resource base engenders significant social cost.

This principle is supported in numerous cultural resource laws in this country. It is the basis for the UNESCO "Convention on the Means of Prohibiting and Preventing the Illicit Import, Export, and Transfer of Ownership of Cultural Property," passed by the General Conference on November 14, 1970 (in *Journal of Field Archaeology* 3: 217–224 [1976]). It is implicit in the directives of numerous federal programs that support or regulate public treatment of our cultural past. It is fundamental to the "Basic Principles of Archaeological Resource Management" adopted by the Society for American Archaeology (Knudson 1982). Within all these statements is a basic "leap of affirmation" that requires no validation or verification. It is the basic principle behind all professional archaeological decision making.

The cultural past includes tangible and intangible elements, "historic properties" and "traditional lifeways" (National Research Council 1982). Thus, archaeologists making decisions about the archaeological elements of the cultural past must make those decisions relative to concerns about prehistory and history, historical architecture and engineering, ethnography and folklore.

As further corollary to the basic principle of the value of conservation, we can state that the entire community has a broad responsibility to support such conservation of a part of the "public wealth." Thus, archaeologists function first as members of the general community, secondarily as concerned specialists.

A second statement of principle relates situation ethics to archaeological decision making:

> The long-term goal is conservation of a resource base for the good of the human community, for the preservation of knowledge and objects as they hold value for long-term cultural coherence. It is not conservation of an individual site or building per se, or focus on a specific research topic out of context of its relationship to the overall cultural needs of the human community.

A third proposition relates to archaeological participation in public policy development and implementation:

> While an important human value, cultural resources are only one aspect of a human social and economic system, and all resource management decisions must be made relative to the broader system; to ignore this broad public context is unethical. Thus, archaeological resources should be managed within a more inclusive context of cultural resources and, further, within the context of national, state, and local public multiresource policies and programs.

Note that in this discussion the concept of "archaeological resource management" does not apply only to federal land-management programs or construction agencies that affect archaeological sites; it also applies to federal programs in basic research (such as those funded by the National Science Foundation or through the Historic Preservation Fund) that relate to the use of our prehistoric and historic residues.

A fourth proposition posits that:

> Archaeologists have a responsibility to make ethical decisions about the management of cultural resources (especially the archaeological component of that resource base) because of (1) their membership in a human community that shares a value of cultural conservation; (2) their personal commitment (and accrued benefit through salaries) to the derivation of knowledge from the archaeological resource base, which generally involves the partial destruction (consumption or use) of that resource base; and (3) their technical knowledge of feasible alternatives for the resolution of environmental or economic conflicts that involve cultural resources.

Archaeological decisions about which sites to excavate or conserve represent the public interest in that they affect the broad human community. Generally, such decisions are based on ethical principles. When they relate to publicly owned sites or projects that involve public funds, they are also guided by public governmental policies and programs. Thus, finally

> Archaeologists have a responsibility to participate in the development of public policies about cultural resource management and programs that implement those policies in order to fulfill the ethical propositions stated above. They must do so in the context of broad cultural resource management interests and multiresource use, using practical tactics and strategies oriented to long-term principles for the greatest public good.

A corollary to this is that nonparticipation in the development of public policies does not follow ethical propositions. If no archaeologists participate in the development of public archaeological policy and programs, nonarchaeologists will develop the latter. The resource base may or may not receive any protection or fiscal support.

The Development of Archaeological Public Policies and Programs

Most archaeologists, traditionally trained as field and laboratory scholars, are overwhelmed with the apparent complexities of federal laws, regulations, programs, and guidelines. This section introduces some of the basic elements in this system and suggests some of the ways archaeologists can participate.

Congress and the Administration

Public policies and programs are basically defined in a two-faceted political arena: the legislative branch and the administrative branch. The functions of Congress are threefold. As the representative body, Congress has the responsibility for formulating basic policies of the federal government. This is done through the process of *authorizing* legislation, such as the National Historic Preservation Act of 1966 as amended, which includes a statement of basic national policy and outlines a program for implementing that policy. Similarly, the American Indian Religious Freedom Joint Resolution of 1978 (92 Stat. 469) is a definition of authority and policy. Authorizing legislation usually includes within it an administrative directive stating that the appropriate Administration official (e.g., Secretary of the Interior) will develop regulations, standards, and/or guidelines to implement the statement of policy and authority as outlined in the authorizing legislation. It also will include the authority to spend funds in support of defined programs, usually with an annual spending limit. It does not actually provide those funds, however; it only authorizes them.

Complementary to the authorizing laws is *appropriations* legislation, which provides the fiscal support for any authorized programs. Based on the federal revenues (from taxes, fees, etc.) that are projected to be available in any year, appropriations laws actually allocate real dollars to the authorized programs within the ceiling limits. The first draft of an appropriations budget is provided to Congress by the Administration, based on the latter's practical experience and program (read "policy") goals. Congress then makes its appropriation decisions based on a compromise between standing authorities and present funds, budgets, and Administration desires. If no dollars, or fewer than have been authorized, are appropriated to support programs, obviously the intent of the authorizing legislation cannot be fulfilled. For instance, the Archaeological and Historic Preservation Act of 1974 (PL 93-291, "Moss-Bennett"bill [88 Stat. 174], as amended in 1978 (PL 95-625), reauthorized the expenditure of $4 million in fiscal 1980, and $5 million in each of the next two fiscal years. However, no money was appropriated for either 1981 or 1982. Thus, affecting public policies and programs as they are defined by Congress means participating in the development of both authorizing and appropriations legislation.

A third function of Congress, which receives little general attention but is an important element in policy implementation, is to *oversee* the Administration's fulfillment of Congressionally designed policies and programs. This task is generally given to authorizing committees. In the House of Representatives, for instance, the House Interior Committee's concern about federal management of archaeological resources led to the Committee Chairman's 1980 request to the General Accounting Office for a formal review of federal archaeology programs. The resulting report to Congress, entitled "Are Agencies Doing Enough or Too Much for Archaeological Preservation? Guidance Needed" (Report CED-81-61), involved professional archaeologists as consultants and has been a basis for Society for American Archaeology discussions with the Department of the Interior about the need for more administrative direction. In addition, professional archaeological participation in the House Agriculture Committee's Forest Subcommittee overseeing of U.S. Forest Service programs brought more attention to cultural resource management within that agency.

It is the Administration, then, which has the responsibilities and opportunities to implement Congressional policy. In doing so, it may slowly or even dramatically modify those policy statements as they come up against the real world of economic priorities. As Dodd and Schott (1979: vi) note, in recent years, studies have emphasized public policy as a "continuum ranging from legislative proposals to administrative implementation"; their analysis of the interrelationships between the two ends of the continuum is instructive. The way a specific interest group learns to understand and influence policy decisions along this continuum is well presented in an analysis by Vietor (1980), in which he notes (p. 9–10):

> Even more than legislation, administrative policy making occurs beyond the purview of the public, often appearing to be the disembodied output of a faceless bureaucracy. In most accounts of the political economy, one is left with the impression that after the legislative battle ends, unnamed bureaucrats implement the fully articulated policy impartially and without influence from pluralist pressures. But as the modernizing process has shifted more and more responsibility for complex policy from legislators to administrators, the political process has been subtly altered in several fundamental ways. More crucial decisions are made in secret, without the knowledge of the electorate or the approval of their representatives. The personal values and ambitions of individual, unelected civil servants have a greater influence on important public policies. And, finally, technocratic resources—data, expertise, and financial strength—afford corporations [or special interest groups, such as a professional society] a unique role in lengthy implementation procedures.

For the past several years, the National Conference of State Historic Preservation Officers has had an ongoing program to collect information about state preservation programs supported with federal funds. The conference has presented these data to both Congress and the Administration, and thus has been a critical factor in the maintenance of the state matching grants program of the Historic Preservation Fund despite Reagan Administration opposition. Through this input, the conference has shaped Congressionally approved funding and influenced U.S. Department of the Interior programs as well.

Let us examine one further example of archaeological community assistance in the implementation of public policy. Planning for the allocation of U.S. Forest Service resources is done under the guidance of the National Forest Management Act of 1976 (90 Stat. 2949). This act has no explicit recognition that national forest lands hold archaeological resources. Regulations about *how* to plan (how to implement the authorized policy) were promulgated as 36 CFR 219. By providing public comment to draft versions of these regulations, and asking supportive Congressmen to transmit those comments to the Forest Service nongovernment archaeologists were able to support the efforts of in-house agency archaeologists to include an explicit requirement for cultural resource management planning in all U.S. Forest Service plans.

The political process is its own American subculture. Each branch has its structures, functions, personal roles and operational styles. Such an anthropological perspective was described recently by Weatherford (1981), and somewhat more positively by Stepick (1982). Learning to participate in this subculture is akin to learning the traditional anthropological process of acculturation. This understanding will enable archaeologists to be effective "lobbyists" or participants representing their special interests and expertise in all the appropriate arenas of federal policy development and implementation.

Those who ultimately make all the decisions about public programs operate in a web of complex factors where it is difficult to extract the pertinent data from the noise, to set priorities among equally unknown interests. They therefore welcome other individuals whom they can meet on a face-to-face basis and upon whom they can rely as a credible voice of a credible constituency. They are dependent upon acquiring information that they can believe. The archaeologists who have been successful leaders in shaping public policy as it reflects archaeological interests have done their homework and known their facts, have been personable and relaxed when dealing with people with other interests, and have been open to discussions of compromise or negotiation when necessary and appropriate. They have had credibility both within the archaeological community and outside of it, with governmental policy makers as well as with other interest representatives. If archaeologists do not participate as actual members of the political process subculture, the subculture will make its decisions without consistent consideration of archaeological concerns.

Other Interest Groups

The need to understand and take into account the nonarchaeological context within which decisions about archaeological public policy are made merits further emphasis. In order to be effective facilitators of public policy decisions, it is necessary for each special interest to understand the other interests—their goals, strategies and tactics, and constituencies. Not only is there a finite number of archaeological sites to be studied, but there is also a limited pool of dollars with which to manage these resources. In addition to the fiscal crunch, there are valid competing interests for the use of the same pieces of land on/in which the archaeological resources are found. These may be as basic as the perceived competition between the restoration architect who wishes to put a new foundation under a Victorian commerical building and the historic archaeologist who sees the ground surrounding the building as the container of an earlier archaeological record meriting conservation. At the extreme end of the continuum, it is the competition between the need for strip-mined coal to offset Near Eastern oil imports and the need for conservation of significant elements of the Chacoan archaeological complex. The American Mining Congress, the National Association of Manufacturers, the Edison Electric Institute, and the Society for American Archaeology each have valid concerns and needs that merit consideration in the development of public policy. Effective development of archaeological interests comes only when there is understanding and appreciation of the needs of other interests.

John Gardner (1981: 23) has noted: "Our pluralistic philosophy invites each organization, institution, or special group to develop and enhance its own potentialities. *But the price of that treasured autonomy and self-preoccupation is that each institution concern itself also with the common good.* This is not idealism; it is self-preservation [italics in the original]."

Archaeology as a Special Interest Group

Over the past century, archaeology and archaeologists have been perceived as a special interest group (cf. King et al. 1977: 24–44) by the nonarchaeological community, including the historic preservationists concerned with the built environment and the cultural anthropologists concerned with the ethnic identity. Until recently, however, it has not been apparent that archaeologists have seen themselves as a cohesive and responsible public community. True, individuals have provided significant leadership in specific instances in developing public policy, and organizations such as the Society for American Archaeology have provided strong support for scholarly standards as well as for the 1945–1976 Committee for the Recovery of Archaeological Remains (Guthe 1952: 6; McGimsey 1982). But there appears to have been little self-conscious participation in the development of the archaeological community as an entity with coherent public policies, morale, and binding values (whether in academia, public agencies, or private industry).

The proliferation of archaeological resource assessment and protection projects during the past decade, as part of the general recognition of the need for broader environmental (including historic preservation) concerns, has created a diversified population of people identifying themselves as "archaeologists." The diversity and resulting fractionation of professional groups have weakened the sense of community among archaeologists. To be effective participants in the development and implementation of public policy in the 1980's and beyond, individual voices must demonstrate that they represent a significant constituency with coherent values and directions. Thus, a situationist ethical stance requires the development of more coherent statements of desired archaeological policies and programs *within* the archaeological community before such are presented for negotiation among competing interests in the halls of Congress and the Administration. Community recognition of the need for such rapprochement has been developing recently; examples include the informal organization of a Coordinating Council of National Archaeological Societies and the ad hoc "Report of the Conference on the Future of Archaeology" from an April 1982 meeting in Minneapolis (Wildesen 1982). It is an ethical necessity to develop in-group consensus, so that public policy positions are truly representative of archaeological community values when presented outside that community.

Archaeologists as Individual Participants in Public Policy Development and Implementation

The basic principles posited at the beginning of this essay are common to the archaeological community. However, the ethical strategies and tactics used by a practitioner to effect those goals must vary pragmatically depending on the practitioner's specific job or role at any given moment. For instance, an archaeologist in a senior administrative position in a federal agency accepts with the job contract the responsibility to carry out Administration policy as that is defined at the highest administrative level. The federal archaeologist who has learned to operate effectively within the bureaucracy will have frequent opportunities to use that expertise and credibility to affect senior policy decisions about archaeological resources, and often will be able to be an informal liaison between the bureaucracy and the nongovernmental archaeological community.

Academic archaeologists, whether oriented toward basic or applied research and service, are part of the "invisible sector" (Gardner 1981: 33) of nonprofit institutions which has more opportunity to provide independent policy leadership. That sector's emphasis on individual initiative and responsibility is strong for the development of professional community leadership, as reflected in the presidential roster of the Society for American Archaeology. At the same time, the emphasis on individualism and research may not select for the attributes and experience necessary to lead a community toward broad consensus and political pragmatism. In complement, cliental archaeologists from the private sector may be more knowledgeable about the anthropology of other interests and about the practical solutions to perceived conflicts. Each of these varying roles provides constraints and opportunities for the political activism of individual archaeologists, a basic context within which personal traits and interests must function.

In the long run, up-front political leadership of the archaeological community probably must come from those who have relatively less economic reliance on competing interests, yet who also have a thorough understanding and appreciation of those interests so as to be able to make pragmatic, relative decisions about policy directions and provide active representation of community interests. Such a leader can present an ethical posture that identifies with the ideal goals of the archaeological community. However, leadership functions only when supported by a coherent community stance, and the latter is the accumulation of individuals who have thought through ethical decisions about public policy and participated in the melding of individual perspectives into a group position.

Specific Ways of Participating in Public Decision Making

The individual archaeologist is responsible for two decision-making activities: (1) participation in the development of intracommunity positions and (2) support of these positions among nonarchaeologists. Both activities are most effective if they are oriented to long-term goals and take into account the validity of competing interests (i.e., the situations within which decisions are made).

There are a number of ways individual archaeologists can participate in the development of public policy:

1. Join one or more professional or avocational archaeological societies and participate in the development of their position statements.
2. Keep informed about current events, through networks such as the Society for Historic Archaeology Newsletter, or the Society for American Archaeology's Committee on Public Archaeology.
3. When federal regulations, guidelines, and/or standards for the conduct of archaeological work are published in draft for public review (in the *Federal Register*), review those drafts and provide comment to the responsible agency as well as the society leadership.
4. When legislation that affects archaeological resources is under review (e.g, National Science Foundation appropriations, historic preservation authorizations), write and/or call House Representatives and Senators. In general, keep in touch with their offices and make them aware of archaeological interests.
5. When conducting publically supported archaeological research, recognize that all such activity involves public policies and goals, not just individual interests. Seek out opportunities to interact with representatives of other interest groups who compete for funds and administrative personnel; learn more about their concerns and priorities, and discuss with them the reasonable and pragmatic goals of archaeology.

An Historical Perspective on Ethical Decision Making and the Politics of Archaeology

As prehistorians, historians, and/or anthropologists with a diachronic perspective on understanding human activities and behaviors, it is appropriate for us to review our historic involvement in the development of public policies of resource protection and management. The following review will look at several historic points of ethical decision making in public policy to identify (1) the archaeological goal; (2) opposition to it, if any; and (3) the compromises necessary to reconcile the goal and the opposition.

Pre-1975 Political Activism

During the first three-quarters of this century, strong public protection of archaeological resources was established in federal laws and programs—almost in a vacuum of concerted political action by a national archaeological community. Programs were developed piecemeal, prior to the development of a coherent and explicit ethic of public responsibility for archaeological materials and in lieu of significant competition by other interest groups for the same dollars. The original perspective on preservation tended to be elitist, focusing on the best examples of architecture and artifacts; this has gradually matured into the concept of a broad scientific and humanistic resource base meriting consideration. Leadership was provided on an individual basis, first from faculty members and researchers in the few graduate programs in archaeology that had been established at major educational institutions, and later from archaeologists involved in publicly funded (non-NSF) programs.

The history of the Antiquities Act of 1906 (34 Stat. 225) is best presented by Lee (1970). That legislation was first introduced to Congress in 1882, with a petition identifying the goal as the preservation of antiquities and ruins "as they furnish invaluable data for the ethnological studies now engaging the attention of our most learned scientific, antiquarian, and historical students" (Lee 1970: 10). The recognition of the general public nature of such scientific information was undoubtedly implicit in the archaeological position statements on the various bills that were drafted in this 24-year campaign, but the stated goal was consistently limited to scientific value. The mechanism for protection was withdrawal from public sale, complemented by government-regulated permits for scientific excavation of withheld sites. Competition developed as people interested in establishing a national park system saw the withdrawal mechanism as a means of reserving lands for public recreational use. At the same time, a major political faction did not want to see the public lands "locked up" in large parks, since large forest reserves had only recently been taken out of the private domain. Lee's description of the legislative history of the Antiquities Act of 1906 does not suggest that the archaeological community had any stake either in seeing the reserved areas identified as parks or in having the former include large areas; hence, it was not really a compromise to accept the concept of small national monuments as antiquarian reserves. The specific goal of site protection was achieved with minimal compromise because it encountered no basic conflict.

Guthe (1952) and Brew (1962) have provided a brief description of the development of public archaeological programs during the 1930's. These involved relatively large archaeological rescue programs supported by public dollars, thereby implementing the basic goals of cultural conservation as set forth in this essay and elsewhere in this volume. There were no broad Congressional statements of public policy underlying these funded program activities, however. Conflicts with economic development, especially water projects, were real but were not perceived to be contests; archaeological resources merited some protection, but not expensive protection that would be in any way commensurate with the real scientific or humanistic value of the resources. The public perception of the need for flood control and water resource development was so overriding as to discount most other interests. Thus, the development of Civil Works Administration archaeological projects and the Tennessee Valley Authority salvage program in 1933–1934, and subsequent Public Works or Works Progress Administrations in the late 1930's, received some scientific guidance from the National Research Council (NRC) and the Smithsonian Institution (Guthe 1952: 5–6) but no explicit Congressional authorization of the merits of archaeology. Throughout the 1930's, archaeologists worked toward their goal of scientific data conservation by making pragmatic decisions about the use of public funds and resources without debating national priorities. The competition for money, under a time constraint, made such debates moot. At the same time, the Historic Sites Act of 1935 was sponsored by preservationists concerned about the built environment, apparently without consideration of its interrelationship with archaeological resources or support from the archaeological community. An implicit ethical decision was being made to deny the broader context of archaeological resources. However, it was during this period (1935) that the Society for American Archaeology was founded "to promote and to stimulate interest and research in the archaeology of the American continents; to encourage a more rational public appreciation of the aims and limitations of archaeological research" (Society for American Archaeology 1974: 669).

The two decades following World War II were a period of extensive national development of reservoirs, highways, and pipelines, and eventually led to the first Congressional mandates for a policy of archaeological conservation since the turn of the century. The impetus for this mandate, which came from an alliance of archaeological researchers and Administration construction agency staff, solidified in the 1940's after the experiences of Depression-Era public archaeology.

Administrative recognition of the need for a more coherent national program for archaeological data recovery was apparent in a meeting of representatives of the Corps of Engineers, Bureau of Reclamation, Smithsonian Institution, and Department of the Interior (National Park Service) at the Bureau of the Budget in July 1945, at which "It was the consensus that archaeological salvage work was a legitimate concern of the Federal Government, that appropriations for the work could properly be requested by the construction agencies, and that the salvage work should be handled by the National Park Service and the Smithsonian Institution (Lehmer 1971: 7)." This consensus was undoubtedly strongly influenced by communications between professional archaeologists such as those in the Society for American Archaeology and those on the Committee for the Recovery of Archaeological Remains (CRAR, established by the American Council of Learned Societies and the Society for American Archaeology), and construction agency administrators—a very pragmatic and ethical way of affecting political decisions and programs. A 1947 ruling from the Bureau of the Budget (Lehmer 1971: 7) underscored the lack of legislative authority for the financing mechanism of this program by instructing the construction agencies to fall back on authorities of the Historic Sites Act of 1935 to support the salvage work. However, none of the archaeological community during this period, including the members of CRAR, appeared oriented toward acquiring a broad archaeological preservation mandate from Congress. Archaeologists did go to Congress for appropriations to support the program, but not for strong authorization. Individual scholars were accustomed to using face-to-face personal interactions to reach what were truly national goals, just as the archaeological community was accustomed to working under charity conditions. Perhaps the lack of a strong perception of the national public cultural value of archaeological information beyond its scientific research interests supported the acceptance of lack of financial support for resource protection and management programs. There was apparently no perceived need for a Congressional policy statement.

Reliance on face-to-face administrative solutions to national archaeological conservation needs continued into the early 1950's, with considerable success. Throughout this period archaeological practitioners and administrators within and outside of federal agencies were articulating an ethic of the national relevance of the archaeological information base as expressed in the basic proposition of this essay. They were not making it explicit in broad national forums or in Congress, but they were implementing it. For instance, in the early 1950's Jesse Nusbaum, the Consulting Archaeologist for the U.S. Department of the Interior, negotiated with El Paso Natural Gas Company for its support of salvage of the archaeological resources on USDI-administered lands that were endangered by the company's proposed pipeline construction. Based on USDI and company readings of the Antiquities Act of 1906, it was agreed that the company had a responsibility to preserve the information value of resources it affected on public lands (Wendorf 1962: 48–50). Further, in 1955 the Federal Power Commission began to require that archaeological resources affected by private dam construction involving public land or license be surveyed and salvaged (Wendorf 1962: 39). Public policies about archaeological values were being developed almost on a case-by-case basis, relatively apart from the scenes of Congressional policy making and in lieu of significant economic competition by individual archaeologists who shared an ethic of public concern.

But economic and political competition was rapidly becoming more complex, and a new generation of archaeologists began to participate in publicly funded archaeology and in a new approach to an archaeological resource base rather than to individual important sites (Wendorf 1962: 82). It is notable that many of these archaeological activists were not residents in major academic or research programs, which tended to disdain the public ethic as it was developed. Professional archaeological participation in the promulgation of authorizing federal archaeological legislation was reinstituted for the first time since 1906 with the successful efforts to add preservation-enabling language to the Federal-Aid Highway Act of 1956 (72 Stat. 913). That legislative statement began with a casual conversation at a service club luncheon—a typical face-to-face personal communication that established an alliance of concerns. This account and others that follow point out the importance of casual conversations and other incidences that might seem to be of little consequence at the time.

In 1953, at a service club luncheon speech describing the success of the archaeological salvage program for El Paso Natural Gas Company in New Mexico, program director Fred Wendorf mentioned the concomitant destruction of archaeological sites during the building of U.S. 66 near Gallup. Sitting in the luncheon audience were two important highway department personnel: C. O. (Pete) Irwin, the New Mexico Chief Highway Engineer, and W. J. (Spike) Keller, the New Mexico engineer for the Federal Bureau of Public Roads. Postluncheon discussions led to the development of a federally run New Mexico highway salvage program in 1954. At the same time the U.S. Forest Service in New Mexico began a program of highway salvage, complementing both the USDI's requirements for pipeline salvage and the New Mexico highway program. A 1955 challenge for payment of a U.S. Forest Service salvage project was reviewed by the U.S. Comptroller General;

Wendorf (1982: personal communication) has provided this summary of the ensuing decision and legislation:

> It turned out, however, that the head of the federal highway agency at that time, a man named C. D. Curtis, was also interested in archaeology and of course he knew the Solicitor General and arranged for me to have a personal interview to plead my case. We wound up on a very important decision (which is reproduced in Wendorf 1962: 97–99). It was the first direct statement that federal funds for construction projects could and should be used to preserve our historical heritage. C. D. Curtis then suggested, because as he said "Solicitor General's opinions can be changed," that we provide a more permanent base for archaeological salvage on highways by including archaeology in the Federal Aid Highway Act of 1956 which was then in the process of being drafted. With the help of Spike Keller and Pete Irwin, the New Mexico Congressional delegation got behind this idea (Senator Chavez was chairman of the public works committee and John Dempsey was the vice chairman of the house public works committee—thus we had important leverage). It was arranged that the staff would call me and I would provide the language which was to be written into the bill, which I did. It was at this point that a special committee for highway salvage archaeology was authorized by the Society for American Archaeology with me as chairman. We set about organizing a national effort to support including archaeology in the federal highway bill. . . .

Of course, it passed with the federal highway bill and the program got under way.

This description of the 1956 legislation is typical of the campaigns for passage of the Reservoir Salvage Act of 1960 (74 Stat. 220) and the Archaeological and Historic Preservation Act of 1974 ("Moss-Bennett," P.L. 93–291 [88 Stat. 174]). Individual archaeologists (e.g., J. O. Brew, Carl Chapman, Richard D. Daugherty, Charles R. McGimsey, III, Raymond Thompson) with personal ties to individual Congressional offices and with strong concerns about public archaeological policy provided leadership in developing campaigns for stronger authorizing legislation for a national archaeology program. They worked with small committees within the Society for American Archaeology and the Committee for the Recovery of Archaeological Remains, and all relied on a strong Congressional sponsor to move the legislation through the House and Senate without having to demonstrate broad grassroots support for the bills. The ethical goal was the implementation of a national program of archaeological resource preservation; the competition was relatively muted since the reservoir, pipeline, and highway salvage programs had been in place in some areas for years; and the negotiations were still minimal.

The goal was still relatively limited, however—while there was a consideration of a broad archaeological resource base, including small lithic scatters as well as deeply stratified sites or those with striking prehistoric architecture, the focus was on salvage of archaeological remains rather than participation in an ethic of preservation of a wider cultural heritage. The Wilderness Act of 1964 (78 Stat. 890), with its definition of wildernesses as lands "untrammeled by man" (Sec. 2[c]) was passed after a 10-year campaign that had not piqued the interest of archaeologists. The National Historic Preservation Act of 1966 (80 Stat. 915) was passed with the deliberate noninvolvement of the archaeological community (King et al. 1977: 34–35), though the Society for American Archaeology did have a committee reviewing the legislation. The Housing and Urban Development Act of 1966 (80 Stat. 1279), the Wild and Scenic Rivers Act of 1968 (82 Stat. 906), the National Trails System Act of 1968 (82 Stat. 919), the National Environmental Policy Act of 1969 (83 Stat. 852), and the Forest and Rangeland Renewable Resourcs Planning Act of 1974 (88 Stat. 476) received no attention from the archaeological community until after they were passed. There was no broad understanding of the significance of these programs in the conservation or destruction of thousands of prehistoric and historic archaeological resources in cities, forests, and the area of any federally permitted development project. During these years each of these programs developed its own constituency and its own articulate interest group, and the competition began to increase for the allocation of scarcer federal and private dollars and priorities. Each of these interest groups had its own ethical posture, and the statements of these postures often conflicted with a preservation ethic at first encounter.

Post-1975 Political Activism

The mid-1970's marked a threshold in the development and implementation of public archaeological policy and, hence, in the manner in which archaeologists ethically participate in such decision making. By that time, the Moss-Bennett legislation was beginning to be implemented, and the U.S. Department of the Interior's Interagency Archaeological Services was beginning to influence many other federal agencies. The regulations supporting Section 106 of the National Historic Preservation Act were published and required compliance; the National Environmental Policy Act was being implemented across many federal agencies; E.O. 11593 required federal land-management agencies to complete broad surveys of their prehistoric and historic archaeological and architectural resources. All of these had to be integrated with the requirements of the plethora of planning laws that Congress was passing, which not only authorized but required federal agencies to plan how they were going to allocate their budgetary and personnel resources among competing resource management issues. The Federal Land Policy and Management Act of 1976 (90 Stat. 2743), the National

Forest Management Act of 1976 (90 Stat. 2949), the Surface Mining Control and Reclamation Act of 1977 (91 Stat. 445), and the Soil and Water Resources Conservation Act of 1977 (91 Stat. 1407) set goals and priorities for managing a multifaceted resource base of both renewable and nonrenewable entities, and archaeologists found themselves in the middle of the competition.

How have we archaeologists handled our political decisions since 1975? There have been two basic ways; one relies more on individual archaeologists' interests and personal ties to agencies and Congress, and the other relies more on individuals backed up by strong national grassroots support. In most cases, significant compromises with other interests have had to be negotiated and accepted. Let us look at three cases in completing our historical review of archaeological political ethics.

The Archaeological Resources Protection Act of 1979 (93 Stat. 721) began with a strong push from concerned individual archaeologists. Steven LeBlanc, Dee F. Green, and Raymond Thompson were all very upset by the government's inability to get significant prosecutions under the Antiquities Act of 1906, in the midst of increased commercial looting of sites in the Southwest. Thus, they committed themselves to the passage of a stronger legislative statement of a national archaeological policy. Archaeologists had recently campaigned for reauthorization for funding of the Moss-Bennett program and hence had strong supporters among both staff and members of the House and Senate Interior Committees. The concerned archaeologists were the first drafters of the proposed legislation; they worked without any agency or organization sponsorship, but they readily received support for their legislative campaign from the Society for American Archaeology, the Society of Professional Archaeologists, the American Society for Conservation Archaeology, and the newly formed Coordinating Council of National Archaeological Societies (CCONAS). Archaeologists did not solicit support for ARPA from other elements of the historic preservation community, as they perceived the matter more narrowly. The legislation ran into some serious competition from commercial collectors and treasure hunters (including the metal detector industry), and negotiations between the competing interests had to be negotiated by Congressional staff members in consultation with the archaeological leadership. To reach the goal of generally stronger protection, the original drafters of the legislation had to accept (1) a definition of "archaeological" materials which excluded materials less than 100 years old (a 50-year-old threshold had been requested); (2) a definition of archaeological resources that did not explicitly discuss "context"; (3) exclusion of the surface collection of arrowheads as a criminal activity; (4) allowance of permitting authority to a governor rather than to the federal land-management agency; and (5) more explicit consultation with Native Americans. In return, the legislation provided a legally defensible definition of "archaeological resources," strong criminal penalties, and the opportunity to sue for civil damages. The legislative campaign solicited broad grassroots support through personal networks, CCONAS, and the Society for American Archaeology's *Committee on Public Archaeology* and *COPA Communications*, which provided a timely newsletter soliciting review comments. A significant portion of the national archaeological community commented on the various drafts of the legislation and supported its passage with letters to Congress. At the same time, the individuals who had first drafted the legislation—who had the personal contacts and credibility with the Congressional staff, and who had committed a significant amount of their personal and professional time to the passage of the legislation—also had the final responsibility of accepting the compromises listed above.

Passage of the Archaeological Resources Protection Act (ARPA) of 1979 was based on the development of a true national archaeological constituency, was oriented toward the protection of a broad resource base rather than individual sites alone, and matured in a milieu of legislative negotiation and compromise. It still came down to the ethics, credibility, and efforts of the individual archaeological supporters to get it passed.

A final example of ethical decisions in recent archaeological public policy making is the passage of the National Historic Preservation Act Amendments of 1980, drafted by Congressman John Seiberling (D-OH), who had been one of the major supporters of ARPA. The bill was a major restatement of the 1966 act; it codified the participation of State Historic Preservation Officers in the federal historic preservation program as well as the survey and evaluation mandate of E.O. 11593, and it reauthorized the Historic Preservation Fund for another five years. The original wording was developed by the more traditional historic preservation community and was oriented more toward the historic built environment, with little sensitivity to archaeological resource base implications.

The involvement of archaeologists in the drafting of the bill and the campaign for its passage was a logical development of the political awareness of the archaeological community through the last three decades. There was strong individual concern and leadership in developing a national position on the legislation; there was strong support by the national archaeological societies (particularly the SAA in its support for a Legislative Coordinator) through the Coordinating Council of National Archaeological Societies; and there was nationwide grassroots support through Communications and Alerts of the SAA's Committee on Public Archaeology.

In working for passage of the 1980 amendments, the archaeological leadership closely coordinated its efforts with those of the National Trust on Historic Preservation, the National Conference of State Historic

Preservation Officers, and Preservation Action (a national lobbying network) to develop a statement that represented a broad heritage conservation perspective. The ethic of cultural conservation, as stated in the beginning of this essay, achieved explicit formulation and acceptance. While the National Conference, the National Trust, and Preservation Action were negotiating with the Conference of Mayors and League of Cities about the impact of the proposals on local preservation programs, the archaeologists had long conversations with the National Forest Products Association, the National Cattleman's Association, the American Mining Congress, and especially the representatives of Western states with vast public lands. The archaeologists translated the goal of historic conservation into a cultural resource management program acceptable to other resource management interests by setting forth the ethic postures of public responsibility presented herein. A general goal was shared by all elements of the broad heritage conservation community, but each special interest within that community had to make an effort to keep the attention on the goal and not get lost in problems of terminology (e.g., "archaeological properties" versus "historic properties").

When testimony was needed in House and Senate hearings, there was broad representation from across the archaeological and historic architectural communities, and from the folklife preservationists. Throughout the campaign, the archaeological community consistently matured in its understanding of its responsibilities in participating in the development of public policies affecting the cultural heritage resource base. Archaeologists across the country participated by writing letters, making telephone calls, and getting out votes for the bill's passage in subcommittee or committee. Some became personally acquainted with the staff of their Senator or Representative, or even with the Congressperson. All of these efforts further articulated and implemented the ethics of public participation.

There was a point of competition in the development of the National Historic Preservation Act Amendments of 1980 that exemplifies the ethical propositions presented herein. In mid-September 1980, prior to markup of the bill by the House Interior Committee's Subcommittee on National Parks and Insular Affairs, opposition arose to the then-present ability to nominate properties to the National Register of Historic Places without the consent of the property's owner. Under the federal tax laws as they were then written, there could be significant tax penalties or disincentives for the demolition or major modification of properties listed on the National Register of Historic Places. At the same time, there were numerous instances of the Register nomination of privately owned historic buildings by state review committees without notification or consent of the private owners, who later suffered a tax penalty if they did not conform to the protection guidelines. Some believed that these Register practices jeopardized the traditional American concept of the sanctity of property ownership, as supported by Constitutional limits on governmental authority to regulate the use of privately owned property without paying compensation to the owners (the "taking issue" [Bosselman et al. 1973]). At the same time, those tax penalties provided significant protection for historic properties that contribute to the overall architectural heritage of our nation. In the closing days of the 95th Congress, a line was drawn and the either/or decision was made by the opposition—either negotiate this issue or lose the bill. Since the bill had to pass on a "unanimous consent" calendar due to its late scheduling, there were few options.

The solution was to limit the ability to nominate privately held properties to the National Register of Historic Places when owners actively objected, but to preserve the ability to determine a privately held property eligible for such nomination in lieu of the owner's consent. Thus, the proscription against federal undertakings' adversely affecting sites on *or eligible for* the National Register was retained, which was judged to be the more important aspect of federal management of prehistoric and historic archaeological and architectural resources in the long term.

Summary and Conclusion

Over the past century, the ethics of archaeologists' participation in the development and implementation of public policy appears to have changed little. That is, the ethical position has been consistent, though there have been changes in how we have carried out those ethics. The decisions have been generally consistent with a situation ethics approach though not explicitly understood as such. They certainly have been pragmatic. Until the last decade or so there has been relatively little open competition for the economic resources needed to conduct archaeological salvage programs, or general planning and management projects. At the same time, archaeologists have been rather inarticulate about the importance of archaeological resources in a broad value of conserving our cultural heritage. Until recently most have not believed it appropriate to invest significant amounts of money in salvage or protection programs. Prior to the 1970's archaeologists developing public policies were able to work successfully within the Congressional system as individuals or small cadres of people. With the growing complexity of Congress and the Administration, that is no longer possible—individuals are still the key, but they must be backed by an identifiable, credible, coherent constituency to have entree to or affect the system. We still can and must shape public policy about the management of archaeological resources; if archaeologists do not participate in this policy and program development, others will.

27

Concluding Remarks

Ernestene L. Green

THE CONCLUSION to a book on ethics can take at least two forms. It can be a list of caveats—don't intentionally destroy data, don't knowingly harm a colleague, do one's best to protect the resource—or it can focus on major issues raised in the text. This conclusion takes the latter route, reviewing the ethical concerns most critical to the profession today. Following the outline of the book, they are divided into responsibilities to the profession and responsibilities to the public.

As the historical and comparative background provided in the first essay demonstrates, archaeology is not the only discipline to wrestle with problems of professional ethics; nor is it the only one to see changes over time in critical issues. Wildesen's and Davis's essays identified an important question for the profession: To whom are we accountable? We are currently using two systems of ethical accountability. The more traditional one is the guild system, or "band of brethren," whereby we are accountable to ourselves rather than to a formal organization. Professional responsibilities are transmitted to the next generation verbally, and the ethical structure is not formalized as a written code or set of standards.

Without abandoning the traditional system, in the past decade we also have begun to implement a more formal structure, consisting of a written code of ethics and standards of performance (see third, fourth, and fifth essays in this volume). Those who have publically endorsed the code and standards by joining SOPA have made themselves accountable to the society and its members for maintaining these standards. At this time one cannot predict whether the two systems will merge, continue to operate simultaneously, or whether one will supercede the other. However, experience has shown the pitfalls of using an accountability system based in one milieu (i.e., academia) to guide our actions in another (i.e., business/government).

A basic question that has bedeviled both the physical and social sciences is: Can scientific endeavors be separated from our system of ethics and values, or does the latter at least in part determine the direction and approach of our investigations? Winter concludes that humans cannot separate their moral codes and values from scientific research and that therefore it is essential to understand how our values affect our investigations. First we must identify our values in our research imperatives.

As archaeology has expanded out of the academic world, it has faced a number of ethical dilemmas related to resource management in government and business. Fragmentation into research interests and resource management is a critical concern to the profession today.

A basic issue here is: To whom do we owe our loyalties, to the discipline or to the client for whom the work is performed? This dilemma is not unique to archaeology. Although the opinions expressed in this volume vary, none excludes responsibility to the discipline. As Raab indicates, the prevailing feeling is that the appropriate behavior is to serve both the client and the discipline—good archaeology is the best product for the client. From an ethical perspective, this is certainly the best approach, and it is often possible. But as Fitting points out, what choice do we make when the client's interests differ from or conflict with those of good archaeology? The appropriate actions depend on the specifics of the situation, but a guiding principle should be to avoid action that sacrifices significant resources in any way. The ethical decision in such a case would be loyalty to the discipline.

Research design, site selection, and significance determinations were considered in the light of ethical responsibilities. A theme that ran through all of the essays on these topics was the "conservation ethic." It is surprising how rapidly the concept of conservation has been accepted since its first introduction in the literature (Lipe 1974). The conservation ethic states that, insofar as it is possible, the resource should be preserved for future use rather than being impacted now by any disturbance (i.e., archaeological excavation as well as disturbance by land-management activity).

Several factors have combined during the past decade to foster the rapid and wide acceptance of the conservation model. Because of land modification projects and vandalism, the resource base has been disappearing more quickly during the past 30 years than ever before. Also during this period, there has been a great deal of change in both the kinds of questions asked about the data and in the techniques of extracting, analyzing, and interpreting them. We have become impressed with the need to save the resource base for future investigations.

The concept of conservation is integrated into most aspects of archaeology today. For example, it is the basis of several of Plog's criteria for selecting a site for excavation and is essential to the ethics of contract archaeology, as Fowler discusses. Dunnell integrates the conservation model into his discussion of significance. On this matter, at least, there is general agreement. Conservation of the resource is a professional responsibility and a widely accepted archaeological ethic.

During the past couple of decades, there has been increasing emphasis on problem orientation and research design to guide the collection, analysis, and interpretation of archaeological data. There is general agreement that, if the project is generated for archaeological research purposes, it would be professionally unethical not to proceed according to a research design. This approach to research is so prevalent today that several professional societies include the provision in their guidelines of professional responsibilities. (See "Toward an Understanding of the Ethics and Values of Research Design in Archaeology," in this volume.) Traditionally, this approach begins with definition of a research problem; next the research is designed or planned; finally, promising locations are selected for investigation.

Coincident with the increasing emphasis on research design has been the growth of cultural resource management as a subfield within the discipline. There are at least two foci of agency management of cultural resources. One is the location and management of cultural sites for their own value. Another is the protection of resources already selected for, and therefore possibly threatened by, land-management projects. In the latter case, the survey and investigation of the cultural data are dependent upon work generated by other management projects. Areas for survey are not selected according to a research design. The same principle applies to sites found during the survey. If the sites must be salvaged, this work is generated by other management requirements, not by an archaeological research project.

This process raises several ethical issues. Can the problem-orientation/research-design approach be effectively applied to cultural resource management? Is it ethical to do so, or not to do so?

Two opposing opinions are expressed in this volume. Raab argues that all archaeological work, including that in cultural resource management, should be planned and guided by a research design. Not to do so, he maintains, would be unprofessional and unethical. This is the opinion most often expounded in the profession today.

Dunnell states that, since cultural resource management projects are generated by agency demands rather than research problems, this work cannot be problem-oriented in the current scientific sense. To pretend that it is, Dunnell maintains, is a sham and unethical. He suggests that the purpose of a cultural resource management project should be to yield a representative sample of the data in the area of investigation.

Resolution of this issue lies in differentiating among kinds of agency projects. Occasionally a land-management agency will decide that, in order to manage cultural resources for their scientific values, it needs a study of the research values of these sites. A problem-oriented, designed research project should emerge. An example is the Chevlon project in the Apache-Sitgreaves National Forest (Plog, this volume). Unfortunately, work of this kind is scarce, especially in these days of reduced budgets.

Some projects generated by land-management activities involve thousands of acres. Examples include dams/reservoirs such as the current Dolores Project in Colorado and defense constructions such as the MX Project and other special one-time projects (Fowler, this volume). In my opinion, archaeological investigations of such large acreages can be designed to focus on one or more research questions and a research design to guide the work can be written. True, the first step here is an agency decision to proceed with a project, but the data from large acreages will bear upon numerous potential research problems. With a knowledge of the archaeology of the area and the kinds of resources that the land contains, research questions can be identified and the work designed to address these problems. This approach is practical and desirable for agency management; it would seem unethical not to follow it.

The real dilemma concerns projects involving small parcels, the location of which is determined by agency activities. Examples include land exchanges, road construction, small timber sales, and range projects. Often small pipelines and transmission lines also fall into this category. Many of these projects are in the sampling mode described by Dunnell. The only way they can be related to a research problem is to be subsumed under a preconceived research framework. This approach is being used now by some agency units (e.g., the Southwest Region of the Forest Service).

Perhaps the most wrenching ethical challenge in archaeology today is posed by the legal requirement to determine the significance of sites on public land. If a site is not deemed significant it will probably be destroyed eventually by construction activity. Coupled with this is the difficulty of evaluating significance from surface data and the knowledge that advances in the field may make seemingly unimportant material very valuable in the future. These considerations often result in a conservative interpretation of significance—when in doubt, call the site significant. Such interpretation can lead to mistrust by managerial officials who have become aware that almost any site can be judged significant.

Several authors suggest solutions to this problem. Dunnell points out that much of the problem lies in a change over time in the framework used to assess values. Legal documents are grounded in humanistic values rather than the scientific values so prevalent in archaeology today. Dunnell feels that significance decisions should be seen as sampling decisions because they determine which element of the record will survive. Rather than develop research questions to judge a resource's significance, he would preserve a certain percentage of each kind of resource.

Expressing the more traditional approach, Plog lists two criteria to consider in significance evaluations: the quantity of the particular kind of site, and the amount of previous investigation. Like others in this volume, he specifies that research questions should be formulated before data recovery and that the investigator should state beforehand what kind of information would be considered significant.

A basic problem with this approach is that it is hard to construct any but the most general research problems in areas of little previous investigation. Fron the perspective of traditional archaeology, sampling is the logical first step. Only after the data are available can research questions be formulated and significance statements framed. The second step, then, is construction of a framework for future significance evaluations.

The essays on economics and contracts examined special problems connected with the business of archaeology. As archaeology has expanded out of the academic world, it has faced a number of new ethical dilemmas. Indeed, Fitting feels that economic issues are the source of most ethical controversies in the discipline.

Intentionally not reporting sites located by a survey or understating their significance is a falsification of data that deserves special mention because of its potential occurrence in contracted work. When a development company or government agency supports a survey because of legal requirements only, the organization tends to view cultural resources as impediments to development. This attitude may be transmitted to the survey archaeologists. Though it is highly unethical, occasionally a field investigator has been more interested in pleasing the employer than in accurately stating the survey results.

The opposite—falsely overstating significance or reporting nonexistent sites—is equally unethical. The essays herein (Dee Green, Fowler, Fitting) indicate that this type of falsification is the more frequent one. Its usual purpose is to expand contracting profits by recommending unneeded work. Since the organization hiring the archaeological contractor usually lacks the in-house expertise to evaluate the specialist's recommendations, there is a conflict of interest for the contractor whose recommendations determine his or her future workload. We like to think that the profession polices itself against this practice. However, overestimates are difficult to prove because the transgressor can obscure the issue by claiming differences of professional judgment.

Fowler brings out another dilemma in contracted work. When a potential contractor knows that the technical specifications or scope of work for a project is inadequate, should he or she bid on the original stipulations or point out the inadequacies to the purchasing organization in the hope that changes will be made? The ethical behavior is not to bid knowingly on an inadequate scope of work. There are numerous cases in which the scope of work was altered by the contracting organization because a potential bidder pointed out problems. On the other hand, a contract is morally and legally binding. It is unethical for a contractor to agree to certain work for a specified price knowing that the bid is inadequate. There are also risks to accepting a contract with the unstated intention of requesting cost-overrun monies. Unless factors outside the archaeologist's control (such as weather) cause the overrun problems, it is likely that the contracting organization will require adequate completion of the designated work, even if the contractor loses money on the project.

Another current issue in archaeology concerns the increasing vandalism and looting of cultural sites. All archaeologists would agree that these activities are highly unethical, as is failure to report vandalism to the appropriate officials. As Dee Green points out, however, opinions about the appropiate penalties for vandalism and looting range widely.

In addition, there are questions of ethics regarding the archaeologist's role in an antiquities trial. Is it correct to assume, as most archaeologists do, that the defendant is guilty unless proven innocent? Does the defendant have the right to expert archaeological testimony, i.e., is it ethical for an archaeologist to counsel and testify for the defense? Is it ethical, as legal procedure requires, to give a monetary valuation to a site?

There are no cookbook steps to reach ethically correct answers to these questions, but there are some considerations and guidelines to help one decide on a course of action. Most archaeologists approach an antiquities trial with a biased mind—they have preconvicted the defendant. Archaeologists' emotions about the resource as well as the history of antiquities trials in the past 15 years are two reasons for the prejudice. Among land managers, archaeologists have the reputation of being more emotionally attached to the resource than any other specialist. This is understandable. Through years of training and experience, archaeologists have learned that interpretations are as good as the accuracy and completeness of the data; that the data are fragile and irreplaceable; and that time, weather, and human actions have already damaged the resource so that data are partial at best. Since vandalism and theft destroy the data further, and the loss is occurring at an increasingly rapid rate, it is understandable that archaeologists are biased against someone accused of destroying the resource base.

The history of antiquities trials further contributes to the prejudice against the defendant. The first well-known antiquities case (the Diaz case) was dismissed on a technicality, not because the defendant was innocent of theft. There are other instances in which charges were dismissed for the same reason, or because the judge or jury felt that, although illegal, pothunting was more like a recreation sport than a crime. In addition, federal agencies and the Department of Justice do not bring a case to trial today unless the evidence is so strong that there will be no question of guilt. This leads archaeologists to presume that a defendant is guilty, even though this is contrary to the presumption of innocence on which our justice system is founded.

Is it ethical for a professional to counsel the defense in an antiquities trial? Legal procedures are more complex than most archaeologists realize. The defense needs expert technical information about such things as the definition of a site and artifact, about the Archaeological Resources Protection Act, about archaeological field and laboratory procedures, and so on. It is quite possible for an archaeologist to provide this kind of information to defense lawyers without condoning the defendant's alleged crimes. In fact, there are instances in which the archaeological consultant to the defense, upon learning the facts, advised the defendant to plead guilty. Thus, each person must base his or her response to a defendant's request for legal assistance on the facts of the particular case and the nature of the request. Simply advising the defense does not imply that the archaeologist condones the alleged crime. Of course, testimony by an archaeologist in support of theft or vandalism of cultural resources is clearly unethical.

Is it unethical to put a dollar value on a site for the purpose of antiquities prosecution? Some archaeologists reason as follows: for scientific purposes, the site cannot be assigned a dollar value; since the purchase or sale of artifacts is unethical, an interest in the dollar value of artifacts is, at the least, not good form. The implied extension of this thought process is that placing a monetary valuation on sites is likewise not proper. Circumstances have changed in the past couple of decades. We now have the legal mechanisms to thwart theft and vandalism of cultural resources on federal land. Because the legal procedure, and, hence, the protection of resources require that a dollar valuation be made of the sites and artifacts, it is unethical *not* to estimate the monetary value of a site. To refuse to make such an estimate aids those who would destroy the resource.

Another change in the past few decades is the increase in the archaeologist's responsibilities to the public. There is a strong positive value today in bringing archaeology to the lay public. Archaeologists have moved from an almost exclusive focus on the profession and its practitioners to the realization that they need the public both to protect the resource and, ultimately, to foster the profession. (See Fagan, Frison, and McGimsey, this volume.)

One reason for the change has been the focus on public lands by legislative action and government management. Archaeologists have become used to the idea that archaeological resources on public lands belong to all Americans and are held in public trust. We increasingly feel a responsibility to inform the public about America's archaeological heritage. Second, archaeologists realize the long-term benefits of public involvement. For example, we call on the lay person to help protect sites from looting and vandalism; we encourage the public's help as advocates for the resource vis à vis land development and land-management activities; we seek lay benefactors as other funding sources decrease. Our ethical responsibility to the public is not limited to this country. As

Healy discusses, when we use the archaeological resources of another country, we have a responsibility to inform those citizens of the results of our investigations.

In this volume, "public" is used as a general term to refer to all non-archaeologists, including individual special-interest groups. The special-interest group that has made the most impact on archaeology recently is that of the Native American. With their increased political involvement during the 1970's, some Native Americans began to assert that excavation of Indian remains violated their religious ethics. This position came as a shock to archaeologists, as it threatened both the scientific ethic of freedom of inquiry and the source of most archaeological investigation in the United States. What emerged was a clash between two value structures.

Meighan points out that there is more than one opinion among Native Americans on this subject. Positions range from the extreme view that any excavation of any prehistoric or historic Indian materials is unethical, to the opposite view that archaeological work is not only acceptable but yields valuable information about a tribe's past. Most common is the intermediate stance, that the unearthing of burials and religious objects is unethical.

Likewise, there is a difference of opinion on the issue among archaeologists. Meighan mentions that at one time some archaeologists in California agreed with the extreme Indian position that excavation of any Native American remains is unethical. This would be rare among archaeologists today; for an archaeologist to agree to this position would be tantamount to forsaking the profession. There are two common ethical stances today.

The first states that, since a basic tenet of archaeological ethics is freedom of inquiry and preservation of data, to prevent investigation of any aspect of culture or to rebury excavated material before it is thoroughly studied violates professional ethics. Moreover, one special-interest group should not be allowed to destroy resources that belong to the heritage of all Americans. The second position, which grows out of situational ethics, is to agree to less than full investigation of all remains. (See Adams and Ferguson, this volume.) In order to be allowed to work on reservation land, some archaeologists agree to avoid burials and other (religious) materials, as specified by the host tribes. A variant is to avoid burials when they can be related to extant tribes.

If the alternative is no investigation, it is appropriate to adjust to accommodate the host's requirements, as long as the veracity of the interpretations is not compromised. In all the examples cited in this volume, particular classes of data were avoided, but the interpretations of the data were not directly compromised. Moreover, Indian hosts provided information about the history and use of artifacts which would never have been forthcoming if archaeologists had not been willing to accommodate to the demands of the situation and the wishes of the people involved. In summary, the long-held ethic of total freedom of investigation can legitimately be adjusted to meet certain specific circumstances without transgressing professional ethics.

Political action can be intimidating to archaeologists because it requires an unfamiliar set of skills and knowledge. Yet, recently, legislative action by a few professionals has resulted in benefits to the entire profession. Though no one would be censored for not participating in the legislative process, there is a positive value to reaching out to the public in this way.

The expansion of the discipline during the past few decades has witnessed an increasing diversity in archaeological ethics and values. Perhaps this volume will help to crystallize and focus some of the concerns so that we may come to grips with the issues that confront us today. It is hoped that this first volume on ethics in archaeology will not be the last, but rather, will serve to stimulate further discussion. We must decide whether we design the route or whether its curves and turns occur by happenstance.

References

ADAMS, R. E. W. (1974), Report of the Secretary: Native American-Archaeologists Relationships. *American Antiquity* 39:668.

ALLAND, A., Jr. (1967), *Evolution and Human Behavior*, The Natural History Press, Garden City.

American Anthropological Association (1973), *Professional Ethics*, Washington, D.C.

American Association of Museums (1973), Museum Association Makes Settlement on Human Remains. *Anthropology Newsletter* 14:9

—— (1978), Human Remains and Sacred Objects. *Museum News*, March–April 1978.

ANGEL, L. & SUCHEY, J. (1982), Proposed Resolution on Reburial. Typescript. American Academy of Forensic Science Anthropology Section.

Anonymous (1935), The Society for American Archaeology Organization Meeting. *American Antiquity* 1:141–151.

BANDELIER, A. F. (1881) Report on the Ruins of the Pueblo of Pecos. Papers of the Archaeological Institute of America 1:37–133.

—— (1892), Final Report of Investigations Among the Indians of the Southwestern United States. Papers of the Archaeological Institute of America 4:1–591.

BARBOUR, I. (1980), Paradigms in Science and Religion. In *Paradigms and Revolutions: Applications and Appraisals of Thomas Kuhn's Philosophy of Science*, ed. G. Gutting, University of Norte Dame Press, Notre Dame.

BARD, K. (1982), An Interview with Robert Horchow. *Early Man* 33.

BASTIDE, R. (1973), History of Applied Social Anthropology. In *Applied Anthropology*, by R. Bastide, Harper & Row. Reprinted in *Readings in Anthropology 77/78 Annual Editions*, The Dushkin Publishing Group, Inc., Guilford, Connecticut.

BEATTY, W. C., Jr. (n.d.), Report of Native American Reactions to Archaeological Investigations for the Kerckhoff Hydroelectric Project, Fresno and Madera Counties. MS. submitted to Pacific Gas and Electric Company, San Francisco, Laboratory of Archaeology, California State University, Fresno.

BENEDICT, R. (1946), *Patterns of Culture*, Houghton Mifflin, Boston.

BINFORD, L. R. (1962), Archaeology as Anthropology. *American Antiquity* 28:217–225. Reprinted in *An Archaeological Perspective*, by L. R. Binford, 1972:20–32, Seminar Press, New York.

—— (1964), A Consideration of Archaeological Research Design. *American Antiquity* 29:425–441. Reprinted in *An Archaeological Perspective*, by L. R. Binford, 1972:135–162, Seminar Press, New York.

BLALOCK, H. M., Jr. (1964), *Causal Inferences in Non-experimental Research*, University of North Carolina Press, Chapel Hill.

BOBROWSKY, P. T. (1982), Aggregation versus Reductionism in Cultural Resource Evaluation: Arguments in Favor of Site Integrity. In *Directions in Archaeology: A Question of Goals*, ed. P. D. Francis & E. C. Poplin, Archaeological Association of the University of Calgary, Calgary, Alberta.

BOSSELMAN, F. et al. (1973), *The Taking Issue*, Washington, D.C.: Council on Environmental Quality.

BREW, J. O. (1962), Introduction. In *A Guide for Salvage Archaeology*, by F. Wendorf, pp. 1–32, Museum of New Mexico Press, Sante Fe.

—— et al. (1947), Symposium on River Valley Archaeology. *American Antiquity* 12(4):209–225.

BRIM, J. A. & SPAIN, D. H. (1970), *Research Design in Anthropology*, Holt, Rinehart and Winston, New York.

BRUHNS, K. (1977), Seizure of Pre-Columbian Antiquities in San Francisco. Journal of Field Archaeology 4:460–462.

BUIKSTRA, J. E. (1981), A Specialist in Ancient Cemetery Studies Looks at the Reburial Issue. *Early Man* 3:26–27.

—— & GORDON, C. C. (1981), The Study and Restudy of Human Skeletal Series: The Importance of Long-Term Collection, *Annals of the New York Academy of Sciences* 376, New York Academy of Sciences.

BUMSTED, M. P. (1980), CRM and the Physical Anthropologist. *American Association for Conservation Archaeology Newsletter* 7(2).

BURCAW, G. E. (1975), *Introduction to Museum Work*, American Association for State and Local History, Nashville.

BURNHAM, B. (1974), *The Protection of Cultural Property. Handbook of National Legislations*, The International Council of Museums, Paris.

California Indian Legal Services (n.d.), Recommendations of the Luiseno Tribe Concerning Interstate 15's Archaeological Sites. Presented to Caltrans on June 17, 1977, Escondido, California.

CAMPBELL, D. T. & STANLEY, J. C. (1966), *Experimental and Quasi-Experimental Designs for Research*, Rand-McNally, Chicago.

Canadian Association of Physical Anthropologists (1979), Committee Report: Statement on the Excavation, Treatment, Analysis, and Disposition of Human Skeletal Remains from Archaeological Sites in Canada. *Canadian Review of Physical Anthropology* 1:32–36.

CARROLL, L. (1960), *The Annotated Alice's Adventures in Wonderland and Through the Looking Glass*, Clarkson N. Potter, Inc., New York.

CASSELL, J. (1980), Ethical Principles for Conducting Fieldwork. *American Anthropologist* 82:28–41.

CERAM, C. W. (1971), *The First Americans*, Alfred Knopf, New York.

CHALK, R. et al. (1980), *American Association for the Advancement of Science Professional Ethics Project: Professional Ethics Activities in the Scientific and Engineering Societies*, Washington, D.C.

CHAMPE, J. L. et al. (1961), Four Statements for Archaeology. *American Antiquity* 27:137–138.

CLARK, G. (1957), *Archaeology and Society*, Methuen and Co., London.

CLARY, D. A. (1978), Historic Preservation and Environmental Protection: The Role of the Historian. *The Public Historian* 1:61–75.

COCKRELL, W. A. (1980), The Trouble With Treasure—A Preservationist View of the Controversy. *American Antiquity* 45:333–339.

COGAN, M. L. (1955), The Problem of Defining a Profession. In *Ethical Standards and Professional Conduct*, ed. B. Y. Landis, *Annals of the American Academy of Political and Social Science* 297.

COLLINS, R. B. (1980), The Meaning Behind ARPA: How the Act is Meant to Work. Miscellaneous Paper No. 33, *Cultural Resources Report* 33, USDA Forest Service, Southwestern Region, Albuquerque.

Committee on Ethics and Standards (1961), Four Statements for Archaeology. *American Antiquity* 27:137–138.

Convention on the Means of Prohibiting and Preventing the Illicit Import, Export and Transfer of Ownership of Cultural Property (1976), *Journal of Field Archaeology* 3:217–224.

CORDELL, L. S. (1979), *A Cultural Resources Overview of the Middle Rio Grande Valley, New Mexico*, USDA Forest Service, Albuquerque.

Court of Appeals for the Sixth Circuit (1980), *Sequoyah* v. *TVA*. 620 F.2d 1164.

CUMMINGS, G. B. (1955), Standards of Professional Practice in Architecture. In *Ethical Standards and Professional Conduct*, ed. B. Y. Landis, *Annals of the American Academy of Political and Social Science* 297.

CUNLIFFE, B. (1981), Introduction: The Public Face of the Past. In *Antiquity and Man*, ed. J. Evans et al, Thames and Hudson, London.

DANCEY, W. S. (1981), *Archaeological Field Methods: An Introduction*, Burgess, Minneapolis.

DANIEL, GLYN E. (1950), *A Hundred Years of Archaeology*, Gerald Duckworth & Co., London.

—— (1967), *The Origins and Growth of Archaeology*, Galahad Books, New York.

DARWIN, C. (1876), *The Descent of Man*, D. Appleton and Co., New York.

DAVIS, H. A. (1972), The Crisis in American Archaeology. *Science* 175:257–272.

—— (1982), Professionalism in Archaeology. *American Antiquity* 47:158:162.

DEAVER, S. (n.d.), American Indian Religious Freedoms Act and Montana Archaeology. MS. Professional Analysts.

DEETZ, J. (1968), Cultural Patterning of Behavior as Reflected by Archaeological Materials. In *Settlement Archaeology*, ed. K. C. Chang, pp. 32–41, National Press, Palo Alto.

DEKEMA, J. (n.d.), Letter from District Director of Transportation to C. Meighan and other archaeologists relative to Highway 15 construction, Billings, Montana.

Dickens, R. S., Jr. & Hill, C. E. (1978), Cultural Resources: Planning and Management. *Social Impact Assessment Series* 2, Westview Press, Boulder, Colorado.

Dodd, L. C. & Schott, R. L. (1979), *Congress and the Administrative State,* Wiley & Sons, New York.

Dodge, W. A. & Ferguson, T. J. (1977), The Zuni Archaeological Enterprise: A New Concept in Conservation Archaeology. Paper presented at the 42nd Annual Meeting of the Society for American Archaeology, New Orleans.

Donaldson, B. et al. (1981), Three Out of Four Ain't Bad: Another Case of Cops 'n' Robbers. *Arizona Archaeological Council Newsletter* 5:13–16.

Drinker, H. S. (1955), Legal Ethics. In *Ethical Standards and Professional Conduct*, ed. B. Y. Landis, *Annals of the American Academy of Political and Social Science* 297.

Dunnell, R. C. (1981), Americanist Archaeology: The 1980 Literature. *American Journal of Archaeology* 85:429–445.

—— & Dancey, W. S. (1978), Assessment of Significance and Cultural Resource Management Plans. *American Society for Conservation Archaeology Newsletter* 5:2–7.

—— (1983), The Siteless Survey: A Regional Scale Data Collection Strategy. *Advances in Archaeological Method and Theory* 6.

Durkheim, E. (1933), *On the Division of Labor in Society*, Macmillan, New York.

Eriacho, W. & Ferguson, T. J. (1979), The Zuni War Gods, Artifact or Religious Beings: A Conflict in Values, Beliefs and Use. Paper presented at New Directions in Native American Art History, University of New Mexico, Albuquerque.

Evans, C. & Meggers, B. J. (1973), United States "Imperialism" and Latin American Archaeology. *American Antiquity* 38:257–258.

—— et al. (eds.) (1981), *Antiquity and Man*, Thames and Hudson, London.

Fairfax, S. R. (1980), Self-Preservation through Heritage Conservation: A Jaundiced View of HCRS Regulatory and Legislative Initiatives. Paper presented at the Western States Heritage Conference, Tucson.

Farb, P. (1968), *Man's Rise to Civilization as Shown by the Indians of North America from Primeval Times to the Coming of the Industrial State*, Dutton, New York.

Ferguson, T. J. (1979), Application of New Mexico State Dead Body and Indigent Burial Statutes to a Prehistoric Mummified Body. Paper presented at the 44th Annual Meeting of the Society for American Archaeology, Vancouver, Canada.

—— (1981a), Rebuttal Report, Prepared for the Pueblo of Zuni, *Zuni Indian Tribe* v. *United States*, Docket No. 161–79L, before the United States Court of Claims, Vol. I.

—— (1981b), The Emergence of Modern Zuni Culture and Society: A Summary of Zuni Tribal History, *A.D.* 1450–1700. In *Protohistoric Period in the North American Southwest, A.D. 1450–1700,* ed. D. R. Wilcox & W. B. Masse, Arizona State University Anthropological Research Paper 24, Tempe, Arizona.

—— (1981c), The American Indian Religious Freedom Act and Zuni

Pueblo. Paper prepared for the American Society for Ethno-History Annual Meeting, Colorado Springs.

FEWKES, J. W. (1896), Preliminary Account of an Expedition to the Cliff Villages of the Red Rock Country, and the Tusayan Ruins of Sikyatki and Awatobi, Arizona, in 1895. Smithsonian Institution, *Bureau of American Ethnology, Annual Report*, 1895, pp. 557–588, Washington, D.C.

—— (1898), Archaeological Expedition to Arizona in 1895. Smithsonian Institution, *Bureau of American Ethnology, Annual Report*, 22, part 1, Washington, D.C.

FEYERABEND, P. K. (1970), Consolations for the Specialist. In *Criticism and the Growth of Knowledge*, ed. I. Lakatos & A. Musgrave, Cambridge University Press, Cambridge.

FISHER, J. J. (1977), Archaeologists Hit Rich Vein of Federal Funds. *Kansas City Times,* April 11 (Part 1 of 4 parts; others published April 12, 13, and 14, 1977).

FITE, W. (1924), *Individualism,* Longmans, Green, and Co., New York.

FITTING, J. E. (1973), Plumbing, Philosophy, and Poetry. In *The Development of North American Archaeology*, ed. J. E. Fitting, Anchor Press/Doubleday, Garden City, New York.

—— (1978), Client-Oriented Archaeology: A Comment on Kinsey's Dilemma. *Pennsylvania Archaeologist* 48:12–15.

—— (1979a), Archaeological Research as Business. In *Scholars as Contractors,* ed. W. J. Mayer-Oakes & A. W. Portnoy, U.S. Department of the Interior, Heritage Conservation and Recreation Service, Washington, D.C.

—— (1979b), Comments on Types of Archaeology. In *Scholars and Contractors*, ed. W. J. Mayer-Oakes & A. W. Portnoy, Department of the Interior, Heritage Conservation and Recreation Service, Washington, D.C.

—— (1979c), Further Observations on Archaeology as a Business. In *Scholars as Contractors,* ed. W. J. Mayer-Oakes & A. W. Portnoy, Department of the Interior, Heritage Conservation and Recreation Service, Washington, D.C.

—— (1982), The New Melones Project: Murphy's Law in Operation. *Contract Abstracts and CRM Archaeology* 3(1):14–19.

—— (1984), Economics and Archaeology. In *Ethics and Values in Archaeology,* ed. E. L. Green, Free Press, New York.

FITTS, W. T., JR., & FITTS, B. (1955), Ethical Standards of the Medical Profession. In *Ethical Standards and Professional Conduct*, ed. B. Y. Landis, *Annals of the American Academy of Political and Social Science* 297.

FLANNERY, K. V. (1982), The Golden Marshalltown: A Parable for the Archaeology of the 1980's. *American Anthropologist* 84:265–278.

FLETCHER, J. (1966), *Situation Ethics, the New Morality*, The Westminister Press, Philadelphia.

FLEXNER, A. (1915), Is Social Work a Profession? *School and Society* 1:904.

FORD, J. L. et al. (1972), Site Destruction Due to Agricultural Practices. *Arkansas Archaeological Survey*, *Research Series* 3.

Fowler, D. D. (1982), Cultural Resource Management. *Advances in Archaeological Method and Theory* 5:1–50.

—— et al. (1980), *MX Cultural Resources Studies. Preliminary Research Design.* Woodward-Clyde Consultants, San Francisco.

Fowler, J. M. (1974), Protection of the Cultural Environment in Federal Law. In *Environmental Law*, ed. E. L. Dolgin & T. C. P. Gilbert, West Publishing Co., St. Paul, Minnesota, pp. 1466–1517.

Frazer, J. G. (1914), *The Golden Bough*, Macmillan, London.

French, L. & White, M. (n.d.), Cherokee Attitudes Toward the Use and Display of American Indian Artifacts.

Gardner, J. (1981), *Leadership: a Sampler of the Wisdom of John Gardner*, University of Minnesota, Hubert H. Humphrey Institute of Public Affairs, Minneapolis.

Gardner, M. (1960), Introduction and Notes. In *The Annotated Alice, Alice's Adventures in Wonderland and Through the Looking Glass*, Clarkson N. Potter, Inc., New York.

Gladwin, H. S. et al. (1937), *Excavations at Snaketown: Material Culture.* Medallion Papers 25, Globe, Arizona.

Glassow, M. A. (1977), Issues in Evaluating the Significance of Archaeological Resources. *American Antiquity* 42:413–420.

Glueck, G. (1981), Hoving Tells of Adventure for the Met, *The New York Times*, Monday, September 28.

Goodyear, A. C. et al. (1978), The Status of Archaeological Research Design in Cultural Resource Management. *American Antiquity* 43:159–173.

Gordon, G. J. (n.d.), Letter from the Heritage Conservation and Recreation Service to the Advisory Council on Historic Preservation and others (March 24, 1978).

Gorman, C. F. (1981), A Case History: Ban Chiang. *Art Research News* 1:10–13.

Grayson, D. K. (1978), Aspects of Archaeological Research Management. In *Scholars as Managers*, ed. A. W. Portnoy, Interagency Archaeological Services, Washington, D.C.

Green, E. L. (1975), Is This Site Worth Saving? New Arguments for the Preservation of Cultural Resources. MS.

Green, D. F. (n.d.), Management of High Altitude Cultural Resources. In *High Altitude Adaptations in the Southwest*, ed. J. C. Winter, Cultural Resource Management 2, USDA Forest Service, Southwestern Region, Albuquerque.

—— (1980), Prosecuting Under ARPA: What to Do Until the Regulations Arrive. Miscellaneous Paper 34, *Cultural Resources Report* 33, USDA Forest Service, Southwestern Region, Albuquerque.

—— & Davis, P. (compilers) (1981), *Cultural Resources Law Enforcement: An Emerging Science.* 2nd Ed., USDA Forest Service, Southwestern Region, Albuquerque.

—— & LeBlanc, S. (1979), Vandalism of Cultural Resources: The Growing Threat to Our Nation's Heritage. *Cultural Resources Report* 28, USDA Forest Service, Southwestern Region, Albuquerque.

GUMERMAN, G. J. (1973), The Reconciliation of Theory and Method in Archaeology. In *Research and Theory in Current Archaeology*, ed. C. L. Redman, Wiley-Interscience, New York.

GUTHE, C. E. (1952), Twenty-Five Years of Archaeology in the Eastern United States. In *Archaeology of Eastern United States*, ed. J. B. Griffin, The University of Chicago Press, Chicago, pp. 1-12.

GUTTING, G. (1980), Introduction. In *Paradigms and Revolutions—Applications and Appraisals of Thomas Kuhn's Philosophy of Science*, ed. G. Gutting, University of Notre Dame Press, Notre Dame.

HANSEN, J. F. (1976), The Anthropologist in the Field: Scientist, Friend, and Voyeur. In *Ethics and Anthropology Dilemmas in Fieldwork*, ed. M. A. Rynkiewich & J. P. Spradley, Wiley & Sons, New York.

HARRIS, M. (1968), *The Rise of Anthropological Theory*, Thomas Y. Crowell, New York.

HAURY, E. et al. (1950), *The Stratigraphy and Archaeology of Ventana Cave, Arizona*, University of Arizona Press, Tucson.

HAWKES, J. (1968), The Proper Study of Mankind. *Antiquity* 42:255-262.

HEALY, P. F. (1981), Interim Report to the Canadian International Development Agency on the Trent University-Royal Ontario Musuem-CIDA Training Program in Archaeology and Culture Resource Management in Belize, 1978-1981. MS. on file, Department of Anthropology, Trent University.

Heritage Conservation and Recreation Service (1980), Resource Protection Planning Process. *Heritage Conservation and Recreation Publication* 50, U.S. Department of the Interior, Washington, D.C.

HILL, J. N. (1966), A Prehistoric Community in Eastern Arizona. *Southwestern Journal of Anthropology* 22:9-30.

—— (1972), The Methodological Debate in Contemporary Archaeology: A Model. In *Models in Archaeology*, ed. David C. Clarke, pp. 61-107, Methuen and Co., London.

HILL, T. E. (1950), *Contemporary Ethical Theories*, Macmillan, New York.

Historic Green Springs Inc. v. *Bob Bergland* (1980), *ORDER*. Civil Action 77-0230-4.. U.S. District Court for the Eastern District of Virginia, Richmond Division.

HOLDEN, C. (1977), Contract Archaeology: New Source of Support Brings New Problems. *Science* 196:1070-1072.

HOLE, F. & HEIZER, R. F. (1973), *An Introduction to Prehistoric Archaeology*, Holt, Rinehart and Winston, New York.

HOLMES, B. E. (ed.) (1980), *A Cultural Resources Survey of the Zuni River from Eustace Reservoir to Bosson Wash, Zuni Indian Reservation, McKinley County, New Mexico*. MS. on file, Zuni Archaeology Program, Pueblo of Zuni.

—— & FOWLER, A. P. (1980), *The Alternate Dams Survey, An Archaeological Sample Survey and Evaluation of the Burned Timber and Coalmine Dams, Zuni Indian Reservation, McKinley County, New Mexico*, Zuni Archaeology Program, Pueblo of Zuni.

HUXLEY, T. H. (1929), *Evolution and Ethics*, D. Appleton & Co., New York.

JENNINGS, J. D. (ed.) (1978), *Ancient Native Americans*, W. H. Freeman, San Francisco.

JERMANN, J. V. (1981), *Archaeology, Space, and Sampling: Methods and Techniques in the Study of Pattern in Past Cultural Activity*. Ph.D. dissertation, University Microfilms, University of Michigan, Ann Arbor.

JOHNSON, E. (1973), Professional Responsibilities and the American Indian. *American Antiquity* 38:129–130.

JOSEPHY, A. M. (ed.) (1961), *Book of Indians*, American Heritage series, Simon and Schuster, New York.

—— (1968), *The Indian Heritage of America*, Alfred Knopf, New York.

JUDD, N. M. (1954), *The Material Culture of Pueblo Bonito*, Smithsonian Miscellaneous Collections 124.

KEATINGE, R. W. (1980), Archaeology and Development: The Tembladera Sites of the Peruvian North Coast. *Journal of Field Archaeology* 7:467–476.

KEEL, B. C. (1977), Grant-Contracts: Mutually Exclusive Paradigms. Paper presented at 34th Annual Southeastern Archaeological Conference, Lafayette, Louisiana.

—— (1979), A View From Inside. *American Antiquity* 44:164–170.

KELLEY, J. C. (1981), Southwest Protohistoric Conference: Discussion of Papers by Adams, Ferguson, Snow, and Wilcox, In *The Protohistoric Period in the North American Southwest, A.D. 1450–1700*, ed. D. R. Wilcox & W. B. Masse, Arizona State University Anthropological Research Paper 24, Tempe, Arizona.

KEMENY, J. G. (1959), *A Philosopher Looks at Science*, D. Van Nostrand Co., Princeton.

KERLINGER, F. N. (1964), *Foundations of Behavioral Research*, Holt, Rinehart and Winston, New York.

KIDDER, A. V. (1924), An Introduction to the Study of Southwestern Archaeology. Papers of the Southwestern Expedition, Phillips Academy 1, New Haven, Connecticut.

KING, M. E. (1980), Curators: Ethics and Obligations. *Curator* 23:10–18.

KING, T. F. (1971), A Conflict of Values in American Archaeology. *American Antiquity* 36:255–262.

—— (1977), Resolving a Conflict of Values in American Archaeology. In *Conservation Archaeology: A Guide for Cultural Resource Management Studies*, ed. M. B. Schiffer & G. Gumerman, Academic Press, New York.

—— (1980), Nobody Knows the Trouble I've Seen: Responses to "The Trouble with Archaeology," Part 2. *Journal of Field Archaeology* 7:245–257.

—— (1982), Future Directions: A Personal Perspective. *American Society for Conservation Archaeology, Report* 9:31–37.

—— & LYNEIS, M. M. (1978), Preservation: A Developing Focus of American Archaeology. *American Anthropologist* 80:873–893.

—— et al. (1977), *Anthropology in Historic Preservation*, Academic Press, New York.

KINSEY, W. F., III (1977), One Archaeologist's Dilemma: A Personal View. *Pennsylvania Archaeologist* 47:42–44.

KIRK, R. (1975), *Hunters of the Whale*, William Morrow, New York.

KNUDSON, R. (1982), Basic Principles of Archaeological Resource Management. *American Antiquity* 47(1):163–166.

KROEBER, A. L. (1940), Introduction. In *Essays in Honor of John R. Sevanton*, Smithsonian Miscellaneous Collection, Vol. 100, Washington, D.C.

KUHN, T. (1962), *The Structure of Scientific Revolutions*, Revised and enlarged 1970, University of Chicago Press, Chicago.

LADD, E. J. (1980), Sacred Areas and Sites. In *A Cultural Resources Survey of the Zuni River from Eustace Reservoir to Bosson Wash, Zuni Indian Reservation, McKinley County, New Mexico,* ed. B. E. Holmes, Zuni Archaeology Program, Pueblo of Zuni, pp. 78–83.

LARGE, A. J. (1977), Public Archaeology: Like It or Not, You are Paying for Digs, *The Wall Street Journal*, August 12.

LEAR, D. (1981), Civil Responsibilities Under the Federal Collections Act of 1966. In *Cultural Resources Law Enforcement: An Emerging Science*, 2nd ed., comp. D. F. Green & P. Davis, USDA Forest Service, Southwestern Region, Albuquerque.

LEE, R. F. (1970), *The Antiquities Act of 1906*. National Technical Information Service, U.S. Department of Commerce (PB 200 042), Springfield, Virginia.

LEHMER, D. J. (1971), *Introduction to Middle Missouri Archaeology*. [Anthropological Papers 1.] National Park Service, Washington, D.C.

LEMASTER, D. C. (1982), How Can a Professional Association Influence Policy-Making? *Journal of Soil and Water Conservation* 37(5):264–266.

LEVI-STRAUSS, C. (1967), *The Scope of Anthropology*, Jonathan Cape, London.

LEVY-BRUHL, L. (1905), *Ethics and Moral Science*, Constable and Co., London.

LINDSAY, A. J., JR., & WILLIAMS-DEAN, G. (1980), Artifacts, Documents, and Data: A New Frontier for American Archaeology. *Curator* 23:19–29.

LIPE, W. D. (1974), A Conservation Model for American Archaeology. *The Kiva* 39:213–245.

——— & LINDSAY, A. (eds.) (1974), Proceedings of the 1974 Cultural Resource Management Conference. *Museum of Northern Arizona Technical Series* 14. Flagstaff, Arizona.

LONGACRE, W. A. (1970), Archaeology as Anthropology: A Case Study. *Anthropological Papers of the University of Arizona*, 17, Tucson.

MACAULAY, D. (1977), *Motel of the Mysteries*, Houghton Mifflin, Boston.

MACDONALD, W. K. (ed.) (1976), Digging for Gold: Papers on Archaeology for Profit. *Technical Report 5*, Museum of Anthropology, University of Michigan, Ann Arbor.

——— & TOWNSEND, A. H. (1976), Problems in the Organization and Growth of Corporate Archaeology. In Digging for Gold: Papers on Archaeology for Profit, ed. W. K. MacDonald, *Technical Report 5*, Museum of Anthropology, University of Michigan, Ann Arbor, pp. 35–51.

MACIVER, R. M. (1955), The Social Significance of Professional Ethics. In *Ethical Standards and Professional Conduct*, ed. B. Y. Landis, *Annals of the American Academy of Political and Social Science* 297.

Malibu Creek State Park (n.d.), Contract Proposal and Scope of Work, Department of Parks and Recreation, Sacramento (1981).

Malinowski, B. (1944), *A Scientific Theory of Culture*, Roy Publishers, New York.

Maquet, J. (1964), Objectivity in Anthropology. *Current Anthropology* 5:47–55.

Martin, P. S. (1974), Early Development in Mogollon Research, In *Archaeological Researches in Retrospect*, ed. G. R. Willey, pp. 3–29, Winthrop, Cambridge.

Matheny, R. T. & Berge, D. L. (eds.) (1976), Symposium on the Dynamics of Cultural Resource Management. *Archaeological Report* 10, USDA Forest Service, Southwestern Region, Albuquerque.

Mayer-Oakes, W. J. (1974), President's Message. *American Association for Conservation Archaeology Newsletter* 1(2):1–5.

——— (1978), Applied and Basic Research in Archaeology: Implications for Archaeology as Part of the Scientific Community. In *Papers in Applied Archaeology*, ed. J. Gunn, Center for Archaeological Research, University of Texas, San Antonio.

McAllister, M. E. (1979), Pothunting on National Forest Lands in Arizona: An Overview of the Current Situation. In *Vandalism of Cultural Resources: The Growing Threat to our Nation's Heritage*, ed. D. F. Green & S. LeBlanc. *Cultural Resources Report* 28, USDA Forest Service, Southwestern Region, Albuquerque.

McGimsey, C. R., III (1972), *Public Archaeology*, Seminar Press, New York.

——— (1982), A Proposal for an Investigation into the Feasibility of Establishment by the National Research Council of a Committee on Archaeological Resources and Research. MS. on file, National Research Council, Washington, D.C.

——— & Davis, H. (eds.) (1977), *The Management of Archaeological Resources. The Airlie House Report*, Society for American Archaeology, Washington.

McGuire, R. H. & Schiffer, M. B. (ed.) (1982), *Hohokam and Patayan: Prehistory of Southwestern Arizona*, Academic Press, New York.

Meighan, C. W. (1982), Archaeology: Science or Sacrilege? MS. on file, Institute of Archaeology, University of California, Los Angeles.

Meiszner, W. C. (1982), CRM Archaeology: Federal Variations. *Contract Abstracts and CRM Archaeology*, 3(1):44–47.

Mellaart, J. (1959), The Royal Treasure of Dorak. *Illustrated London News*, November 28:754 ff.

Merriam-Webster, A. (1966), *New World Dictionary*, Merriam Co., Springfield, Mass.

Meyer, K. (1973), *The Plundered Past. The Story of the Illegal International Traffic in Works of Art*, Atheneum, New York.

Michigan Compiled Laws Annotated (1977), Dead Human Bodies. Section 750.160.

Miller, D. (1980), Archaeology and Development. *Current Anthropology* 21:709–726.

Monypenney, P. (1955), The Control of Ethical Standards in the Public

Service. In *Ethical Standards and Professional Conduct*, ed. B. Y. Landis, *Annals of the American Academy of Political and Social Science* 297.

MOORE, W. E. (1967), Economic and Professional Institutions. In *Sociology*, ed. N. J. Smelser, Wiley & Sons, New York, pp. 273–328.

MORATTO, M. J. & KELLY, R. E. (1977), Significance in Archaeology. *The Kiva* 42:193–202.

—— (1978), Optimizing Strategies for Evaluation of Archaeological Significance. *Advances in Archaeological Method and Theory* 1:1–30.

MORGAN, L. H. (1877), *Ancient Society*, Holt, New York.

MUSCARELLA, O. W. (1977a), Unexcavated Objects and Ancient Near Eastern Art. In *Mountains and Lowlands: Essays in the Archaeology of Greater Mesopotamia*, ed. L. D. Levine & T. C. Young, Jr., *Bibliotheca Mesopotamica*, 7:153–207, Undena Publications, Malibu.

—— (1977b), "Ziwiye" and Ziwiye: The Forgery of a Provenience. *Journal of Field Archaeology* 4:197–219.

NADER, L. (1976), Professional Standards and What We Study. In *Ethics and Anthropology Dilemmas in Fieldwork*, ed. A. Rynkiewich & J. P. Spradley, Wiley & Sons, New York.

NAGEL, E. (1967), The Nature and Aim of Science. In *Philosophy of Science Today*, ed. S. Mossberger, pp. 3–13, Basic Books, New York.

NAGIN, C. (1981), First, the "Hot Pot"—Now, an "Uncup." *New York*, December 7:61–74.

NASH, J. (1976), Ethnology in a Revolutionary Setting. In *Ethics and Anthropology Dilemmas in Fieldwork*, ed. M. A. Rynkiewich & J. P. Spradley, Wiley & Sons, New York.

National Park Service (1981), *Cultural Resource Management Guidelines (NPS–28)*, National Park Service, Washington, D.C.

National Research Council (1982), *Assessing Cultural Attributes in Planning Water Resources Projects*. Environmental Studies Board, National Research Council, Washington, D.C.

News and Views (1981), *Newsletter of the Department of Parks and Recreation*, Sept. 1981, p. 3, Sacramento.

NICKENS, P. R. et al. (1981), A Survey of Vandalism to Archaeological Resources in Southwestern Colorado. *Cultural Resource Series* 11, Colorado State Office, Bureau of Land Management, Denver.

North Carolina General Statutes (1981), The Unmarked Human Burial and Human Skeletal Remains Protection Act, Chapter 70, Article 3.

NOVICK, A. L. (1980), Introduction. Symposium issue: the curation of archaeological collections. *Curator* 23:7–9.

NURKIN, G. (1982), The Conservation of Archaeological Resources: the Federal Legislation. *Contract Abstracts and CRM Archaeology* 3(1):48–58.

OAKLEY, C. B. (1981), Major Theft in Moundville, Alabama. *Journal of Field Archaeology* 8:498–503.

ODUM, H. T. (1971), *Environment, Power and Society*, Wiley-Interscience, New York.

OLIVAS, E. (1977), Letter "To Whom It May Concern," by Chairman of the Business Council, Santa Ynez Indian Reservation (Dec. 14, 1977).

ORTNER, D. & PUTSCHAR, W. G. J. (1981), Identification of Pathological Conditions in Human Skeletal Remains. *Smithsonian Contributions to Anthropology* 28. Smithsonian Institution, Washington, D.C.

PATTERSON, L. W. (1978), Basic Considerations in Contract Archaeology. *Man in the Northeast* 15–16:132–138.

PEDEN, W. (ed.) (1955), *Notes on the State of Virginia*, University of North Carolina Press, Chapel Hill.

PELTO, D. & PELTO, G. H. (1978), *Anthropological Research* (2nd ed.), Cambridge University Press, Cambridge.

PENDERGAST, D. M. (1981), *Excavations at Altun Ha, Belize, 1964–1970* 1, Royal Ontario Museum, Toronto.

——— & GRAHAM, E. (1981), Fighting a Looting Battle: Xunantunich, Belize. *Archaeology* 34:12–19.

PHILLIPS, B. S. (1966), *Social Research, Strategy and Tactics*, Macmillan, New York.

PLOG, F. (1974), *The Study of Prehistoric Change*, Academic Press, New York.

——— (1980), The Ethics of Archaeology and the Ethics of Contracting. *Contract Abstracts and CRM Archaeology* 1:10–15.

——— (1981), *Cultural Resources Overview, Little Colorado Area, Arizona*, USDA Forest Service, Albuquerque.

POKOTYLO, D. L. (1982), Contract Archaeology and Academic Research: Crisis, What Crisis? In *Directions in Archaeology: A Question of Goals*, ed. P. D. Francis & E. C. Poplin, Archaeological Association of the University of Calgary, Calgary, Alberta.

POPPER, K. R. (1970), Normal Science and Its Dangers. In *Criticism and the Growth of Knowledge*, ed. I. Lakatos & A. Musgrave, Cambridge University Press, Cambridge.

POWELL, J. W. (1891), *Indian Linguistic Families of America North of Mexico. Smithsonian Institution, Bureau of American Ethnology, Annual Report*, 100, 7, Washington, D.C.

PRIEST, J. (1833), *American Antiquities and Discoveries in the West*, Harpers, New York.

Pueblo of Zuni (1982), *Zuni Comprehensive Plan, 1981 Update*. Pueblo of Zuni.

QUIMBY, G. I. (1979), A Brief History of WPA Archaeology. In *The Uses of Anthropology*, ed. W. Goldschmidt, American Anthropological Association, Washington, D.C.

RAAB, L. M. (1977), The Santa Rosa Wash Project: Notes on Archaeological Research Design Under Contract. In *Conservation Archaeology*, ed. M. B. Schiffer and G. J. Gumerman, pp. 167–182, Academic Press, New York.

——— (1979), Research Design and Resolution of Problems in the Contract Archaeology Process. In *Scholars As Contractors*, ed. W. J. Mayer-Oakes & A. W. Portnoy, U.S. Department of the Interior, Washington, D.C.

——— (1981), Getting First Things First: Taming the Mitigation Monster. *Contract Abstracts and CRM Archaeology* 2: 7–9.

——— (1983), Toward an Understanding of the Ethics and Values of Research Design in Archaeology. In *Ethics and Values in Archaeology*, ed. E. Green, Free Press, New York.

——— & Klinger, T. C. (1977), A Critical Appraisal of Significance in Contract Archaeology. *American Antiquity* 42:629–634.

——— (1978), A Reply to Sharrock and Grayson on Archaeological Significance. *American Antiquity* 44:328–329.

——— et al. (1980), Client, Contracts, and Profits: Conflicts in Public Archaeology. *American Anthropologist* 82:539–551.

——— (n.d.), Cultural Resource Management in the University: Getting What We Deserve. *Journal of Field Archaeology* (in press).

Redman, C. L. (1973), Multi-Stage Fieldwork and Analytical Techniques. *American Antiquity* 31:61–79.

Rieth, A. (1970), *Archaeological Fakes*, trans. D. Imber, Barrie and Jenkins, London.

Rippeteau, B. E. (1979), Antiquities Enforcement in Colorado. *Journal of Field Archaeology* 6:85–103.

Robertson, B. P. (1980), *Archaeological Survey for a Buried Telephone Cable in Zuni Pueblo for Universal Telephone Company of the Southwest, Zuni Indian Reservation, McKinley County, New Mexico.* MS. on file, Zuni Archaeology Program, Pueblo of Zuni.

Rosen, L. (1980), The excavation of American Indian Burial Sites: A Problem in Law and Professional Responsibility. *American Anthropologist* 82:5–27.

Rouse, I. (1939), *Prehistory in Haiti, A Study in Method*, Yale University Publications in Anthropology 21, New Haven, Connecticut.

Rowe, J. H. (1979), *Archaeology As a Career*, Archaeological Institute of America, New York.

Rynkiewich, M. A. & Spradley, J. P. (1976), *Ethics and Anthropology Dilemmas in Fieldwork*, Wiley & Sons, New York.

San Luis Obispo Telegram Tribune, December 17, 1977, San Luis Obispo, Calif.

Santa Barbara News Press, November 6, 1981, Santa Barbara.

Scheffler, I. (1967), *Science and Subjectivity*, Bobbs-Merrill, Indianapolis.

Schiffer, M. B. (1976), *Behavioral Archaeology*, Academic Press, New York.

——— & Gumerman, G. J. (eds.) (1977), *Conservation Archaeology: A Guide for Resource Management Studies*, Academic Press, New York.

——— & House, J. H. (eds.) (1975), The Cache River Archaeological Project: An Experiment in Contract Archaeology. *Arkansas Archaeological Survey, Research Series* 8.

——— & ——— (1977), Cultural Resource Management and Archaeological Research: The Cache Project. *Current Anthropology* 18:43–68.

Schoeninger, M. J. & Peebles, C. S. (1981), Notes on the Relationship Between Social Status and Diet at Moundville. *Southeastern Archaeological Conference Bulletin* 24.

Setzler, F. M. (1943), Archaeological Explorations in the United States, 1930–1942. *Acta Americana* 1:206–220.

Sharrock, F. W. & Grayson, D. K. (1978), Significance in Contract Archaeology. *American Antiquity* 44:327–328.

Smith, M. A. (1955), The Limitations of Inference in Archaeology. *The Archaeological Newsletter* 6:1–7.

Smith, W. et al. (1966), The Excavation of Hawikuh by Frederick Webb Hodge, Report of the Hendricks–Hodge Expedition, 1917–1923. *Contributions from the Museum of the American Indian, Heye Foundation 20,* New York.

——— (1977), Society for American Archaeology Constitution and By-Laws. *American Antiquity* 42(2):308–309.

Society for American Archaeology (1948), By-Laws of the Society for American Archaeology. *American Antiquity* 2:148.

——— (1974a), New Presidential Statement, Annual Meeting. *American Antiquity* 39:652–653.

——— (1974b), By-Laws of the Society for American Archaeology. *American Antiquity* 39(4):669–673.

——— (1977), By-Laws of the Society for American Archaeology, as amended May 1975. *American Antiquity* 42:308–312.

——— (1982), Report to the Executive Committee of the Society for American Archaeology. Typescript.

Society for California Archaeology (1981), Resolution on Treatment and Reinterment of Human Remains (passed by Executive Board of the Society for California Archaeology, Nov. 14, 1981).

Society of American Archivists (1979), A Code of Ethics for Archivists. *Society for American Archaeology Newsletter* (July), pp. 11–15.

Society of Professional Archaeologists (1976), Organization and Incorporation Notice.

——— (1981), Code of Ethics and Standards of Performance. *Directory of Professional Archaeologists*, pp. 3–6.

——— (1982), *Directory of Professional Archaeologists*, 7th ed., Washington University, St. Louis.

Spencer, H. (1895), *The Principles of Ethics* I, D. Appleton and Co., New York.

Spradley, J. P. & Rynkiewich, M. A. (1976), Preface. In *Ethics and Anthropology Dilemmas in Fieldwork*, ed. M. A. Rynkiewich & J. P. Spradley, Wiley & Sons, New York.

Sprague, R. (1974), American Indians and American Archaeology. *American Antiquity* 39:1–2, Salt Lake City.

Squier, E. G. & Davis, E. H. (1848), Ancient Monuments of the Mississippi Valley. *Smithsonian Contributions to Knowledge* 1, Washington, D.C.

Stephen, A. M. (1936), *Hopi Journal*, 2 vols., ed. E. C. Parsons. Columbia University, Contributions to Anthropology, vol. 23, New York.

Stephens, J. L. (1841), *Incidents of Travel in Chiapas and Yucatan*, Harpers, New York.

Stephenson, R. L. (1963), Administrative Problems of the River Basin Surveys. *American Antiquity* 28:277–281.

STEPICK, A. (1982), Anthropology and Congress: A Review Essay of Jack Weatherford's "Tribes on the Hill." *Human Organization* 41(4):366–369.

STRUEVER, S. & HOLTON, F. (1979), *Koster,* Anchor/Doubleday, New York.

STUART, G. E. & GARRETT, W. E. (1981), Maya Art Treasures Discovered in Cave. *National Geographic* (August) 160:220 ff.

SUCHEY, J. A. & SHERMIS, S. (1975), California Archaeology, Osteology, and the Excavation of Ancient Human Remains. MS., University of California, Los Angeles.

TAINTER, J. A. & GILLIO, D. (1980), *Cultural Resources Overview, Mt. Taylor Area, New Mexico*, USDA Forest Service, Albuquerque.

TAMPLIN, M. J. (1981a), Problems in Development Archaeology. Paper presented at the Conference on "Directions in Archaeology: A Question of Goals," University of Calgary, Calgary, Alberta.

—— (1981b), Archaeology and Culture Resource Management. Paper presented at 10th Annual Meeting of Canadian Archaeological Association, Calgary, Alberta.

TAYLOR, P. (1958), Social Science and Ethical Relativism. *Journal of Philosophy* 55:32–43.

TAYLOR, W. W. (1967), *A Study of Archaeology*, Southern Illinois University Press, Carbondale.

THOMPSON, J. E. S. (1963), *Maya Archaeologist*, University of Oklahoma Press, Norman, Oklahoma.

THOMPSON, R. (1956), The Subjective Element in Archaeological Inference, *Southwestern Journal of Anthropology* 12:327–332.

—— (1958), Modern Yucatecan Maya Pottery Making. *Memoirs* for the Society for American Archaeology, 15.

—— (1978), Beyond Significance. *American Society for Conservation Archaeology, Newsletter* 5:15–21.

TOULMIN, S. (1970), *Reason in Ethics*, Cambridge University Press, Cambridge.

TRIGGER, B. G. (1980), Archaeology and the Image of the American Indian. *American Antiquity* 45:662–676.

TYLOR, E. B. (1871), *Primitive Culture: Researches Into the Development of Mythology, Philosophy, Religion, Language, Art, and Custom*, J. Murray, London.

U.S. v. *McClain*, 545 F. 2d, 988 (5th Cir. 1977).

U.S. Air Force (1981), MX Missile Project. Deployment Area Selection and Land Withdrawal/Acquisitions DEIS. Department of the Air Force, Washington, D.C.

U.S. Code (1980a), An Act for the Preservation of American Antiquities. 1906. Title 16, Secs. 431, 433.

—— (1980b), Historic Sites, Buildings, and Antiquities Act, 1935. Title 16, Secs. 461–467.

—— (1980c), Reservoir Salvage Act, 1960; Amendments 1974, 1978. Title 16, Sec. 469.

—— (1980d), National Historic Preservation Act, 1966. Title 16, Sec. 470.

—— (1980e), National Environmental Policy Act, 1969. Title 42, Sec. 4321 *et seq*.

—— (1980f), Executive Order 11593. Protection and Enhancement of the Cultural Environment. Title 16, Sec. 470.

—— (1980g), National Historic Preservation Act Amendments of 1980. Title 16, Sec. 470.

U.S. General Accounting Office (1979), Uncertainties over Federal Requirements for Archaeological Preservation at the New Melones Dam in California: Report by the Comptroller General of the United States.

—— (1981), *Are Agencies Doing Enough or Too Much for Archaeological Preservation? Guidance Needed.* CED-81-61.

U.S. Supreme Court (1896), *United States* v. *Gettysburg Electric Railway Company*. 16 U.S. 668ff. (1896).

Vietor, R. H. K. (1980), *Environmental Politics and the Coal Coalition*, College Station, Texas A&M Press.

Vitelli, K. D. (1982a), Mail Order Antiquities. *Journal of Field Archaeology* 9:121–122.

—— (1982b), To Remove the Double Standard: Historic Shipwreck Legislation. *Journal of Field Archaeology*: 10.

Vogel, J. C. & Van De Merwe, N. J. (1977), Isotopic Evidence for Early Maize Cultivation in New York State. *American Antiquity* 42:238–242.

Wagner, H. A. (1955), Principles of Professional Conduct in Engineering. In *Ethical Standards and Professional Conduct,* ed. B. Y. Landis, *Annals of the American Academy of Political and Social Science* 297.

Ward, A. E. (1982), Navajo Graves: An Archaeological Reflection of Ethnographic Reality. Center for Anthropological Studies, Albuquerque.

Wassaja (1975a), July, 1975. American Indian Historical Society, San Francisco.

—— (1975b), August, 1975. American Indian Historical Society, San Francisco.

—— (1976), February, 1976. American Indian Historical Society, San Francisco.

Watson, P. J. et al. (1971), *Explanation in Archaeology: An Explicitly Scientific Approach*, Columbia University Press, New York.

Wauchope, R. (1965), *They Found the Buried Cities*, University of Chicago Press, Chicago.

Wax, M. L. & Cassell, J. (1979), Fieldwork, Ethics, and Politics: The Wider Context. In *Federal Regulations: Ethical Issues and Social Research*, ed. M. L. Wax & J. Cassell, Westview Press, Boulder, Colorado.

Weakly, W. (1977), Federal Project Planning: The Bureau of Reclamation. *Issues in Archaeology, Report Special Issue* 5(2–3), Advisory Council on Historic Preservation, Washington, D.C.

Weatherford, J. M. (1981), *Tribes on the Hill: an Investigation into the Rituals and*

Realities of an Endangered American Tribe—the Congress of the United States, Rawson Wade, New York.

Weinland, M. (1981), Archaeological Significance: A 10-Year Review of Nominations From Kentucky. *American Society for Conservation Archaeology, Report* 7:12–19.

Wendorf, F. (1957), The New Mexico Program in Highway Archaeological Salvage. *American Antiquity* 23(1):74–78.

—— (1962), *A Guide for Salvage Archaeology*. Museum of New Mexico Press, Santa Fe.

—— (1979), Changing Values in Archaeology, *American Antiquity* 44:641–643.

White, L. A. (1959), *The Evolution of Culture*, McGraw-Hill, Inc., New York.

White, P. T. (1982), The Temples of Angkor: Ancient Glory in Stone. *National Geographic* 161:552–589.

Wilcox, U. V. (1980), Collections Management with the Computer. *Curator* 23:45–54.

Wildesen, L. E. (1979), Coming of Age in Applied Archaeology. *Reviews in Anthropology* 6:373–385.

—— (1980), Getting Us All Together: Cultural Resources Contracting in the Pacific Northwest. Proceedings of the American Society for Conservation Archaeology Symposium on the Ethics of Contracting.

—— (compiler) (1982), Report of the Conference on the Future of Archaeology. MS. on file, Society for American Archaeology, Washington, D.C.

Willey, G. R. (1953), Prehistoric Settlement Patterns in the Viru Valley, Peru, *Bureau of American Ethnology Bulletin* 155.

—— & Sabloff, J. A. (1980), *A History of American Archaeology*, 2nd Ed., W. H. Freeman, San Francisco.

Williams, G. (1951), *Humanistic Ethics*, Philosophical Library, New York.

Williams, L. R. (1977), Vandalisms to Cultural Resources of the Rocky Mountain West. *Cultural Resources Report* 21, USDA Forest Service, Southwestern Region, Albuquerque.

Winter, J. C. (1980), Indian Heritage Preservation and Archaeologists. *American Antiquity* 45:121–131.

—— (n.d.), Letter to Governor Brown concerning Excavations in San Jose (March 25, 1978).

Woodall, J. N. & Perricone, P. J. (1981), The Archaeologist as Cowboy: The Consequence of Professional Stereotype. *Journal of Field Archaeology* 8:506–509.

Woodbury, N. & McGimsey, C. R., III (compilers) (1977), The Crisis in Communication. In *The Management of Archaeological Resources*, ed. C. R. McGimsey, III & H. A. Davis, Special Publication of the Society for American Archaeology.

Woodward, B. L. et al. (1981), *Patterns of Site Vandalism on the Tonto National Forest, Arizona*. Paper presented at the 1981 Annual Meetings of the Society for American Archaeology, San Diego, California.

WRIGHT, J. V. (1982), Archaeological Cultural Resource Management—Preserving the Past for What Purpose? In *Directions in Archaeology: A Question of Goals*, ed. P. D. Francis & E. C. Poplin, Archaeological Association of the University of Calgary, Calgary, Alberta.

WRIGHT, K. & REID, J. J. (1979), Adverse Impacts of Vandalism. In *Reports of Historic Preservation Survey and Planning*, by University of Arizona Field School, Grasshopper Region, Fort Apache Indian Reservation, Phase II, June, July and August, 1979, ed. J. Jefferson Reid. MS. on file, Department of Anthropology, University of Arizona.

WRIGHT, M. J. (1982), Boop Bop Dittum Dottum Wattum Chew: How to Evaluate Site Significance Within Fresh Water Reservoirs. In *Directions in Archaeology: A Question of Goals*, ed. P. D. Francis & E. C. Poplin, Archaeological Association of the University of Calgary, Calgary, Alberta.

ZIMMERMAN, L. J. & ALEX, R. (1981a), Digging Ancient Burials: The Crow Creek Experience. *Early Man* 3:3–10, Center for American Archaeology, Evanston, Illinois.

——— (1981b) How the Crow Creek Archaeologists View the Question of Reburial. *Early Man* 3:25–26.

Index